W9-AXJ-423

THE LUNATIC GIANT IN THE DRAWING ROOM

JAMES HALL

The Lunatic Giant in the Drawing Room

THE BRITISH AND AMERICAN NOVEL

SINCE 1930

Indiana University Press Bloomington, London

SECOND PRINTING 1969

Library of Congress catalog card number: 68-14602

Manufactured in the United States of America

Contents

Acknowledgments

I am grateful to the following for permission to quote:

SAUL BELLOW. From *Dangling Man* and *The Victim*: Vanguard Press, Inc. and Weidenfeld & Nicholson Ltd. From *The Adventures of Augie March*, *Seize the Day*, and *Herzog*: The Viking Press, Inc., Weidenfeld & Nicholson Ltd., and Saul Bellow.

ELIZABETH BOWEN. From *Bowen's Court*: Longmans, Green & Co. Ltd. and Alfred A. Knopf, Inc. From *The House in Paris* and *Death of the Heart*: Jonathan Cape Ltd. and Elizabeth Bowen.

WILLIAM FAULKNER. From *The Hamlet*: Random House, Inc. and Chatto and Windus Ltd.

IRIS MURDOCH. From *Sartre, Romantic Realist*: Bowes & Bowes and Yale University Press. From *Under the Net*, *An Unofficial Rose*, and *The Unicorn*: Chatto and Windus Ltd. and The Viking Press, Inc.

ROBERT PENN WARREN. From *All the King's Men*: Harcourt, Brace & World and Eyre & Spottiswoode.

ERIC AUERBACH. From *Mimesis*: Princeton University Press.

Preface

The book is about six novelists who have explored beyond the existing formulations of experience. The title suggests a starting point, the main chapters a testing of new and revived hopes. The chronology reports a story of developing perspectives over thirty-five years. Hopefully the whole will give the general reader an over-all view of the period and the professional fresh perspectives on known work. Since it is unrealistic to expect any reader to have just finished all the novels dealt with, I have tried to include enough detail to indicate or recall the nature of each book. Individual chapters look for the new turn where it occurs—in a body of work, two or three major successes, occasionally in a single novel.

I have had good and errorless advice from several friends—David C. Fowler, A. C. Hamilton, Robert B. Heilman, Dr. Roger C. Hendricks, Donald Kartiganer, Roger Sale, and Arnold Stein. My wife, Carol, who teaches the novel besides being a poet, contributed not only sensitivity to language and symbol but detailed interpretations. Miss Dorothy Smiley's typing of the manuscript was also an excellent job of editing, and Miss Laurie Glass typed revisions well and expeditiously. A grant from the University of Washington Graduate School helped with the manuscript preparation. Beyond specific indebtedness lies the large gratitude of any instructor to his students, whose willingness to take seriously a given framework encourages him and whose occasional impieties force him to recognize his simpler obsessions.

I am grateful to the editors of *ELH* and the *Humanities Association Bulletin* for permission to reprint parts of the chapters on Iris Murdoch and Faulkner.

J. H.

July, 1967

THE LUNATIC GIANT IN THE DRAWING ROOM

ONE

What Happened?

By the late Middle Ages poets in Western Europe had developed a sophisticated psychological romance. Suddenly, inexplicably, a simpler mode set itself up as the avant-garde. *Piers Plowman* led, according to one distinguished medievalist,* to a still simpler and more popular form, the morality play. Now, suddenly enough, moralists like Sartre and Camus, morality dramatists like Brecht, Beckett, and Ionesco have superseded the most complex psychological romance ever written—the early twentieth-century novel.

Faced with this reversal a few honest critics have retired from the present, lamenting the triviality of poetry, the poverty of theater, and the death of the novel. More have regretted the disappearance of the hero. Worst of all, history may sustain their estimate of the past thirty-five years compared to the preceding thirty. A real problem that cannot be talked away does exist: can people who think as we have come to think write good novels?

* David C. Fowler.

Some naïveté, of course, prejudices the question. The hero, like innocence, has been disappearing since *The Iliad.* At certain times writers must rejuggle their idea of him and may be looking more than finding. The stresses of the past quarter century have created a pressure to codify once more the wisdom of the race, to sort among the new irrationalities for a tenable ideal of individuality—an "identity"—and a course which promises more than survival. The great occurrence of recent years has not been the hero's disappearance, however, but his reconstitution: mind as a set of forces, with possibly definable speed and direction, has replaced mind as fluid consciousness.

Beyond doubt, the 1930's formed contemporary ideas of personality in the novel and the war reenforced them. The most visible legacy of the period has been a revival of the will to do something—even when the components of *something* have proved unclear. This wary revival, haunted by the modern image of the fractured self, did not occur when conditions became better, as *The Wasteland* had forecast, but when they became worse. So far nothing like a nineteenth-century enthusiasm for the will has developed—merely a renewed interest in it as a possibility at all. Yet the metaphysical and moral probing has helped produce a different kind of novel. In opposition to what most of us learned to value in school, character has become more representative, and action has often carried whatever complexity the novel has. From Kafka through Camus to Golding, the hope for answers available to a planning intelligence has pushed the personae of novels away from sensitive consciousnesses, watching decay proceed at a bearable pace, toward representative forces colliding in conflicts that will resolve themselves one way or another.

The logic seems inescapable, whatever the consequences to art forms, and the moral case for the new kind of writer solid. The complaining tone of early twentieth-century fiction—sometimes gentle, sometimes fierce—about a world the novelists never made and the spoken or unspoken demand for an Energizing Principle to compel the activity of all good men implied leisure. If Godot did not appear immediately, people could wait. Since 1930, though, writers have had to accept not only their predecessors' picture of the self—irrational, indecisive, angry, apathetic, terrified—but more insistent incursions on privacy and more ambiguous attitudes to events. At the same time, they have had to discard that equivalent of the physicists' "ether"—a new Energizing Principle—and think of their lives, if controllable at all, as products of individual effort. Naturally, something has happened to the leisure value of a rich inner life. When the mind must depend on its own analyses of situations and organize itself on a course which may or may not ever prove right, it comes to think of itself more as a force than as a reservoir of percepts and feelings. Yet this very centering of energies raises an esthetic problem inseparable from the human one: people do have reasons for thinking their less useful emotions interesting.

Nothing so simple as the extremes of the two generations occurred at once, but around 1930 recent images of the world and the self began to meet their own contradictions at the same time that new demands faced them. A structure of feeling built up by the early twentieth century had acquired enough prestige to begin shaping readers and newer writers. (The many later novels trying to reconcile fathers and sons suggest the chances for a continuity unwanted thirty years before.) Though everyone knows in a way what this structure was, only another book could define it accurately. Here naming a few of its influential components may give a recognizable starting point.

Most people can agree on one first-generation strategy for dealing with commercial civilization. Many writers' theories of history and personality contrast unity of being with "multiplicity," "anarchy," and "a thousand lost golf balls." Novelists as well as poets locate this unity somewhere in the past—the Middle Ages, the seventeenth century, the eighteenth century, grandfather's time, memory, and of course myth. But the writers tend to play with history or myth. Their sense of loss and deprivation can equally well appear a contrast between contemporary practice and the best ideals of man.

Yet the real attitude toward multiplicity was not so clear-cut as the formula. The artists were themselves engaged in multiplying possibilities. Doing so was, in fact, their strongest basis for confidence. In many, a vision of expanding the inner world by sensitive perception consoled for defects outside, though raising for the future dangers of finding another anarchy within. In the short run the new guidelines being tested in literature—from psychology, anthropology, history, physics, and philosophy—seemed reasonable guarantees against getting lost inside the enhanced self. An exploring spirit cushioned whatever real despair existed. As Lionel Trilling puts it, novelists like Joyce, Proust, Virginia Woolf, and Mann encouraged a taste for pure spirit and a distaste for things and conditions. Yet Joyce and Mann, in particular, recognize the vulnerability of their vision and protect it with irony and wit.

Postwar novelists like Huxley, Fitzgerald, Hemingway, and Waugh contributed an increasing love for intensity in its own right. Valid experience must ring on the nerves. As portraits of the artist or the contemplative give form to the hope of expanding sensitivity, so party-goers with their coteries become questers for intensity, preservers of wartime excitement amid the unsuitable conditions of peace.* And in America these natural avatars of the period's ideal take on the disguise of other energy-heroes—gangster, tycoon, hunter.

The first generation in fact offered extraordinary variety, but some stances appealed more directly than others. By 1930 a few had coalesced enough to give a reasonably cohesive picture of the world and of ideal personality. (D. H. Lawrence, ill and inner, intensely alive in the art colony at Taos and scornful of the daily English world, was "living the myth" of his generation.) But putting all the many senses of self into a barrel labeled Sensitivity-with-Intensity would require a capacious barrel. In fact, are not the differences so great as to negate any real common spirit? It is often the business of literary historians to say so; but they have the advantage of knowing how the story came out, of not being engaged in the immediate battle to make a new literature and a new view of life prevail. The point here is a different kind of truth: young writers and readers did not at the time set out at once to draw

* My *Tragic Comedians* (Bloomington: Indiana University Press, 1963) discusses this development at length.

distinctions in depth. They responded to a general spirit, making up their own mixtures. They liked an idea of personality that seemed not only more adequate than the preceding ones but more inspiring. And again everyone knows in a way what it was. A receptive, transforming, waiting consciousness committed to experiencing intensely and in depth, and excited by a wealth of new ways for looking within and without—for of course this new intelligence, though it thought about itself, also took in the world selectively and changed it too.

The second-generation novelists did not set out to revolt against this agreement. They respected it. They merely drew the assignment of living longer and seeing how the package worked. Even before 1930, Faulkner's *The Sound and the Fury* had given the alarm that withdrawal could lead to bewilderment and terror. By the time Hesse published *Steppenwolf* in 1933 the first generation had ended —just as it began to impose itself on public consciousness. (For all the new sociology, novelists in the thirties still thought themselves going to school to the experimentalists who had preceded them. The reputations of Joyce, Proust, Mann, Yeats, and Eliot solidified. Criticism evangelized and explicated in their behalf. Young people all over the West began using them to correct their elders.)

Hesse was actually codifying previous discoveries, but his cool clarity shows a shift of concern, a perspective unavailable in the heat of the day. Steppenwolf himself is a model contemplative hero, withdrawn not only from faith in the activities of people around him but from even nominal participation. He keeps a diary, stays up late thinking, travels light, and moves on when involvement threatens. Or did. When a girl draws him into contact with other people, he steps through a looking glass and finds in himself the prime component of the once and future hero. He discovers aggression. The contemplative man kills his girl, snipes at automobiles, sets armies in motion, all without apparent purpose. Earlier novelists had portrayed aggression. Hesse merely makes it a direct consequence of the ideal of sensitivity—and puts it at the end of his story.

Faulkner and Hesse deal with a contradiction becoming apparent in one great first-generation dream: its inherent passivity had increased resentment without admitting or dealing with it. The depression added more active issues and heightened awareness of individual frustration by making it seem universal, omnipresent, and enduring. Bad times not only increased impatience, but gave it moral standing. And in annihilating the prestige of the existing social management, they made many feel that mind and will *must* be brought to bear on simply getting along. Fear helped make revolutionary rationalism seem natural. But many people still meant to use it in order to live like portraits of the artist. The inherited ideal of personality did not change overnight; it meant to become involved only enough to underwrite its continuance. It did not want to sacrifice any of its new spirituality for the sake of control.

But putting new value on aggressiveness and mind cut squarely across the acquired conscience based on the inner life. Increasing bitterness sped up the cycle of anger-and-fear. And aside from results, aggressiveness began to pose problems in its own right. For results could not be put aside or postponed in the leisurely manner of the first generation. So the attempt to make a working team of sensitivity and will proved far more difficult than making one out of sensitivity and mind. Applying knowledge turned out to be harder than gaining it. Without meaning to, out of apparent necessity, the second generation began to set up a personal ideal with directly contradictory aims: to be as private, sensitive, and imaginative as Stephen Dedalus—but more fun-loving—and as moving and shaking as Voltaire.

However, simply shifting from the artist to the problem-solver as protagonist could not satisfy the human demand. Not only would the change be too abrupt for always conservative rebels, but, since problems resist and multiply to infinity, the image lacks appealing self-reference. It sounds too much like middle management. So to give continuity amid detail the novelists began edging cautiously backward toward an idea of heroism. Walter Houghton's excellent book has shown how much the Victorians needed heroes and hero-worship. Caught in an analogous position, between a preceding self-exaltation and a necessity to make society work, contemporary novelists began trying not only Victorian characters but Victorian forms. In some way the demand for problem-solving had to be met without falling back into the ennui of the humdrum from which modernism had rescued us.

Fortunately, the ideal had persisted nicely. No one need have truck with the nineteenth century. The first generation had used its new romantic science of anthropology to transform hero-worship as well as religion into myth. In actual use during the twenties, it emphasized *distance* between heroism and actuality. Percival and the London observer are a long way apart; so are Ulysses and Bloom. Eliot's affections lean toward Percival, Joyce's toward Bloom, but they agree on distance. Only Yeats and Graves were wild enough to believe that myth and occurrence somehow correspond, and both had to take very long views. Myth appeals to contemplation of how things go, but has too little touch with events to give much guidance in action. When novelists began asking their characters to act, they had to find ways of reducing the distance—by giving body to myth and rescuing event from its stereotype of boredom.

So our age has seen the end, for the moment, of grand gesture. To replace myth in the gap between ideal and real, some contemporaries have compromised on theatricality. When this effect turns up, as it will presently, in novels as different as *Death of the Heart*, *All the King's Men*, and *The Power and the Glory*, it must be serving a crucial purpose in the emotional economy of a generation. One aim, of course, has been to keep significant conduct above the level of everyday without letting it get out of touch with the power of platitude and humdrum. If myth evolved into drama in Greek times, it also has within the memory of living men, and with comparable results. The hero's passion leads the chorus, but the chorus is there to counsel and oppose. Forty years ago no one needed its advice.

Recently an able critic, Robert Langbaum, has proved by logic that the modernist ideal of individual fitting more or less smoothly into mythical role had to eventuate into tragicomedy.* My book, *The Tragic Comedians*, showed merely that it had. But not exactly by finding mythical roles—at most by looking for them. For attempting to unite the antitheses without a religious leap creates the peculiar rhythm of recent fiction—jerky, one-step-forward-half-a-step-sidewise, trying awkwardly to integrate provisional roles rather than confident of having found continuity in the right one. Agreement on the nature of pain and of a muddling ideal character has made the comic novel possible in this age. To the amalgam of the sensitive and heroic man, the comic novelists add a catalyst, the unconfident confidence man. He wants to exert will without being sure that it will prevail—or even compete with others of like mind. In Huxley, Waugh, Henry Green, and Cary, the unconfident confidence man brings the *degree* of expediency necessary to make things go—in so far as they do. Vitality in the character reflects, too, some hope that we understand cultural patterns and promises enough to have the future partially in hand.

The more serious novelists cannot take straight the faith in energy and resilience that the unconfident confidence man represents. Their novels spell out what agreements exist, dwell on the difficulty in maintaining them, and note their inadequacy at best. So for a time their form of expressing energy becomes a theatrical heightening of representative character and event, and their form of seeking direction an edging toward allegory. But this path, once found, does not continue in straight lines. The questionings, accident reports, revisings, and mutations make up the interest of the story. And after 1950 theatricality diminishes.

My discussion of the tragicomic novelists implied a relation between cultural patterns and change which the "serious" writers lay out more precisely. However complex, the pattern never really fits even as it develops; it gains its cutting edge by emphasizing and omitting. It functions well or dramatically enough to make elisions seem insignificant and those disturbed by them old-fashioned, but, as the formulae age, new events and feelings not foreseen by their

* "The Mysteries of Identity: A Theme in Modern Literature," *American Scholar*, vol. 34 (1965), 569-587.

makers emphasize inadequacies. The twentieth century has wanted to have things both ways. It has driven for change, for control of events in the name of "rational" improvement, and it has, like any other age, wanted to cling to familiar patterns. Only when conditions and responses shift so much that the ideas, habits, and assumptions become false over too large an area does the general agreement break. In the meanwhile people stretch familiar schemes—and protagonists—as far as they can go. An age like ours assimilates as much as possible to its inherited hero and has not reached a time of revolutionary dissatisfaction. Endless tension between cultural pattern and sought change, results—and creates a sense that the times are shifting too rapidly for the human spirit.

The discussion so far applies more closely to British and continental literature than to American. No significant portraits of the artist as such appeared in this country before 1930. The similar impulse expressed itself through tycoon, hunter, gangster, and, ultimately, psychiatrist. But the active spirit behind the American transformation has by now become international—and so has the surviving portrait of the artist. The much-resented Americanization of Europe has been taking place in the novel too, though—for whatever consolation it may give our allies—the Europeanization of America has advanced even more rapidly. The kind of novel being written abroad came to America with Faulkner, Dos Passos, and Wolfe in the thirties, when new forces were already pressing on it, and the kind of novel being written in America came to England at the same time with Graham Greene.

This increasing internationalism makes it important to include both British and American in tracing recent developments. The tendency to merge does not, however, obliterate one deep difference: the effect of class upon aggression. British class values, under attack but surprisingly resistant, offer comfort, safety, style—the sense of life as bourgeois theater in which a person can be well-regarded by others qualified to judge. Class emphasizes intelligence, group agreement on projects only half-satisfactory to any individual. Modern British comic novelists use and resist it in the name of vitality, personality, and the awkwardness of fitting its shifting fashions. For, as Powell and Hartley show, fashion is its mode of operation and its necessary illusion. By contrast, American angry comedy seeks to channel aggression with far less regard for the look of the act and far less trust of others' opinion.

Conspicuous representatives—Mayfair, big politicians, tycoons, great country gentlemen—form the class image, not rank-and-file members. Englishmen too are willing to go to Hell, but they want to do it in good company. What a high-level coterie or committee can agree on limits action, and such decisions always have a self-preserving instinct. Fictional heroes often want to go beyond this consensus, but they can go less far than Americans without feeling the threat of emotional illness. So English novelists have a place for eccentrics as representative of individual whim, but not for Ahabs or Hucks, who can get far out and still feel themselves representing true sanity. American novelists imagine secret sharers all over the country. No committee or coterie has the *moral* right to set standards. (In England, even Lawrence had to have his visible disciples. So does Leavis. Here only Southerners, who have a class sense, can establish coteries.) In short, class involves a technique for channeling aggression, and even so strong-willed a novelist as Elizabeth Bowen and so emancipated a one as Iris Murdoch reflect its sense of reality in a way that no contemporary American novelist does.

Finally, this book is a companion piece to my earlier one. *Together* they try to define main directions in the form over the past thirty-five years. For Englishmen tragicomedy has proved preeminently sucessful in this generation, and something similar promises to dominate the immediate future in America. By and large, only Englishwomen and Americans have been able to write the serious novel in recent times. So the British novelists treated in this book may strike readers as less clearly outstanding than their American counterparts. But, after we have taken patriotic satisfaction in the intensity and depth of our men, we ought to credit the British with their own virtue—a breadth of writing so evenly matched that everyone will have his own candidates for the epithet of "major."

What do the six writers discussed here—Elizabeth Bowen, Faulkner, Warren, Greene, Bellow, and Iris Murdoch—have in common that makes them superior? My original basis of choice was simply that they seemed to me the best. Something like Leavis' standard of range and maturity might have rationalized the decision. (Possible inclusions like Angus Wilson and Ivy Compton-Burnett lack the range of the novelists treated.) But, once chosen, they all turn out to be explorers, writers trying to go beyond existing formulations. They all show an uncommon pressure to set directions for experience while giving the fullest expression to disorder. They all show steadiness in the face of threat, with no Orwellian "history as nightmare," no easy Beckett resignation, no Durrell vacations. They stick, their minds keep working, and they sometimes roll Sisyphus' rock a little way up the hill. Their differences stand out beyond their similarities and the book tries, first of all, to emphasize individuality.

But my aim is not to separate novels into bins labeled Sensitivity and Aggression or to subsume all conflict under these massive headings. I want instead to show what happens when a structure of feeling with a powerful hope and a compelling literature behind it meets new and not readily reconcilable aspirations. And what happens when the rough initial adjustments meet their inherent and unpredictable obstacles, when new or revived hopes develop before the dust from the first battles can settle. This sort of knowledge cannot come from definition and classification, however careful, but only from following struggles in the novels themselves. So the book focuses on motion in time and within novelists, not on abstract ordering of experience whose essence has been disorder. Even more than the human image then and now, my subject is the forces that go into producing the *ex post facto* composite. If their conflicts in the novels are accurately described, then *x* and *y* might substitute for *sensitive* and *aggressive*. The book aims to tell about literary occurrences and seeks no quarel over the summarizing language.

The question of how good these second-generation writers are will come in more meaningfully in the last chapter, when individual critiques have established more bases for judgment. Meanwhile we can begin from the going agreement, which does not quite accept the death of the novel but reveres ancestors. An attitude mixed out of suspicion, curiosity, and half-hearted loyalty to our team will do. But one fact may be worth keeping in mind: the great accomplishment of the first generation depends heavily upon its European members—and its poets. With the question resticted to the novel in English, decline may be less certain.

The story begins with a newly won ideal meeting its own contraditions in a world suddenly even less engaged than before in perpetuating fluid, sensitive consciousness.

Beginnings in Endings

TWO

The Giant Located: Elizabeth Bowen

Elizabeth Bowen casts a warm cold eye. Though still alive, she comes down to us with a reputation already frozen: a conservative fallen among avant-gardists, another Jamesian, a British Edith Wharton. Even the honor she gets as a stylist is suspect. It suggests good housekeeping—picking up and arranging the pieces scattered by more headlong predecessors.

In actuality Miss Bowen is one of the few radical explorers in the recent novel. The part of her work that looks conservative really shows her recognition of change. By the time she found herself, in the middle thirties, the revolutionary positions of the previous age were no longer revolutionary. Yet because they still seemed so to many, an elite could adopt them as guides for living—and signs of an intellectual aristocracy. Goals that in writers of the twenties kept fairly separate ways now seemed combinable. Advanced people could think of themselves as valuing deep and complex inner experience, like Proust, Mann, Virginia Woolf, and Joyce, while trying to achieve dramatic intensity, like Hemingway, Huxley, and Fitzgerald. But in practice these ideals were proving less compatible than in imagination. New tensions resulted, and produced their own poets.

Elizabeth Bowen is a born consolidator. She wants no less than a *smooth* mixture of all the best ingredients available. She feels the need not for new alternatives, but for harmonized ones. Virginia Woolf's heroines have soul, but can barely manage a dinner party; Elizabeth Bowen's assume that they have soul, but would not like living in the scatterbrained fashion of Mrs. Ramsay. They value competence and control too. The new novelist thus wants deep feeling to coalesce with style, drama, participation, and, unlike Waugh, will not settle for being half-ashamed of the effort. Ideally, the once revolutionary attitudes would become absorbed experience, enliveners of continuity rather than curious discoveries, domesticated carriers of vigorous hopes. But this intense wish for depth, liveliness, and safety meets within Miss Bowen a clarity about all the obstacles to its fulfilment—and the conflict makes her a novelist.

She knows, for example, what happens when numbers move onto a frontier once visited only by explorers and trappers. The group wants not only law and order, but the amenities of civilization. It needs the recognizable signs that lend a shape, a style, to experience. The wish gives Miss Bowen's scene its power. Her heroines want a "modern" sense of living without sacrificing the continuity or stability won by those who consolidated the values of a landed aristocracy with success in commerce. Where novelists of the twenties often disdain the past and industrial society, she sees no future in flights to the Alps or islands off the coast of Africa and little sustenance in elite London coteries of fellow-intensives. Miss Bowen's most thorough critic, William Heath, sees society as a rude limiter of the sensitive will, but her adults actually love-and-hate commercial civilization. She speaks for those adaptable aristocrats who moved the old furniture into the town house and got rich in the advertising business. And she knows what made them leave the farm. Over and over she shows the purposelessness, ineffectiveness, eccentricity, and insanity remaining in the less adaptable. Her heroines want to maintain or even construct continuity, but they do not foresee giving up London for a return to agriculture. (The author's part-time return to Ireland in later life may say something different.) Miss Bowen's best novels show imaginative energy so confined as to express only a small part of itself and ask, is this enough? They show, too, a resentment at situation so great as to make looking for new worlds—or old ones—impossible. But the sensitive will operates in contemporary circumstances *by choice*. To eliminate the taste for Regent's Park or even the rented flat would be to eliminate reality. Miss Bowen's heroines want to stay and complain.

The force behind this scene of an enlarged continuity comes from superimposing upon it a revolutionary scene—the twentieth-century shift in women's aspirations. Two of Miss Bowen's best novels express dissatisfaction with the role of wife and mother; her heroines find themselves inadequate to it and it inadequate to them. Her third important novel tests the possibility of free woman, man's comrade but not dependent. The books are not *about* this problem; they use it as a given condition for restlessness. And Miss Bowen pictures society's part in the conflict not as rules, but as feelings bred in by people whom the heroine respects, likes, and wants to please. Inner and outer merge—and have merged since birth. Women are expected to be sensitive and warm; they are also expected to make correct choices in marriage. Only a woman novelist realized fully the discrepancy in these prescriptions and put so directly the question that gives Miss Bowen a great part of her historical importance: is sensibility practical?

Her question remains, but by now some of her means have the charm and drawback of seeming old-fashioned. One look at the young heroes of today, with their knowledgeability from the cradle and wisecracking voices, makes the contrast with her soft tone and protected children unmistakable. Actually, these are conventions, not necessarily falser than present ones, but serving a different purpose. The child must be protected artificially to let the inner light dramatize the compromise that adults make in seeking to mix contradictory ideals. But Miss Bowen differs fom her predecessors in her sterner test: she tries some of their ideals on less perfectly equipped people in less suitable circumstances—on civilians who want to live within society rather than on heroic experimenters with mind and life.

Clearer recognition of aggressiveness complicates the problem. To many first-generation novelists, assigning sensitivity to the artist and will to the commercial man seemed to correspond roughly to the facts. But the two are not in the nature of things separate. Miss Bowen has only to give her child characters an unarguable mixture to transform the issue. A heroine who cannot consider the world well lost or console herself that her aches are stigmata has a new set of difficulties. Worse yet, adolescent sensitivity may not remain all promise for the adult. It can become conscience and in Miss Bowen's adults does. When perceptive sensitivity becomes the expected rather than the barely achievable, a norm, adults face a conflict that cannot be resolved by satirizing the middle classes.

So Miss Bowen lays out the elements for a stand-off. Since desirable choices have opened out, compromise among them seems the mature possibility. Yet real compromise cannot occur. In the novels the heart is what it is. It cannot give without ceasing to be heart and becoming policy. It chooses to break first, but—Miss Bowen's stern test—its breaking does not bring time to a stop. The desire to make feelings omnipotent in a world of clashing wills does not go away, but creates new disappointments in new outlets. As Miss Bowen puts the issue in plain prose,

> The outsize will is not necessarily an evil: it is a phenomenon. It must have its outsize outlet, its big task. If the right scope is not offered it, it must seize the wrong. . . . Not the will itself, but its wastedness is the dangerous thing. (*Bowen's Court*)

The novels show that there will be waste.

Miss Bowen had been writing for fifteen years when she published her first book with a real claim on the future—*The House in Paris*. Perhaps this long apprenticeship occurred because she had to absorb so much and find a form for expressing the combination. She may have had to wait, too, for sensitivity-with-intensity to come under attack—not randomly, as in Huxley, but systematically and radically. Eight years before *The House in Paris,* Alberto Moravia had published *The Time of Indifference.* Whether or not Miss Bowen read it, it expressed a going skepticism and weariness. Moravia's hero, a young artist manqué, finds that he simply does not have the feelings the culture has come to expect in his type. Neither his mother's theatricality about her emotions nor his own forced outbursts affect him as they are supposed to. He does not hate the real estate operator who has been keeping her for years and is now trying to seduce his sister. When he nevertheless tries to follow the inherited imperatives of sensitivity and intensity, by shooting the crude fellow, he cannot bring the act off. He cannot love a mother-substitute. In his first and best novel Moravia raises the issue of self-consciousness in sensibility. To what extent is the intense artist merely a cultural stereotype and to what extent is he natural and real?

The House in Paris comes in at this point. Expanding new faiths do not need a metaphysics; maturing ones do. So Miss Bowen, unable to assume what her predecessors had assumed, begins to provide a secular theology for instinctive loyalties. The peculiar carefulness of the novel comes from its will to build the argument from the ground up. Miss Bowen's view about evolution in manners and morals, about discontinuity between the structured life represented by the country and the catch-as-catch-can experience of the city follows a diagnosis already made familiar by Forster, Lawrence, and others. Her originality comes in feeling strongly the new demand—that a morally valuable innerness be reconcilable with a harsh will to self-assertion, that ideals of personal fulfilment somehow work in the world. (Lawrence almost alone among the older writers shows faith in this possibility, and the fact explains a good deal about his posthumous growth in reputation.) *The House in Paris* raises a basic question: are sensitive perception and intensity compatible goals in the world its characters choose to live in and with even more inclusive assertions of the will arising? Is it possible to conserve and consolidate first-generation values with the more comfortable inheritances?

All the complexities of the novel have a simple aim: to make the admittedly unstable yield stability-in-motion. Miss Bowen carries Moravia's question one step further—to turn it upside down. "Indifference" becomes the state of mind that cannot last, and a possibly fruitful tension its natural outgrowth. The process, though, takes two generations. In the first, sensitive passivity, abetted by parents who do not oppose, leads directly to outbreak. In the second, living on the verge of outbreak gives the ten-year-old boy vitality, but brings him into collision with society's will to regulate and channel. An American novelist might find this development plausible without finding it hopeful, but Miss Bowen inherits a British faith in tension between personal and social. And she has the talent to make an American reader feel that energy plus firm containment *may* produce a more admirable human image.

Heath, feeling Miss Bowen's sternness and unwilling to write her down as a thorough pessimist, hazards that she shows some hope of making life an art, but this is too smooth, too Yeatsian and Mannian to fit. The sustaining drive in her work grounds itself on primitive "fact": life demands drama, and will create it out of the suitable or unsuitable materials at hand. This drive turns day-to-day living into continual skirmishing. In more critical times it leads to a deeper drama set in basic experience. Symbiotic relationships developed out of the child's need for support create a permanently unstable situation. Insecurity makes him want to live through them forever, and growth forces him to try breaking through them. Since other people's reponse to this tension vary widely, Miss Bowen sets up drama as vital, natural, *and* complex.

In *The House in Paris* the structure surrounds the crisis of an absentee mother with one day in the life of her actually illegitimate son. Merely by centering on these two Victorian representatives of the outsider, Miss Bowen emphasizes how thoroughly older modes of channeling impulse have survived the revolution in manners. The argument for naturalness proceeds by moving symbiotic relationships in two opposing directions. The ten-year-old boy, who does not remember his mother, has come to Paris believing intensely that reunion with her will harmonize his energies. Though the idea puzzles his new young acquintance, mother to him means completing the self.

> "But what are you going to do in England?" she said.
> "We shall be together."
> Henrietta thought: Which is ordinary, after all. But his manner had made it sound supernatural.

Contrastingly, the enclosed central section, set eleven years earlier, shows the evolutionary process. Passive sensitivity in the mother-to-be leads to the desire for intense experience and turns into a revolt against symbiotic relationships.

The insulated boy furnishes the basic definition for the sensitivity-intensity-will complex. He is a nightmare child whom only Miss Bowen could love—anti-social, self-centered, on the edge of kicking and screaming. His sensitivity is almost entirely painful to him, and Miss Bowen accepts the fact as ground enough for his behavior and charm. He has no feeling for expansive possibilities in his temperament. Though he complains of his adoptive parents, he offers no evidence of mistreatment. He resents instead their permissiveness and tameness—they weep for Shelley, drowned nearby. He asserts without sense of contradiction the child's unlimited claim to support for being himself and the wish for an authority to tell him what to do. For him, sensitiveness represents neither guide nor reproach, but intensity. It simply exists—and wants. (He does not consider, for example, difficulties in meeting a mother for the first time at the age of ten.) In Leopold, Miss Bowen brings a possibility latent in the modern novel out into the open: sensitivity and will may combine in the same character without a saving exit into art, expatriation, sympathy, or humor.

Significantly, the novel chooses to quarrel directly with humor. Already other first-rank British novelists were beginning to meet similar contradictions with comedy; but Miss Bowen does not mean to reduce her values because they are in trouble. For her, comedy avoids the barricade by distracting attention from the problem. It reconciles *conventionally*. So humor is literally foreign to Leopold:

> *The Strand Magazine* had looked a gold mine to Leopold, but its trafficky cover and glazed smell turned out to be richer than its contents. Frowning with scornful mystification, but still reading, he walked, when the women had gone, across to the sofa, where he lay over the magazine on one elbow, turning over the pages with quick brown hands as though he had England here. He pored over the photographs of statesmen and battleships, the drawings of frank girls, butlers, sports-cars and oak-beamed room. The funny stories and pictures brought him to a full stop. His passionate lack of humour was native and untutored; no one had taught him that curates, chars, duchesses, spinsters are enough, in England, to make anyone smile. The magazine perplexed Leopold with its rigid symbolism, Martian ideology.

As will appear, a more knowledgeable hostility to humor had activated his father and provided the sympathetic base for the affair which produced Leopold. He is the seventh son of a seventh son.

All these symptoms form only the periphery of Miss Bowen's sensitivity in action. Skirmishing constitutes the center. The age of ten is, after all, far from being the bottom of the well; Leopold has a great deal more social awareness than some of his behavior suggests. He does know that kicking and screaming can no longer control situations. So he has developed the ultimate practical mode of making his moment-by-moment feelings correspond with their expression; his self-centeredness goes as far as it can without collapsing the social situation entirely. His most telling scenes develop a strategy of skirmish—the art by which Miss Bowen's characters manage to express their intensity without giving up the benefits of civilized intercourse. Conflict flares up over a delicate point, takes sudden turns, threatens to become worse, breaks off suddenly, may end in truce. Leopold works this tactic thoroughly on Henrietta, the little girl with the correct response to loss of a mother:

> "Oh," she said, "she just said your mother lived somewhere else."
> "Somewhere else from where?"
> "From you."
> Leopold stopped rocking, bumped down on his heels, and stood disconcertingly still, his pig-pupilled eyes, set close in, transfixing her so

intently that she thought for a moment he had a cast in them. He said: "So you thought that was funny?"

"Yes, I did," she said boldly. "I did think that was funny."

"If you told that to other people, would they think it was funny?"

"Well, they wouldn't *laugh*, if that's what you mean by funny. I suppose they might think it was rather sort of *peculiar*. But then I promised not to."

"Tell other people?"

"Mmm."

"It's not a secret," said Leopold haughtily.

"Oh, Miss Fisher said it was."

"Did she tell you not to ask me things?"

"How do you mean?" she said, flustered.

Leopold smiled to himself. "She told me not to answer, what*ever* you said. She hopes I won't say anything."

"Then ought you to?" said Henrietta, reproving.

"I don't have to be obedient to Miss Fisher. It's not my fault if you are here while I talk. Look–now your mother's dead so you can't possibly see her, do you still mean to love her, or is that no good now? When you want to love her, what do you do, remember her? But if you couldn't remember her, but heard you could see her, would you enjoy loving her more, or less?"

"I don't see what you mean," said Henrietta, distracted–in fact in quite a new kind of pain. She saw only too well that this inquisition had no bearing on Henrietta at all, that Leopold was not even interested in hurting, and was only tweaking her petals off or her wings off with the intention of exploring himself. . . .

"You see, you and I are just opposites. I *don't* remember my mother, but *shall* see her again." He watched Henrietta closely, to see, as though on himself, the effect of this.

The effect was odd. Henrietta turned down her eyes, smoothed her dress on her knees, and remarked with the utmost primness: "You must be very glad: no wonder you are excited. I am excited, going to Mentone." . . . Her sex provided these gestures, showing how bored she got with someone else's insistence on their own personality. Her dread of Leopold gave way to annoyance. Already she never met anyone without immediately wanting to rivet their thought on herself, and with this end in view looked forward to being grown up.

Even the adjectives and adverbs suggest the speed of these turns—"disconcertingly," "boldly," "haughtily," "flustered," then "reproving," "distracted," "utmost primness." Defensiveness calls up agility and resourcefulness, and can be almost simultaneously aggressive and fearful.

In the first section this little scene of cross-purposes epitomizes Leopold and sets up his disappointment, but in itself shows what Miss Bowen wants to and can do. The strangeness comes from the old game of making the children little adults with all of experience except a central drive blocked off. Their getting on each other's nerves provides immediate action, but in the structure, they separate externally elements in the mother's conflict. Henrietta has already combined her sense of self with the accepted modes of expressing it; Leopold has been miraculously insulated from anything except his sense of self.

Dramatically, the scenes in the Paris house, the home of raw emotion, photograph childhood sensitivity at a given instant and furnish a print for comparison with the motion picture of the mother's story. They define the check point as a mixture of antagonisms and yearnings, eager to be translated into acts corresponding to their intensity. Civilized living modifies this base into a barely controlled volatility which makes communication difficult but exciting. Karen's story shows how the warmth in this mixture leads to expressing the anger—and then seeking to regain the warmth.

Miss Bowen's uneven handling of the middle section locates its dramatic center. The shadowy men contrast bluntly. Karen should marry the absent, acceptable diplomat. She takes as lover a rootless, mother-ridden Frenchman who, though present, often seems not to be. But this is a woman's world; its possibilities and antagonisms fall within that frame. Karen loves and fights her aunt, her mother, and her girl friend—all of them epitomes of available feminine roles.

Karen's sensitivity at the beginning shows development beyond Leopold's. Instead of yearning for a vaguely conceived rescuer, she identifies quickly with other women whose predicaments arouse her fears for herself. Her sympathies act as a force for self-recognition—specializing in unpleasantness. For her, being a woman means that she must wait—for her fiancé's return, in this case—and get tired of it. Because her fiancé does not promise to fulfil her need for the compelling, she identifies with the family legend of passivity, Aunt

Violet—Miss Bowen's version of Forster's wise, dying mother—and looks into the restlessness behind acceptance:

> "One sometimes wishes one had done more," she said.
> "But you being you is enough for anybody."
> Aunt Violet took this with such unmoved stillness and sadness that Karen realized how often it must have been said, and what a stone for bread the remark was. There had been her two happy husbands—apart from everyone else. Letting go of Karen's arm, she sat down on the parapet with her back to the view and began to pull rather helplessly at an ivy stem. "I meant, selfishly," she said. "I was thinking more of myself."
> This was like hearing a picture you had always loved to look at, dearer than a "great" picture, sigh inside its frame. That it should be less sustaining to be than to see Aunt Violet struck you with remorse. . . . All these years she had stood by, uncritically smiling, had she been wanting really, like other women, to be the heart of things, to *be* what was going on? . . . Aunt Violet had spoken of Karen's marriage as, simply, a pleasant plan for tomorrow: having been so much a woman all through her own life, had she hoped her niece might be something more? . . . All your youth, you want to have your greatness taken for granted; when you find it taken for granted, you are unnerved.

Some critics have thought that Aunt Violet's death shocks Karen into outbreak, but actually death merely gives authority to a shock already fully felt. Faced with the monumental object-ness of her social role, she tells Aunt Violet that the world needs a revolution. Aunt Violet thinks it would be bad for Uncle Bill.

Karen recognizes, in other words, the crucial difficulty in the ideal of passive sensitivity: those who do not make their own choices have others make them. The grooved lines of her mother's life stand before her as "their" plan for her. This clear view of her own nature drives her to seek intensity. Lacking an Energizing Principle from outside, she draws on the adolescent reservoir. Her affair with Max tries desperately to recreate feelings from the days when she had boarded at the house in Paris.

> He was the first man I noticed, she thought now.
> She thought, young girls like the excess of any quality. Without knowing, they want to suffer, to suffer they must exaggerate; they like

to have loud chords struck on them. Loving art better than life, they need men to be actors; only an actor moves them, with his telling smile, undomestic, out of touch with the everyday that they dread. They love to enjoy love as a system of doubts and shocks. They are right: not seeking husbands yet, they have no reason to see love socially. This natural fleshly protest against good taste is broken down soon enough; their natural love of the cad is outwitted by their mothers.

Karen's voice merges with the narrator's to say: life is not drama. However, for her the wish to make it drama is life. But her vision of a decisive blow against a low-keyed authority—and against nothingness—fails to recognize how far the grotesques who represent it have got inside Karen herself. Even Max is the anticlimax to an earlier dream, though he does fit the demand by being genuinely complex and intense. "What Naomi said was true, he *did* mind everything; a harsh edge you sometimes felt in his manner being chagrin, perhaps, at minding so much." The affair develops through a shared negative: the two fall in love skirmishing about a sense of humor. Leopold, the intense child, does not comprehend it at all; Max, the intense adult, opposes it on principle.

Max brought out his cigarette-case, opening it thoughtfully. "But how should it waste time to be eighteen? Any year of one's life has got to be lived. Five years hence, you may dislike what you are now."

"I may. But not so much."

"You were more serious then—will you smoke?"

"After tea, thank you—to be serious is absurd; it is useless: what can one do?"

"So you gave that up, since eighteen?"

"I had no sense of humour then."

"Oh, good God!" said Max sharply.

"Why?"

"What you say is deadly. Must everything be funny?"

"One's life is."

"No wonder you get on nicely."

Max identifies humor as society's weapon against uncompromising self-expression—and he will not compromise. Karen does not want to.

The issue also defines the sister-rivalry. Naomi offers her man a

Nurse. She works to comfort Max when he does not want comfort. So she comes down inevitably on the wrong side:

"I think that humour is English courage," she said.
"Ostrich courage," said Max.
"Please," said Naomi, "do not be anti-English—Karen, please eat a bun."
Max ate two mouthfuls of the bun, then said: "Humour is like a silly vow of virginity."
"Max was saying," said Karen, "how well I get on these days."
"You should be glad," said Max, "I wish I got on as well." . . .
"But chaff is English, Max: you are being jolly," she said.
"Max thinks too much of ambition," Naomi said, like a loving young governess.
"So does Karen; she is ambitious to live."
"What old friends we are," said Naomi, "telling each other truths." She refilled the teapot happily.

By comparison, the affair itself is conventionally soggy, with an occasional good touch like the evasive tête-à-tête on French kings:

Outside, the street, empty, reeled in midday sun; the glare was reflected in on the gold-and-brown wall opposite; side by side in the emptying restaurant, they surrounded themselves with wars, treaties, persecutions, strategic marriages, campaigns, reforms, successions and violent deaths. History is unpainful, memory does not cloud it; you join the emphatic lives of the long dead. May we give the future something to talk about.

But this strong wish to see drama break through the daily often threatens the author's control. At best Max has a good deal of daydream in him, and a just-before-bedtime scene turns into unintentional absurdity:

He made her face inland, where the High Street lights rose steadily through the rain and windows studded the hill where many people would sleep tonight.
"I am supposing," he said, "that you know what you are doing. It will be too late when you ask yourself: What have I done?"

The real force of the affair comes from another direction. Karen has asked, what exciting event can be made to happen before the pleasant prison closes in forever? And she has answered, in fact if not in words, that she can express her anger. She plans a one-night revolution that will demonstrate her feeling against Aunt Violet, her mother, and Naomi. So the powerful part of the love story shows her confusion when the most drastic blow she can imagine fails to correspond to the need.

I am let back, safe, too safe; no one will ever know. Naomi and my mother, who would die if they knew, will never know. What they never know will soon never have been. They will never know. I shall die like Aunt Violet wondering what else there was; from this there is no escape for me after all. Max lies beside me, but Naomi sat on my bed in the dark; she was there first and will never go away. I have done what she does not know, so I have not done what I dread. Max said at Boulogne: "One cannot simply act." I thought he meant, must not; what it meant was, cannot. People must hope so much when they tear streets up and fight at barricades. But, whoever wins, the streets are laid again and the trams start running again. One hopes too much of destroying things. If revolutions do not fail, they fail you.

In the logic of the novel, however, Max need be little more than a handy man so long as the woman's relationships seem intense. Naomi—present throughout, colorless, dominated by her sadistic mother, suddenly and amazingly beloved—approaches caricature of the passive, self-sacrificing ideal of woman, the symbiotic prisoner. It is against this ideal that Karen strikes—and in its nature that Naomi helps her. She hands over Max to test her own worthiness to be loved. And not Max's death, but conciliation with Naomi and the mother occupies Karen after the affair. She argues with herself that she did not go to spite Naomi but went because Naomi could never be happy until the threat of love between the two intense figures had been removed. In the last part of the story Karen achieves reconciliation with both mother and friend.

But peace costs. The self can apparently make no meaningful assertion against the symbiotic "plan." Max realizes that in rebelling he has only been fulfilling his adopted mother's scheme, and commits suicide. Karen proves unable to resist her mother's privacy-respecting kindliness. But Miss Bowen sees two sides. The wish that dominates the novel—for mere restless self-expression to make a noise in the world—does work out in the final section. Not only does Max kill himself, but the one-night stand produces Leopold, a far more formidable revolutionary. The shock of his birth kills Karen's mother. Naomi spends ten years feuding with a mother who represents grotesquely the destroying side of the relationship—as Karen's represents the indulging and guiding. The public school diplomat knowingly marries the unwed mother. Best of all, Karen's continuing dissatisfaction forces him to "act on the child's scale" and kidnap Leopold. Karen has made a grander mess than she could have imagined. Restless anger, the novel proves, does not just eventuate into fretfulness. But Karen's inability to accept as life itself the process which led to her outbreak incapacitates her and leaves her on the verge of collapse, veering between acceptance and rejection of the consequences embodied in Leopold. The success of *The House in Paris* does not come from resolving conflict, but from identifying it—defining a meaningful sensibility, its processes, and its barriers.

In its own terms *The House in Paris* downs the Moravia threat. Much of life may be tamed and predictable, but a source of indestructible unselfconscious drama remains—the symbiotic relationships built in before the threat becomes known. These may lead to confusion, which at least has its own excitement, and can lead to withdrawal. The boy and the mother show the same alternating rhythm of wait-and-attack. Waiting is unbearable and attacking, in impatience to devour, turns the attacker back to his symbols of safety. Still, so long as a child cries when his mother does not come, symbiotic drama will stand on the firm soil of the "natural." Life will alternate meaningfully between trying to break free from and to rejoin.

Miss Bowen leaves the novel open at the end. She does see a possibility—not of resolution but of continuing productive tension. The diplomat, though he may be acting on the child's scale in taking Leopold illegally, means to make an adult out of him. Ray not only inherits the shaping-up process, but believes in it enough to put energy into it. While doing his best to make friends, he plans ahead:

So they walked across the big space between the barriers and the buffet staircase, the exits: Ray head down, Leopold looking round him, twirling like a camellia Henrietta's cockade. Leopold took a step and a half to each of Ray's; when anyone barged their way he swerved in to Ray instinctively. Ray strode like a robber with one babe through a wood. Their inappropriateness to each other made people stare. Leopold had in blazing gold round his cap the fierce name of a battle ship. His silence fell in with Ray's as imperfectly as his step—he seemed to be buoyed along.

In the hall outside the turnstile it was quieter. Ray slowed up. "I'm sorry," he said, "I can't stand the noise in there."

"I rather liked it," said Leopold.

(The devil you did. You will notice, we talk where I can talk. You will not quote Mme Fisher, you will not kick me in taxis, you will not shout in houses where they are ill. You will wear a civilian cap, not snub little girls and not get under my feet. There will be many things that you will not like. There are many things that I do not like about you.)

"What I was trying to say," Ray went on aloud, "was: I must telephone—yes, to Versailles, to your mother. She may be beginning to wonder why I am not back. Then I shall get a drink. Then we might get something to eat."

Since no reader can imagine Leopold abandoning his strategy of skirmish and surrendering, prolonged tension is certain. *If* productive too, it might unite in some as yet undefinable way self-expression and social submission. At least a new cycle has begun.

The House in Paris takes hold by fits and starts. *The Death of the Heart,* which has a claim to greatness, sustains its vision of adult wishes challenged by the standard of adolescent ones. Only an exceptional reader, however, can resist the powerful sympathy with the young girl and its pull to make the novel into a melodrama, with the defensive and self-absorbed adults the villains. Anyone who did so would in fact miss the force of the book. A critic can add little to Miss Bowen's accomplishment there but can hope to increase respect for the total meaning—to define what happens while we are sympathizing with the supersensitive heroine.

Few readers have taken seriously Miss Bowen's word that she was writing about grown-ups and drew in the adolescent for contrast. Yet there is no reason not to. *The Death of the Heart* develops, not as an opposition between youth and middle age, but as a double action. The adults' story envelops the adolescent's and the two interweave, Portia to cause an attack of conscience and the adults to make her feel unsupported in a trying time. On a sheer statistical basis, the girl's consciousness dominates only about half the book. She seems to prevail more thoroughly because she is single-minded and because we are often being made aware *of* her when we are not being made aware *through* her. She incarnates the adult problem of sensibility become conscience—and appears almost solely as this through the first of the three sections. What the "innocence" she seems so "ruthless" in behalf of amounts to is a crucial question, but Miss Bowen does not hurry to tell us. Instead she shows its effects.

Probably no one reading the opening pages for the first time will suspect that the novel is not about Anna. She appears as a retired innocent who has built her defenses around marriage. Though they seem less solid than the house by the park, they work after a fashion. Her account of the young sister-in-law to a friend epitomizes two of them:

> "In ways, she's more like an animal. I made that room so pretty before she came. I had no idea how blindly she was going to live. Now I hardly ever go in there; it's simply discouraging."
>
> St. Quentin said rather vaguely: "How annoying for you!" He had screwed round his head inside the folds of his scarf, to consider Anna with abstract attentiveness. For she had this little way of travestying herself and her self-pities, till the view she took of herself, when she was with him, seemed to concert exactly with the view he took of her sex. She wrote herself down like this, obligingly, to suit him, with a touch of friendly insolence. He saw in this overacting a kind of bluffing, which made him like Anna, whom he liked much, more. Her smoothness of contour, her placid derisive smile, her way of drawing her chin in when she did smile, often made him think of a sardonic bland white duck.

Anna's use of humor differs sharply from the resistance of the intense, earnest characters in *The House in Paris*. For her it means, not a conventional obscurantism, but a slightly burlesqued self-recognition. Second, she sees Portia in the room as a figure in a *scene*—whose use baffles the designer.

The double vision here amounts merely to applying Anna's

concept of herself. She has made her whole imposing house a theater and cast herself as the star. Presumably low-sexed, she wants to bask in affection while keeping men off her quilts. Since the failure of her "natural" course, the one Portia will try, she has turned to spiritualizing furniture—estheticism domesticated—and made her drawing room the stage for a witty public personality, with an invited audience of three. Her manner represents a *learned* way of getting along with people whom she needs but would also rather not see. "Life militates against the seclusion we seek . . . in the long run we may not choose our company." So she feels eyes watching her, snaps at the audience, wants total approval, believes she is not getting it and does not deserve it. The discrepancy between the public personality and the doubt gives Portia power over Anna and activates the paranoia that makes up the other side of her exhibitionism.

But what will Portia see if she does have the second sight Anna credits her with and judge if she is in fact a legally installed judge? What are Anna and her husband doing wrong? Or, to put the issue as it appears, what does Anna blame herself for? Essentially, for being herself. Practically, for a list of errors. Not having married the ideal man. Not liking children. Not being approved of by them. Not wanting to see people after having invited them. Not having talent or wide interests. Not being passionate about her husband. For being cool, witty, inhibited, and suspicious—defensive instead of warm, outgoing, trusting, maternal. For being a self-absorbed wife and stepmother instead of the tender mistress whom adolescent imagination had told her she could be.

This masochistic drive toward self-recognition ties into the purposes of Anna's theatricality, but in itself proves unbearable without a more objective view. In the long run Anna's best defense—her effective will to orientation—rests on her ability to listen to St. Quentin. Judged as talk, their long, sometimes stilted conversations are improbable. Judged as a probable character, St. Quentin is impossible. True, he fits a recognizable type—the artist who has left living to his servants—but he is primarily a function rather than a person. He comes on stage when needed and gets off the moment he has said his lines. When he materializes to Portia as the devil in the last act he claims to see no motive for bringing her knowledge. Significantly, he appears at moments of upset. The novel begins with news of the damning diary brought to him, introduces the drawing room scene with him at the tea table, faces Portia with him when she has lost her lover, keeps him late at dinner while Anna and Thomas try to locate the runaway, and gives him the curtain speech.

St. Quentin is the disloyal friend who sees through the act—almost Anna's double. He can interrupt her make-believe with unpleasant realities.

When the door shut, St. Quentin said: "Well, we might do better than that. *You* did not do well, Anna—raving about those bears."

"You know what made me."

"And how silly you were on the telephone."

Anna put down her cup and giggled. . . .

"All the same, I wonder where she got that distinction. From what you say, her mother was quite a mess."

"Oh, the Quaynes have it: one sees it in Thomas, really," Anna said—then, palpably losing interest, curled up at her end of the sofa. Raising her arms, she shook her sleeves back and admired her own wrists. On one she wore a small soundless diamond watch. St. Quentin, not noticing not being noticed, went on: "High foreheads suggest violence to me. . . . Was that Eddie, just now?"

"On the telephone? Yes. Why?"

"We know Eddie is silly, but why must you talk to him in such a silly way. Even if Portia *were* here. 'I'm not here; I never am here.' *Tcha!*" said St. Quentin. "Not that it's my affair."

But he can also interrupt her self-contempt for a fairer view—and for this she needs him. Her talks with him become almost talks with herself, but a clear, detached, analytical self, freed from reproach as an inadequate wife and mother.

At the end St. Quentin articulates the theory of the lunatic giant which explains what excitement and justification adult life can hope for—and what the adults have been working to do when Portia believes them to be doing nothing.

"Clearly not," said St. Quentin. "Look where we all three are. Utterly disabused, and yet we can't decide anything. This evening the pure in heart have simply got us on toast. And look at the fun she has—she lives in a world of heroes. Who are we to be sure they're as phony as we all think? If the world's really a stage, there must be some big parts. All she asks is to walk on at the same time. And how right she is really—failing the big character, better (at least, arguably) the big flop than the small neat man who has more or less come off. Not that there is, really, one neat unhaunted man. I swear that each of us keeps, battened down inside himself, a sort of lunatic giant—impossible socially, but full-scale—and that it's the knockings and batterings we sometimes hear in each other that keeps our intercourse from utter banality. Portia hears these the whole time; in fact she hears nothing else. Can we wonder she looks so goofy most of the time?"

Achieving this controlled volatility without sacrificing the drawing room has been Anna's *raison d'être*.

Other novelists have created sensitive girls in Portia's range at least, if not equal to her. Miss Bowen's claim as a major novelist rests on her added ability to project her vision of living as controlled volatility. Though she regularly shows youthful sensitivity moving toward trauma, her real question appears at the end: after disappointment, what? In her answer, the individual meets defeat in his all-or-nothing effort by stylizing himself into a "realistic," acceptable character which partly corresponds to the emotional self. But the unexpressed parts keep raiding at the edges and breaking through the "theatrical" pose. This mixture meeting others' mixtures creates a conflict of lunatic giants in the drawing room. The problem becomes to exercise the giant enough to provide excitement without allowing him to take over and disable the personality.

Practice presents difficulties. Anna's theatrical temperament has found no adequate drama. As playwright of the town house, she envisions only keeping the scene going with the same cast. Contretemps and occasional epiphanies occur, but the lack of drive to kill the usurper or forestall the future or marry the prince limits excitement. Anna's reverse has inhibited not only action but imagination. She avoids even thinking of activities she does not do well. Her theatricality thus embodies a neurotic response. Probably better ways exist to handle the problems, but Anna's half-adequate mode has meant developing to the highest possible skill Leopold's knack for skirmish. People invade her otherwise empty privacy: they disturb her with a drive for intimacy greater than she wants. But if they did not do so she would be miserable. Having stabilized the foundations of life by marrying Thomas, she is now alert to find raiders whom at some point she means to repel—but not too soon. She knows how far she can go before fear or anger overrides pleasurable excitement. When the alarums become loud enough, she summons her till then idle resources to throw back the invader, but calls off pursuit quickly. She does not want him to go away—only to continue with an understanding of who rules.

These skirmishes differ from those in *The House in Paris* in the professional finish of the performance. A brief scene gets in "natural" feelings, social rules, experience, rehearsed offenses, defenses in depth, outbreaks against the rules, and sudden improvised responses. The survivor has proved his adequacy to the perils of civilized living. The difficulty lies in finding a suitable opposite, for only one who touches Anna's unexpressed emotions will do. Her ego seeking and meeting its beloved opponents constitutes "The World" of the first section. Portia's hostility gains its power by making the ego self-conscious and self-questioning—holding a mirror to the learned defense and making Anna "overact."

Anna has filled the gap between early love and actual marriage with spare bachelors. She already has St. Quentin and Eddie, the captive *enfant terrible.* The first dramatized action brings in Major Brutt, a superb character superbly intergrated into the structure. He arouses Anna's confused resentment of change—both as the aging process itself and as shifting social value. Major Brutt personifies the awkward man—out of touch with the modern world, by-passed by time—but as a war hero and friend of her old lover he is Pidgeon returned in degraded form. He also reenforces the diary's reproach to civilized adults: for Major Brutt's awkwardness consists in not having learned to put a theatrical barrier between feeling and behavior. He *is* what he seems—a decent human being, decorated for bravery, experienced in colonial management, and unemployable. Modern commercial London wants clever, flexible, unscrupulous young men. "Makes of men date, like makes of cars; Major Brutt was a 1914-1918 model: there was now no market for that make." Finally, Miss Bowen knows that shocks are not sought and administered in private. Instead of the selected audience she cherishes, Anna has to conduct her reevaluation of the past before the two people who intensify most her devotion to it: Portia, whose appearance has already brought back too many memories, and her husband, the grumbler who stands in Pidgeon's place.

Miss Bowen's skill with the initial meeting depends on sketching divergent reactions while keeping the main tension on Anna.

Anna and Portia, glum for opposing reasons, waited in the foyer while Thomas went for a taxi. For those minutes, in the mirror-refracted glare, they looked like workers with tomorrow ahead. Then someone looked hard at Anna, looked back, looked again, registered indecision, raised his hat and returned, extending a large anxious delighted hand. "*Miss Fellowes!*"

"Major Brutt! How extraordinary this is!"

"To think of my running into *you*. It's extraordinary!"

"Especially as I am not even Miss Fellowes, now—I mean, I am Mrs. Quayne."

"Do excuse me—"

"How could you possibly know? . . . I'm so glad we've met again."

"It must be nine years plus. What a great evening we had—you and Pidgeon and I—" He stopped quickly: a look of doubt came into his eyes.

Portia stood by, meanwhile. "You must meet my sister-in-law," said Anna at once: "Major Brutt—Miss Quayne." She went on, not with quite so much assurance: "I hope you enjoyed the Marx brothers?"

"Well, to tell you the truth—I knew this place in the old days; I'd never heard of these chaps, but I thought I would drop in. I can't stay I—"

"Oh, you find them lowering, too?"

"I daresay they're up to date, but they're not what I call funny."

"Yes," Anna said, "they are up to date for a bit." Major Brutt's eyes travelled from Anna's smiling and talking mouth, via the camellia fastened under her chin, to the upturned brim of Portia's hat—where it stayed. "I hope," he said to Portia, "*you* have enjoyed yourself." Anna said: "No, I don't think she did, much—Oh, look, my husband has got a taxi. Do come back with us: we must all have a drink. . . . Oh, Thomas, this is Major Brutt." . . . As they walked two-and-two to the taxi, Anna said to Thomas out of the side of her mouth: "Friend of Pidgeon's—we once had an evening with him."

"*Did* we? I don't— When?"

"Not you and I, silly: I and Pidgeon. Years ago. But he really must have a drink."

"Naturally," said Thomas. Putting on no expression, he steered her by one elbow through the the crowd at the door—for whenever you come out, you never avoid the Rush. In the taxi, infected by Major Brutt, Thomas sat bolt upright, looking hard at everything through the window in a military way. Whereas, Major Brutt, beside him, kept glancing timidly at the ladies' faces flowering in fur collars in the dark of the cab. He remarked once or twice: "I must say, this is an amazing coincidence." Portia sat twisted sideways, so that her knees should not annoy Thomas. Oh, the charm of this accident, this meeting in a sumptuous place—this was one of those polished encounters she and Irene spied on when they had peeped into a Palace Hotel. As the taxi crawled into Windsor Terrace, she exclaimed, all lit up: "Oh, thank you for taking me!"

"Thomas only said: "Pity you didn't like it."

"Oh, but I did like being there."

Major Brutt said firmly: "Those four chaps were a blot—This is where we stop? Good."

"Yes, we stop here," Anna said, resignedly getting out.

The bachelor's need for family warmth, the husband's tired annoyance, and Anna's second thoughts strain the social compromise:

It was admirably hot and bright in the study—all the same, indoors the thing became too far-fetched. Major Brutt looked about unassumingly, as though he would like to say "What a nice place you've got here," but was not sure if he knew them well enough. Anna switched lamps on and off with a strung-up air, while Thomas, having said: "Scotch, Irish or brandy?" filled up the glasses on the tray. Anna could not speak—she thought of her closed years: seeing Robert Pidgeon, now, as a big fly in the amber of this decent man's memory. Her own memory was all blurs and seams. She started dreading the voice in which she could only say: "Do you hear anything of him? How much do you see him, these days?" Or else, "Where is he now, do you know?" Magnetism to that long-ago evening—on which Robert and she must have been perfect lovers—had made her bring back this man, this born third, to her home. Now Thomas, by removing himself to a different plane, made her feel she had done a thoroughly awkward thing. The pause was too long: it smote her to see Major Brutt look, uncertain, into his whisky, clearly feeling ought he not, then, to drink this? Ought he not to be here?

Otherwise, he could wish for nothing better. . . . He was the man back from somewhere, out of touch with London, dying to go somewhere after a show. He would be glad to go on almost anywhere. . . . Major Brutt was the sort of man who, like a ghost with no beat, hesitates round the West End about midnight–not wanting to buy a girl, not wanting to drink alone, not wanting to go back to Kensington, hoping something may happen.

The mixture of consciousness, social cliché, shifting point of view, and quick authorial comment shows Miss Bowen near her best. In less than two paragraphs she uses the *habit* of skirmish—of guarded relationships—to set up a clash with disorganized defenses, and all without a major hostility on any side. Presently Major Brutt has Thomas yawning over the tired old love story, Anna overacting, and Portia delighted at hearing about Pidgeon—alive and well elsewhere.

No previous experience is required, however, to feel Major Brutt's moral presence. His honesty, kindliness, and superfluousness haunt the learned response at variance with the wish for empty privacy. A litte later, his unannounced visit brings the shock even to Thomas, the well-insulated husband.

This Saturday afternoon Thomas, home from the office, sat at his study table, drawing cats on the blotter, waiting for Anna to come back from lunch. . . . When he heard the bell ring he looked up forbiddingly (though there was just a chance Anna might have forgotten her key), listened, frowned, put whiskers on a cat, then looked up again. If it had been her, she would ring two or three times. The ring, however, did not repeat itself–though it lingered uneasily in the air. Saturday made it unlikely that this could be a parcel. That it could be a caller did not, at his worst moment, enter Thomas' head. Callers were unheard of at Windsor Terrace. They had been eliminated; they simply did not occur. The Quaynes' home life was as much their private life as though their marriage had been illicit. . . .

In the seconds before Thomas came to his door, Major Brutt may have realised that this was a better house to be brought back to in triumph than to make one's way into under one's own steam. While he looked up the draughtless stairs behind the white arches, some aspirations faded out of his mind. He glanced at the console table, but did not like to put down his hat yet: he stood sturdily, doubtfully. Then a step just inside that known door made him re-animate like a dog: his moustache broadened a little, ready for a smile.

"Oh, *you:* splendid!" said Thomas—he held his hand out, flat open, with galvanised heartiness. "I thought I heard someone's voice. Look here, I'm so sorry you—"

"Look here, I do hope I'm not—"

"Oh, good God, no! I was simply waiting for Anna. She's out at some sort of lunch—you know how long those things take."

Major Brutt had no idea—it had seemed to him more near tea-time. He said: "They must be great places for talk," as Thomas, incompletely resigned, got him into the study, with rather too much fuss. The room now held fumy heavy afternoon dusk—Thomas had been asleep in here for an hour before unscrewing his pen, opening the blotter and sitting down with some of his papers out. "Everyone talks," said Thomas. "I can't think, can you, how they keep it up." He looked at his cats with nostalgia, shut the blotter, swept some papers into a drawer and shut the drawer with a click. That was that, he seemed to say, I *was* busy, but never mind. Meanwhile, Major Brutt pulled his trousers up at the knees and lowered himself into an armchair.

Without intending anything, Major Brutt forces self-recognition on Thomas:

Then he gave Major Brutt a quick, undecided mean look. One had clearly got the idea this Brutt was out of a job: had he not said something about irons in the fire? That meant he was after something. That was why he had come. Now, no doubt, he had something soft in Quayne and Merrett's in view—he would not be the first old buffer who had.

Then, Thomas had a crisis of self-repugnance. Twitching his head away, with a shamefaced movement, from that block of integrity in the armchair, he saw how business had built him, Thomas, into a false position, a state of fortification odious, when he noticed it, to himself.

Only a superior talent could have done the shading and shifting of emotion in these scenes, but Anna's skirmishes with Eddie get even nearer the heart of the theatricality-and-neurosis problem. Major Brutt brings home to Anna and even Thomas emotional continuity as a fact. But Eddie, the third bachelor who fills out the incompleteness of Anna's married stasis, gives her a chance to express herself dramatically in the present. As a professional *enfant terrible,* he acts out feelings that Anna suppresses. His volatility not only provides excitement in itself, but offers the challenge of taming him as the objective correlative of taming the self. And Eddie is just tamable enough and just slippery enough to be the perfect opponent in Anna's game.

The scene that introduces their relation leads directly to his taking up Portia—and the inevitable rivalry between married woman and girl—but Eddie does more than link the adolescent and adult stories. He is a magnificent creation in his own right. Critics have pointed to theatricality as his difficulty, but they might better have said that his difficulties cause his theatricality. His troubles differ from Anna's in intensity and motive. He has one foot in the adult world and one in the child's. So he plays up his "cosmic black moods, which were the things he was principally noted for," but "something abstract and lasting about the residue of his anger had been known, once or twice, to command respect." His action, which makes acceptable emotions that in raw form could never be, has far less margin for error than Anna's. If she fails to merge "policy" and feeling, a quarrel may ensue. If Eddie fails, he loses his livelihood; he is literally surviving on the ability to make his personality the objectification of others' angers. He has discovered early that he can represent confused youth attractively to older women: by enacting his own hostility and self-pity, he appeals to theirs. And he can make his gratitude felt:

> Anna had never cared to be the romantic woman, but now Eddie became her first troubadour. He lent himself, gladly and quickly, or appeared to lend himself, to Anna's illusions about living. He did more: by his poetic appreciation he created a small world of art round her. The vanities of which she was too conscious, the honesties to which she compelled herself, even the secrets she had never told him existed inside a crystal they both looked at—not only existed but were beautiful. On Anna, he had the inverse of the effect Portia's diary was to produce later.

But Eddie survives by something deeper than acting and flattery. He can shift just rapidly enough from hostility to gaiety to get under other people's skins and become an indispensable annoyance.

At the very moment when Anna has tamed him by getting him a job, he can put her on the *qui vive* again:

Eddie brought one hand out of his pocket and pinched a heavy moiré fold of the curtain by which he stood. This half-conscious act was hostile: Anna heard the moiré creak between his finger and thumb.

She did not for a moment doubt that in his own mind Eddie was travestying the scene. Yes, and he showed her he felt he was bought goods, with "Quayne and Merrett" pasted across his back. She said in a light little voice: "I'm glad you're pleased about this."

"Five pounds a week, just for being good and clever! How could I not be pleased!"

"I'm afraid they may want just a little more than that. You really will work, I hope?"

"To do you credit?"

Then, because she did not reply, there was a pause. Eddie swung round at her with his most persuasive, most meaningless smile. "Do come and look at the lake! I don't suppose I shall ever look at it with you in the morning again: I shall be much too busy." To show how immaterial this was, Anna good-temperedly came to join him. They stood side by side in the window and she folded her arms. But Eddie, with the affectionate nonchalance of someone whose nearness does not matter, put a hand on her elbow. "How much I owe you!"

"I never know what you mean."

Eddie's eyes ran over her doubtful face—the light seemed to concentrate in their brilliant shadows; his pupils showed their pin-points of vacuum. "Marvellous," he said, "to have a firm in your pocket."

"When did you first think I might fix this up for you?"

"Of course it occurred to me. But the idea of advertising was so repellent, and to tell you the truth, Anna, I'm so vain, I kept hoping I might get something better. You're not angry, are you, darling? You shouldn't judge people by how they have to behave."

"Your friends say you always fall on your feet."

The remark was another thing that he would never forgive her. After a stonelike minute he said: "If I have to know people who ruin me, I mean to get something out of it."

"I don't understand. Ruin you? Who does?"

"You do, and your whole lot. You make a monkey out of me, and God knows what else worse. I'm ashamed to go back home."

"I don't think we can have done you much harm, Eddie. You must still be quite rugged, while you can be so rude."

"Oh, I can be rude all right."

"Then what is upsetting you?"

"Oh, I don't know, Anna," he said, in a burst of childishness. "We seem to be on an absurd track. Please forgive me—I always stay too long. I came round to thank you for my lovely job; I came here intending to be so normal—Oh, look, there's a gull sitting on a deck chair."

My case for Miss Bowen's double vision rests even more on the quality of these early scenes than on their quantity—hence the liberal quotation. But, if Portia is a figure in an equation rather than a protagonist, what does she do for the novel? First of all, she gives it a living vision of something better than Anna's skirmishes. However hard to define, this vista means enveloping another personality in one's own vague dream of unity—a nonphysical union of souls, without rivalry and antagonism. Portia's vignette for the ideal is her daydream of Eddie sleeping in a hut, his head in her lap. There mother is no rival, Eddie offers no opposing personality, no one laughs at the fragile relationship. Even the imaginary mother who would advise on means and sympathize with defeats is superfluous. Portia sees love as union with an only slightly different self. Fearful of attack, she instinctively attracts a young man who wants to patronize her childishness and will not make love to her. Portia's vision of excitement is the moment of *waiting* to be kissed. In practice, after three pages of quibbling, she has to kiss Eddie—and scares him.

So writing about Eddie in a diary is more fun than being with him. Portia wants all life to consist of tender, potent quiescence and creates turmoil around her because it is instead made up of interruptions. The teacher catches her reading the love letter, Anna finds the diary, the earthy girl's twitching thumb in the movie house dramatizes active sex, rivalries break out at the seashore, and Eddie insists on talking about his "despair." Portia compounds her difficulties by upsetting the possible relationship in upholding the dream one.

But Miss Bowen makes more of Portia than giving her the soprano lyric. After the first section her attachment to Eddie guides the action and her point of view predominates—second-guessed throughout, of course, by the voice of the narrator. This narrator holds a double view—speaks tenderly of Portia's "loving nature" and notes with critical intelligence the "ruthlessness" of "innocence." In the long run, however, the narrator insists so much on our sympathizing that the whole attitude becomes suspect. The scenes themselves do not seem to be saying quite the same thing. After urging us to join Portia, Miss Bowen finally goes so far as to put her beyond our full involvement. We begin to be anxious about sensitive imagination carried to such solipsistic extremes that it must be shot down. Toward the end Miss Bowen approaches caricature of sensitivity as an ideal while still pitying it almost fulsomely—and the maneuver works. To the extent that we join Portia, we share her self-pity and her hatred of Anna, who seems to be causing all the trouble. But in the last section the scene shifts and we see Anna in all her restlessness with her husband, efforts to get Major Brutt a job, fear of losing Eddie to the girl, need for St. Quentin's therapy, and bewilderment at what to do about Portia. In hating Anna we have been hating a part of ourselves. Even more important, Anna's world of defined and half-solved problems relieves the anxiety created by our long self-indulgence with Portia. The cool aristocratic decision to send the housekeeper to pick up the pieces of Portia seems to deal with the emergency, and the long talk between Anna, Thomas, and St. Quentin half-reconciles them and us to the impossibility of desires for omnipotence.

For Portia has trouble only partially because adults fail to meet her demand for human solidarity in defeat. True, the adults distrust her unlimited claim, but they do not interfere with her trying to fulfill it. In fact, they maintain a surprising aloofness. They have confidence in Nature—it will tell Portia without their spending an unpleasant hour doing so. But who could possibly want the "edited" life that Portia observes with such distaste? Anna and Thomas and Major Brutt. Each by his own route has arrived at preferring it to emotional turmoil. To them sensitivity has become threat rather than promise.

But Portia fails mostly because her desire to impose power on others by fitting them to her dream meets stronger resisting powers.

For her, imagination and action do not compartmentalize themselves, as they do in Proust and Joyce; she wants them to be identical. So the great interruption occurs when she meets cruder young people at the seashore. The discovery that some young men have roving hands makes her doubt the purity of Eddie's love. She finds that bold young women not only flirt but fight back hard when attacked. The sensitive boy can get drunk and disorderly. These scenes have been called snobbish and they are, but not just against people with lower incomes and smaller houses. They are snobbish against the physical, the aggressive, the rivalrous, the actively sexual. The cold order of the town house too defends against these—and justifies a fear of the wanted drama. But the scenes are not primarily snobbish in the name of the town house, for Portia has only a slight foothold there; the basic standards are tenderness, honesty, depth of feeling, "the happy passive nature." Threat arises from the aggressiveness which makes Waikiki "the fount of spontaneous living" but is always crowding the "upright rudeness" of its conventions. Mr. Bursley roams the dance floor; Daphne invites fondling, works hard, and righteously says the unforgivable; the episode ends in drunken moroseness. The dominant metaphor for Waikiki is noise.

But Portia and Eddie do not break up because of the casual sexuality at Waikiki, though their quarrel starts there. The usual interpretation blames his theatricality, holds him not a genuine enough person to accept Portia. But Eddie is one of the best character creations in modern literature and carries the one thoroughly unreconcilable note in the novel. He has a real problem: he wants to keep a foot in the "corrupt" adult world, where he works for Anna's husband and needs to be *enfant terrible* to Anna, and the other in the unsullied childhood which Portia represents to him. He cannot make the unsatisfactory adult truce with things as they are nor invite the reader to look beyond adolescence, and he cannot manage the balancing act to either Portia's or Anna's satisfaction. Our last view shows him deserted by the girl and preparing to open the woman's message of rejection. Portia flees because he will not make an exclusive league with her, but in her paranoid fear of being laughed at exaggerates his league with Anna. His conflicting wishes for dependence and independence, survival and regression make his shifts between hostility and friendliness the most rapid in the novel—and him its most volatile and ambivalent character.

Even the narrator joins the love-hate relationship with a ruthlessly snobbish appraisal of Eddie's apartment, "Like the taste of many people whose extraction is humble, what taste he had lagged some decades back in time. . . ." But the actual description shows a more ambiguous attitude:

> If this interior showed any affectation, it was in keeping the bleakness of college rooms—the unadult taste, the lack of tactile feeling bred by large stark objects, tables and cupboards, that one does not possess. The concave seats of the chairs, the lumpy divan suggested that comfort was a rather brutal affair. Eddie's work of presenting himself to the world did not, in fact, stop when he came back here, for he often had company—but he chose by all kinds of negligence to imply that it did. Whatever manias might possess him in solitude, making some haunted landscape in which cupboards and tables looked like cliffs or opaque bottomless pools, the effect (at least to a woman) coming in here was, that this was how this fundamentally plain and rather old-fashioned fellow lived when *en pantoufles*. On the smoky buff walls and unpolished woodwork neurosis, of course, could not write a trace. To be received by Eddie in such frowsty surroundings could be taken as either confiding or insolent. If he *had* stuffed a bunch of flowers (never very nice flowers) into his one art vase, the concession always seemed touching. This was not all that was touching: the smells of carpet and ash, of dust inside the books and of stagnant tea had a sort of unhopeful acquiescence about them. This was not all phony—Eddie did need to be mothered; he was not aesthetic; he had a contempt for natty contrivances, and he did sincerely associate pretty living with being richer than he could hope to be. . . . Thus he kept the right, which he used, to look round his friends' room—at the taste, the freshness, the ingenuity—with a cold marvelling alien ironic eye.

If understanding is a form of love, Miss Bowen's liking for her "cad" is strained but real. Eddie adds greatly to the resonance of the novel, for he suggests that life may never achieve the exciting stability of drawing room skirmishes or become a series of interim reverses like the adolescent's. It may instead be endless, instant shifts between warmth and anger while feeling that "the skies had begun to fall—like pieces of black plaster they had started, still fairly gently, flaking down on his head." To temperaments less cushioned by civilization than Anna's or to less happy passive natures than Portia's, life may seem a frenzied fight on a stage-lighted windy plain.

The magnificently oblique ending takes advantage of all the reverberations the novel has set up. The strategy of making us hate Anna for nonsupport and sexual rivalry pays off. For finally there are no villains, and life is not a melodrama—only inadequate people working inadequate defenses for clashing purposes. Portia's running away will not solve anything, but does achieve part of her aim—it creates an effect. It shows Major Brutt that, however much he wants to sit by a warm family hearth, he will continue to guard his unhappy privacy against even the most impassioned human claim.

> He swiveled round on his chair, as wretchedly as a schoolboy, to look, in glum, dumb, nonplussed communication at his own rubbed ebony hairbrushes, his studbox, his nail scissors—as though these objects, which had travelled with him, witnessed to his power somehow to get through life, to reach a point when one says, It doesn't really much matter. Unhappy on his bed, in this temporary little stale room, Portia seemed to belong nowhere, not even here. Stripped of that pleasant home that had seemed part of her figure, stripped, too, of his own wishes and hopes, she looked at once harsh and beaten, a refugee—frightening, rebuffing all pity that has fear at the root.

And the flight finally does engage the attention of the adults at home. Their tense telephoning shows how much they do accept responsibility for her safety and comfort, if not for her emotions. Their reconstruction of events begins to make Portia understandable to them. (They see that diary snooping could be construed as prying into feelings which the possessor feels unsure whether to cherish or be ashamed of.) Anxiety smokes out the animus behind Thomas' tolerance. His threat to fire Eddie arouses the love behind Anna's rejection:

> "No, you can't do that, Thomas," Anna wildly repeated, pulling her pearls round. "If he is being slack, simply give him a good fright. But

you can't sack him right out of the blue. You've got nothing against him, except being such a donkey."

But St. Quentin sits by to reintroduce the reality principle to the excited parents-by-accident. By recognizing themselves in his not unattractive lunatic giant in the drawing room, they will survive the attack of reenergized conscience to resume the life of skirmish. Portia's battle has actually made them aware of a drama in their own lives forgotten amid the usual self-kicking.

The *Death of the Heart* is a monument, one of a kind. Miss Bowen has not been able to reproduce its effect, nor has anyone else. It shows the dominant hope of half a century greatly diminished. Miss Bowen works through to a painful certainty that had to be achieved before new possibilities could be taken up. If a writer so careful, definitive, and committed to the value can come up honestly with no more than she does, it must have become very vulnerable. For her the old equation works poorly. She feels both sides of the contradiction: every exaggeration in the claims of sensitivity increases the pressure which no conceivable world can satisfy. Her significant gesture in splitting the character of wife and novelist denies the faith that esthetic awareness can override the negatives in living—gives it a role only as consoler. Bereft of that out, every added reliance on inner light exposes the hopeful to shock, and threatens the security he cannot, in real life, abandon. Theoretically, adolescence ought to provide guides for the future; making its prejudices into realities ought to be the aim of a lifetime. But the concept of adolescent sensitivity which Miss Bowen inherited and could not change simply would not serve that purpose. She established a radical discontinuity between youthful hopes for omnipotence and any possible adult living, while at the same time intensifying the reproach for "failure."

The hope Anna holds of making life into an art suggests a finished, singing-golden-bird retrospect which her dynamic skirmishing can aspire to but not achieve. What I have been calling controlled volatility, exercising the lunatic giant on a leash, does indeed represent a hope for making pleasure a little stronger than pain. But the nerves stretch so taut in trying and barriers flash up so quickly that the margin can at best be very narrow. In those less than superbly equipped, the balance will tip the wrong way. The forward-looking question is not whether Miss Bowen hopes—she could not give excitement to the skirmishing if she did not—but whether the aspiration has enough energy left to compete much longer with other and newer aspirations.

Certainly the novel shows working arrangements between character and self. Portia has not yet stylized herself to a character. She is all self and sensitivity. But a considerable range in possible characters does exist. Though Major Brutt is outside present limits, Thomas, St. Quentin, and Anna—all very different—are within them. Eddie may or may not be—he has a chance. He dramatizes the crucial questions. Can the rough fit between character and self work well enough to be lived with? Does the character express enough of what the self has to express to survive or, better yet, live "happily"? At best, the pleasure-pain balance will be close, but all the adults except Eddie have some margin.

Finally, the lunatic giant formulation shows how far the shift of feeling in the century has gone. *The Magic Mountain* had allied sensitivity and illness, but gratifyingly. "Lunatic" stresses a dynamic, distressing, possibly incurable kind of illness. The word suggests doubt about the worth of sensitivity, while the use tries still to transform the threat into a value in active life. But Miss Bowen has enlarged the dangers over the days when sensitivity could be seen primarily as opportunity for self-development.

The Death of the Heart fits the British image: It is about muddling through. Miss Bowen became a serious novelist by taking the problem hard, but her contemporaries, realizing that it had been lived with so long as to become habitual, were beginning to turn it into comedy. When Miss Bowen herself broke through, she became an all too merry widow. In *The Heat of the Day* she arrives at that disaster for the imaginative writer—she solves her problem. The novel is a plain box with a note inside, "I have left home."

Anyone with hindsight can see that such a solution impended. While not wanting to miss the experience of marriage, her best heroines have no special gift for it. They share, on the one side, aggressiveness, and, on the other, weakness in the traditionally feminine nurturing impulse. In so far as it exists, it expresses itself toward men worried about their adequacy, candidates for unusual dependence on women. Karen can thus combine an attack on the official roles with some warmth toward a man who does not fit. With a husband to provide, Anna can keep a passive man to understand her, an outsider to excite her, and a tarnished hero to adore her; but she cannot remain unconscious that, if she is using them, they intend using her. Thomas keeps trying to get out of the study she has dutifully decorated for him into the drawing room or, worse yet, the bedroom. Eddie drops her for Portia after she has got him a job. St. Quentin prefers tea and toast by the fire to hearing her troubles outside in the snow. And Major Brutt wants to relieve his contagious loneliness. Yet Anna's arrangements are the best that the traditions of country living adapted to the modern commercial city can provide. The town house by the park transplants the country house, imperfectly. If the role of well-off wife can give opportunity for self-expression, Anna has it and, with Portia's arrival, has the chance to play mother. She accepts and resents so much her training about place and sensibility—and her own wish for invulnerability—that she will not develop even the interests open to her, much less revolt against the whole position.

A novel that carries such formidable conflicts to the end of the road cannot totally lack interest, if only because we want to know how things came out. Unfortunately, *The Heat of the Day* comes out an inadequately controlled fantasy deficient in felt life. A good deal of honor always goes to the writer who will not repeat his obsolete conflict and tries to get down some sparer truth of the present. Not every novelist moved by time and war, however, has auctioned so much as Miss Bowen. The popular form is the right one, for Miss Bowen has a popular cause, but the love story vehicle, with its crude fantasy of the fortyish divorcee importuned by two men who count, arouses more resistance than automatic sympathy.

But the novel does have two at first puzzling areas of felt life. Scene does more to define the heroine than she herself can do. Miss

Bowen made her way with furnishings; yet here Stella takes ironic pride in her rented apartment in a dissociated locale and the absence of all personal belongings. She savors the gauche lover's seeing her in a "beautiful" rented ashtray. The earlier works do not show the naturalistic novel's enthusiasm for objects as guides to the inner world, but rather a desperate clinging to fine furniture, a determination to notice the polish that only an old servant can put on inherited pieces. Stella has abandoned with relief the effort to spiritualize the material.

Why? Because it means to her the pint-sized outlet for the outsized will—middle-class marriage. Here war both causes and represents a breakup of defined male and female roles. Stella has become a triply emancipated woman. Her important work at the Ministry makes her the equal of any man, the superior to many, and the dependent of none. For this satisfaction she has joyously sold house and furniture. Moreover, the new claim to significance has diminished her interest in family continuity, by reducing her need for ancestral support and childhood promise. She takes a career woman's sincere interest in her son and a day off for Cousin Ned's funeral, but attends left-handedly to both.

The apartment makes up only half the setting. The noise of bombs falling, now close, now far off, completes it and heightens the small drama within. Somehow the blitz seems a good thing for London. For Stella has the Bowen sense of life as waiting for the intense, but this time waiting recklessly for ultimate intensity. Stella happily refuses to abandon her room for the shelters. For once, the sexual threat has its proper accompaniment in the world outside. Best of all, chaos guarantees freedom. So long as those bombs go off, men cannot dominate events. The wishes to make life drama and to avoid being confined by men coalesce.

The other felt life—showing the causes of her lover's treason—also comes from shedding outworn belief, never really believed in but carried along because inherited and not replaced. These scenes attack the effort to transplant the country house into organized urban life. War intensifies organization, until the palely surviving image of the aristocrat as warrior becomes unrecognizable in the bureaucrat. To abandon this hope, Miss Bowen drops her close psychology and tries to write the new novel of forces, where personality becomes subordinated to representative issue, but the form gives her trouble. Though a melodrama of traitors and spies in Eden could conceivably work, Miss Bowen represents too journalistically. There is a blackout, just as we saw in the movies; bombs fall, just as we read in the papers; the spies spy and the traitors betray, just as we read in the men's magazines. While much of the action takes place at night, Miss Bowen's fondness for bright bulbs interferes with her creating the odd lighting that has let novelists of forces like Camus and Iris Murdoch succeed.

Things could not easily be otherwise, for the novel wants, above all, to clarify the already known. Its strangeness comes from the absence of surprise amid all the noise and shocks. Cousin Ned, the Irish landowner, dies suddenly when no one knew he was even in England; but, Irish landowning being what it has become, he has been dead—or removed from reality—for a long time. His funeral becomes an item on the week's agenda. A strange, awkward man appears by night to accuse Stella's lover of betraying secrets to the Nazis. Officially she doubts him, but, as she realizes later, knows from the first that he is telling the truth. She preserves the affair by having the good manners to postpone questions.

Strangely, too, Miss Bowen gives her mature heroine the tensionless love her adolescents had dreamt of earlier. Excitement can come only from doubting its reality, but the novel never convinces that the characters believe in it enough for the question to cut deep. So Robert, the warrior-bureaucrat, turns out to be the enemy of Stella's security and will have to jump off the roof. So Harrison, the intelligence agent, likes planting doubt more than making love. About what might have been expected.

The reasons for perfect love and absence of surprise go together. Robert is to be an ideally attractive betrayer—sensitive, well-mannered, competent, country-bred. If he is not what he seems, neither are his values. He demonstrates the madness that ensues when the portable virtues—manner, ability, sensitivity—become divorced from their pastoral base. He comes alive only in returning home to consider selling the family house, and even in this scene the life is not so much his as his family's. Country living has degenerated into a sister's snappishness and a mother's hostility. Scandalously, the house is revealed as not a family seat, but the last in a series bought and sold by Robert's father in an effort to symbolize a stability impossible among such clashing wills. The weak resistance to selling dramatizes the falsity behind the solid claim. Robert, long alienated from the hope and the clash, near the crisis of his London affairs, absentmindedly says sell.

In the logic of these forces, Stella has been an accomplice in treason so defined. She has thoughtlessly gone her urban, adult, independent way disregarding the old values, the authority of adolescent sensibility, and the traditional feminine role—has preferred being thought faithless rather than deserted and preferred remaining mistress to becoming wife. Robert's crisis makes her see emancipation and alienation as identical, if not too painful. The attempt to carry the idealized refinements of a landed aristocracy into the commercial city seems ended in vacuum with her and a mad rage for order with Robert.

The alternative, doing dirt on the whole outworn hope, appears as sexual degradation. The writer on the original dust jacket worried enough about Harrison, the intelligence agent, to describe him as a "recognizable type." If by that he meant a man anyone would be likely to meet, the words apply doubtfully. But Harrison is recognizable. From behind the seediness there emerge the features of the Bowen boy friend—the twisted, self-tortured, aggressive man, a paler, less self-esteeming Max or Eddie. This active man from Nowhere is the defender of the nation while the correct Robert is its enemy. Harrison offers Stella the appealing chance for degrading heroism. By taking him as a lover she can save Robert. The Bowen women have always had a weakness for such men, as more exciting than the official man, and here the possible heroism of saving the old by joining the functionary adds an attraction.

But in this novel paleness means more than reminiscent features. Heath has pointed out the mechanical means of identifying Harrison as really a man like Robert, even to his being known as Robertson in Ireland, but essentially Harrison is a ghost, the embodiment of Stella's doubt and certainty about lost faiths. (Miss Bowen's inability to make him also seem like a human being signals her difficulties with this kind of narrative.) He appears suddenly at night, whispering temptations in the glare behind the blackout curtains. His information seems consistent, his moves confident. His accusations take root in Stella's suppressed question about love and angry rootlessness.

Several antitheses between old ideals and youthful functionalism accompany the main conflict. The old Irish landlordism flickered out in apathy and insanity; perhaps Stella's son, who *may* survive the war, can restore it by scientific agriculture. The lower class girl, impatient and promiscuous, is fertile. Perhaps her resilience and illegitimate child will mean something. But the war atmosphere that works has nothing to do with these unlikelihoods. Bombs mean waiting, this time not to be kissed, but recklessly waiting in the open for something explosive to happen. At the end, it has happened. The need for men and houses has been blown away, along with a lot of false old imperatives, and Stella can live in the here and now. Her son may or may not be able to restore the estate, but it is not her problem. She has achieved the rather vacant freedom and privacy that Anna wanted.

THREE

Play, The Fractured Self, and American Angry Comedy: From Faulkner to Salinger

When an interviewer in New York asked Henry Green what American writers he would like most to meet, he named only Faulkner. That the British comic "miniaturist" should admire the man of the big claim ought not to have been the surprise it was. For Green and Faulkner both bring more threatened temperaments to the concept of personality laid out by Joyce: a few obsessions absorbing every experience past, present, and to come. The Englishman is a shorthand symbolist, the American a worshiper of size, but they begin from a common base. Both inherit and extend an international modernism.

The agreement to insist upon Faulkner as a unique king, a

national monument, a regionalist, and of course a non-reading American novelist in good standing obscures his importance in the continuity of literature. More important, these universals underestimate his power of penetrating to the center of issues immediately at stake. By the time he began to write well, the first generation abroad had substantially filled in its vision of the fractured self. In the interest of richness it had chosen to kaleidoscope consciousness and in the process had come upon disturbing signs of self-division. The logic of its elected hopes made experience into meaningful moments with waste sad times stretching before and after. But every age is an age of transition and even Faulkner links something and something. He has, as a matter of fact, unusual capacity for looking forward and backward at once: he stands between an overextended and increasingly out-of-touch affection for the fractured self and a succeeding desperation to pull the pieces back together and redirect them, between a leisurely be-still-and-wait and an anxious go-get-'em.

Faulkner transforms the fractured self into fractured structure. More accurately, he clarifies the picture by representing the one in terms of the other. Unlike Green and Elizabeth Bowen, he is not a complex dynamic novelist. He is first of all a radical simplifier, the perfect compartmental mind. He makes literature locally dramatic, ultimately contemplative. His characteristic structure—*The Sound and the Fury, The Wild Palms, Light in August, The Hamlet*—lays out parallel examples walled off from each other's activity and producing their effect by juxtaposition in the reader's mind. Impulse has this aspect, that, and the other one. Though *The Hamlet* presses toward an organized clarity which *The Sound and the Fury* does not visualize at all, both comprehend complexities by fencing off three areas of private property. Faulkner locates and reproduces sides of human nature, but these exist in separate realms of discourse and have little to say to each other. "Spatial form" creates a passive irony about the human condition. Faulkner shows little of Elizabeth Bowen's will toward productive tension between disparate drives.

Thus *The Sound and the Fury* walls off its angry but cheerful idiot, unaware of his conflict and tragic only as seen from outside. Another fenced area contains the mixed-up violent lover, half-aware and highly conscious of himself as a tragic figure. The third pasture holds the practical mind in a comedy of exasperation. The novel has the excitement of frightening, frustrating discovery, newly seen in its tripartite reality. *The Hamlet,* however, has absorbed this triple vision: it reduces horror by eliminating surprise. The distance achieved by living with a way of thought dictates its tragicomic form. Faulkner's last major novel sums up and makes visible the tendencies of a career. (Two lesser works carrying on the story do not alter the fact.)

The concept of character in *The Hamlet* proceeds from and intensifies this pull toward analysis. For Faulkner's people are less like real ones than like forces in the mind, provided with an incredibly complete set of objective correlatives. Thus every character is himself to the hilt—at all times and places. Old Varner, secure in achieved command, always sits in his barrel chair before the Frenchman's Place or rocks on the porch or lies in his hammock. Ratliff is forever planning, playing, being sympathetic. Eula is always Object. Labove does nothing but hunger for her for five years. Flem is always Flem, and, Dickens-style, Faulkner invents a new Snopes for every minute variation. With everyone except Mink, he abandons the standard ambivalence of modern character to intensify a single drive.

To mask this concentration and make event seem more than pattern, Faulkner needs not only his internationally-oriented style, but his country people. Critics who have themselves left the South applaud his decision to stay, often more as a matter of team loyalty than definable gain. Tenant farming provides a scene, of course, for the sense of life as straining for absolutely necessary and absolutely uninspiring goals. For the novelist who loves sound and fury enough to need orientation strongly, though, the country people make better laboratory animals than Bloom or Swann for isolating and classifying strains of modern impulse. Like the very rich, country people are different from us. We are willing to believe that they concentrate themselves into single drives. They thus become larger than we. At the same time we—and the author—can look down on them and comprehend their simpler mechanisms. Both perspectives work to create beautifully disguised paradigms, as available to Caldwell as to Faulkner. (Some patterns, though, work better than others and interact more meaningfully.)

But if Faulkner wants to make the sun sit still for photographs to be enlarged later, he can also make his characters run. Once having laid out the mind and world according to plan, he makes his characters collide within their fenced-off frames of reference. Conflict within each depends on agreement about the most hopeful line of self-assertion—championship games, sex, direct act. The major separations represent unintegratable impulses. And form follows function. Since for Faulkner and his characters man has a natural right to abundance—in energy, emotion, sex, intelligence, life plan—frustration, the normal state, means being deprived of this right and leads to aggression. So technique—the dramatically excessive quantity of biography, environment, and words—repeats moral value. But the collisions within the tripartite structure in *The Hamlet* make a sharp advance toward drama compared to the Joycean comedy of stasis. Stasis remains between game, sex, and revenge; within these realms pressures create active conflicts.

So, though Faulkner takes great steps toward the novel of forces, with its passion to orient and direct, he stops short and creates a unique double effect of stillness and motion. However much the framework may isolate drives, he surrounds his representative figures with so much poetic particularity and subjects them to so much contingency that they transcend their analytic function. And his continuous heightening-lowering language enlarges as it enlivens them. The point calls for considerable illustration later, but, first, a guess about how Faulkner arrived at his summing up and a look at what he forecasts.

In the novels of the absurd that Faulkner's reputation primarily rests on, he comes at the end of a line. Within his predecessors' double view of consciousness—the possibilities of expanded personality and the irony of its relation to the world—he diminishes the first and intensifies the second.

No one need stare hard at some of Faulkner's protagonists to recognize portraits of the artist manqué as we have been defining him, but Faulkner's representation of raw neurosis transforms the picture. Bayard Sartoris and Quentin Compson retain the passivity, but their imaginations have taken the crucial turn toward loving pain—equating it with a central self. Faulkner tests furiously the possibility glided over in the first generation—that, instead of expansively creating its own imaginative order to replace an unfriendly outer prospect, the mind will come to find its excitement in its own disorders. Fear and guilt will become its torturers—and only meaningful intensity. Joyce celebrates Mr. Bloom's flights from pain without testing the danger inherent in the removal. Faulkner twists depth psychology from its curative purpose in order to heighten risk. Like Miss Bowen, he values passive sensitivity highly—sentimentally in Bayard Sartoris—yet must raise the question about its ability to prevail in the world. Depression psychology increases the credibility he can give his answer: it hasn't a prayer. But, because it is the only value modern man can feel, because it cannot abandon its attempt to establish itself minimally, at least, and because its failure in any case produces intensity, his heroes beat their heads against walls better than anyone else's. Somehow he became famous as a writer about violence, but his finest talent is for showing the verge of outbreak. He stretches the nerves as tightly as they will stretch, and keeps them that way interminably.

Faulkner does not, of course, leave the will-filled grandfathers as mere reproaches to modern sensitivities. *Absalom, Absalom* shows how the formula of will went down by failing to calculate the range and force of the emotions. In the present, Joe Christmas' modest efforts to establish himself as a small businessman leave him bewildered by the storm that blows up within and around him. Once discovered, the inner life cannot be downed by remaining ignorant of it. Faulkner's earlier critics, feeling it necessary in the interests of seriousness to deny that he is a sensationalist, made him a moralist, historian, and political scientist. But he *is* a sensationalist —the finest of them all—and his moral contribution comes directly from the fact. He carries passivity, sensitivity, and intensity to the end of the line at Terror. He gives a dramatic force no one else had provided to the bewilderment which half a century of attempting to create values out of "sincerity" had arrived at. And he could no more live with the results than the civilization itself could.

The Sound and the Fury thus both defines one component of the present problem and indicates what road Faulkner represents the end of. For all the energy and running about, the picture of sensitive consciousness is essentially static. Benjy remains kindly, impotent, and confused. Quentin remains esthetic, heated, frustrated at his inability to make his view of himself as rebel against God impose itself on the world. If Quentin represents man angry without an adequate sense of cause, Jason represents rationalist man irritated. Early critics underestimated the love in portraying Jason. He nags for order after having simplified life into action too narrow to satisfy—yet too ambitious to bring off. His story carries the only dramatic action in the novel. He fights both the soft emotionalism around him and its willful search for outlets. Given the bias of the novel for expressing the full range of feeling, he is defeated from the start. The action works mostly to play Malvolio-style jokes on him. Yet Faulkner allots him surprising energy and in the end he seems the least purely representative character. Where Quentin's language is monotonously hepped up and Benjy's tricksy, Jason's energy develops a good deal of flexibility and linguistic range.

Ultimately Jason, the neglected member of the trinity, enables Faulkner to go on beyond his original diagnosis. In it he had removed from sensitivity its force of personal continuity, education, and imaginative play to dramatize it as penned up and bewildered for unspecifiable errors, and unable through intellectual advantage to find an outlet for the resulting anger. Sensitive passivity achieves its ultimate union with intensity, in a vacuum. But Faulkner also shows a drive for control over both this emotionalism and the environment. He embodies the 1930's revival of interest in will through Jason, Sutpen, Ratliff, and Flem Snopes and thereby introduces an element absent in his most direct technical influence, Joyce.

A powerful conviction comes through in *The Sound and the*

Fury: that personality, divided into three parts, cannot be integrated. Unintegrated, it cannot satisfy itself or exert significant force in the world. Yet the very act of drawing the three characters so affectionately—filling each compartment so completely—suggests an ideal integration. Separateness can make sense in the light of an absent but imaginable unity of being, or it can be merely natural fact. What if one character could integrate Benjy's harmless good nature, Quentin's imagination and sensitivity, and Jason's drive for control? Faulkner does not answer that question. (Graham Greene's whiskey priest represents the strongest effort to do so in contemporary fiction.) Faulkner never wants to break through his compartmental thinking, but in *The Hamlet* he resets his fences. He experiments with, What would happen if we transferred some of the animal life from Field B to Field A, some more to Field C? Would not Field B then look different too?

Nothing quite so diagrammatic happens in *The Hamlet*, but one of its shifts leads directly toward the present. In his last major novel Faulkner draws the distinction that has made possible the move from frustrated to irritated heroes. He does not himself forecast any such direction; he merely and characteristically sets the possibilities side by side. Yet the very naming of prospects lays the ground for a tragicomedy achieved by multiplying the possible games and hesitating to go all the way with more dangerous obsessions.

The Hamlet moves enough of the artist into the practical man to make the business deal a game of dramatic art. The sewing machine salesman Ratliff becomes not only the antagonist of Flem Snopes but also a story-teller with enough imagination to feel himself into the character of Ab Snopes, the barn burner. Yet Ratliff shares Jason Compson's irritated concept of life as "strategies for encompassing situations." In the light of Faulkner's earlier work he looks like a dangerous move toward conciliation with society—and is at least a cautious one. The step from tragic perspective to tragicomic becomes possible when Faulkner chooses to take a wider, because more remote, view of his scene. But his choice of scene is crucial to shifting the relationships, and in making it he was much more on his own than contemporary English writers of tragicomedy have been.

For until recently the tragicomic novel in England has had a locatable scene. The class coteries of Huxley, Waugh, and Powell; Cary's bohemians; Hartley's or Compton-Burnett's villages; Henry Green's servants—the range of the immediate past suggests itself in these. Building so good a set of novels on so narrow a scene may be an anomaly, but it may also be one reason for an assurance sharply different from the American uncertainty. Agreement upon scene, reflecting an inherited agreement on issues, has made possible a sort of continuing conversation. Huxley's testing the survival of older attitudes prepared for Waugh's involvement with "Make it new"; Waugh's bright young people set up Henry Green's picture of the party-goers as foggy children; and Green's concern with managing life helped provoke Powell's researches on his circling friends. In England scene and counterstatement provide starting points, make possible economies, adapt tensions already marked as significant. The novelist can begin with a new angle rather than a new world. In the United States, where comedy has always needed naturalization papers, each novel seems to call for a fresh start.

Yet the mere quantity of recent tragicomic fiction makes this hypothesis unlikely. Since *The Hamlet*, a shelf of already old favorites has built up—*The Adventures of Augie March*, *Lolita*, *The Catcher in the Rye*, *The Assistant*, *The Southpaw*, *Catch-22*. If the theorists are right that comedy by definition demands a coherent society, its appearance in force suggests a wider consensus than is normally admitted. Yet whatever agreement exists provides not answers, but subjects for debate. Considered as forerunner and development in a progressing discourse, *The Hamlet* and *The Catcher in the Rye* have enough name familiarity to guarantee that they speak for something and somebody in America.

Even thus limited, the common issue is hard to define. An answer starts not so much from this-versus-that as from a juggling act for which no standard technique has yet evolved. Society in this country certainly has no philosophy or theology and no promise of finding either, but it has a rough-and-ready morality and a few hopes, half-respectable, half-suspect, which it acts on and tries to perpetuate. Of these the most formidable tries to channel sheer aggressiveness, arising from "the exhaustion of weaning," tenant farming, original sin, automation, or whatever, into an acceptable competitiveness. (Only soreheads challenge the value of Little Leagues.) But many in the society would like to soften this training with decency, humanity, friendliness, community; and novelists have normally sympathized with them—though as aware as football coaches of the obstacles.

The problem of making this mixture work has been around for a long time and is not necessarily comic. (C. P. Snow is rarely funny.) But another hope, always somewhat suspect in this country but now widely available, adds a dimension. While waiting for channeling to produce its miracles, people look for activities enlivening, enriching, exciting but not too exciting, maybe only entertaining. The exact adjective is hard to find, but hard-working people with some margin do not wait on adjectives. They do not mean to do anything so foolish as some of Huxley's, Hemingway's, Fitzgerald's, and Waugh's characters—abandon the job for play. They only want the fringe benefits.

The comic novel presents a ready medium for examining this juggling act. Comedy presumably began with festival, and play has been one root of the English success—whether in Joyce's internal games, Huxley's by-passing of the stuffy, Waugh's revolutionary styles, Green's pleasure-and-pain, Cary's moral fun, or Powell's revisiting past party-going. The traditional English respect for leisure has made easier these novelists' efforts to establish modes and rationales for play—for in a disciplined society it must have a rationale—but American novelists have also begun to raise the question of how to enrich and enliven the old ethic, yet retain a moral direction too valuable to discard in a day when new ones are not easy to come by.

The newer novelists show some agreement on where the balancing act becomes critical. They locate, in all sorts of places, the point at which society's *preparation* of the individual—its effort to pass on its going values—collides most sharply with his own eccentricities, odd desires, and miscellaneous angers. The school, the Chicago streets, wartime Italy, the baseball diamond, and the crossroads from which a town's significant citizens arise have served similar purposes. This kind of training camp locates an increased respect for the power of society to impose and transmit its attitudes —so that competitiveness, for example, becomes not merely an outside force but a part of identity and conscience for the hero. The individual shaping process becomes the future for society itself. Behind the apparently neutral scene of diamond or country store lies respect for a social power more moderate, but not necessarily less effective, than that of *1984* or *Brave New World*.

The Hamlet marks a turning point for other novelists as well as for Faulkner and is a classic modern blend of comedy and pain. Steinbeck's *Tortilla Flat*, almost contemporary with it, takes the traditional view of primitives as outside the competitive society, living well on nothing a year. No incurable hangovers result from wine; no ambitions disturb friendships; no arguments to the self about decency occur, for the flatlanders are decent by definition. But in *The Hamlet* the conflict between competitiveness and humanity becomes central, with the old Faulknerian motifs of subsistence agriculture and violence stemming from helpless rage as forces just below the surface. By setting an archaic, pastoral scene, Faulkner comes to some terms with competitiveness in the only way possible for him—by finding it deep in the history of peasant society and individual growth, and hence as traditional as Sartorises.

In *The Hamlet* Faulkner wants to express a revolutionary spirit without losing the benefits of nature and continuity. So he dignifies rebellious anger while celebrating frozen hopes and orderly evolution. (The Southern critics who emphasize his conservatism and the Northerners who play up his radicalism can both be right.) This quarrel with the self begins from its extremes.

The single enlivening element which the culture supports is competitiveness mixed with some fellow feeling. Old Will Varner stands for this tradition and Ratliff, who sees no new way, wants to be the true son. ("There are only two people who can handle Flem

Snopes and Jody Varner ain't one," he brags.) The ritualized episodes in the opening section tell of almost knightly man-to-man combats—Ab's with the horse trader, Jody's with Flem, Ratliff's with Flem—while the tone of familiarity proves how much the community accepts these grown-up games for both excitement and status. They dramatize life and establish masculinity in a society where few other assertions can succeed.

Though the scene is provincial, these showdowns turn on a value taken seriously in the world at large. Rituals and all, they come close to burlesquing Hemingway's contests of champions. Ab is the county champion at horse trading, his adversary the regional one. Ratliff is the playful manipulator, Flem the time-and-motion-study one. Comedy follows from the dream of proving absolute superiority. In the nature of things a man successful in these games cannot stop until he overreaches—tests himself against an invulnerable foe. Emotions handicap human beings, but not pros. The runaway mules get Ab overexcited. Ratliff depends too much on intelligence: his first contest with Flem runs double reverses so tricky that few readers can follow them. Much of the pleasure comes from sheer play of mind, and the comic tale always reaches its climax with the balloon bursting. For Ab the air literally goes out of his repurchased horse. The crucial signature on Ratliff's note turns out to be the idiot Ike's, the Texas ponies race all over the county. Masculinity proves almost but not quite assertable. The protagonist provides a comedy of irritation.

Though Faulkner's geography of old attitudes adds up to a new one, his mode is embellishment rather than insight. The leisurely pace of the stories—their willingness to take time loading up the separator—builds comfortably around the already foreseen and hence already cushioned reverse. Nobody expects Ab to beat the trader. Compared to the sharpness of Waugh, Henry Green, or Cary, Faulkner is barely funny at all. The British writers specialize in the unexpected perception or cross-purpose. Faulkner produces a relaxed faith that such disappointments have occurred before and will occur again without unbearable effects—and with a good deal of anticipatory excitement. Life can be lively without ceasing to be fairly safe.

But this outlet for the oversize will can work even as well as it does only for the talented. For most the problem of humanizing subsistence remains. In the next two sections of the novel Faulkner explores reversals both more exciting and harder to bear. Not much in Frenchman's Bend can be loved and had; yet people want to do more than endure. His men, unlike Lawrence's, cannot withdraw from the public world into the familial, for it is the women who disappoint and deprive them, yet bind them to the job. Everybody wants Eula and nobody we know can have her; Mrs. Mink traps Mink in his time of loneliness and becomes his burden; Mrs. Houston draws Houston back from Texas with unfulfillable promise; Mrs. Armstid drags Armstid back toward her vision of subsistence. Ike, deprived of his cow, caricatures a universal disappointment that reenforces a universal anger.

Nevertheless, for all this practical knowledge, the Eula section celebrates sex—not as fulfillment or community, simply as exciting force. More accurately, her story celebrates frozen anticipation. Maximum tension, not anything that can happen, produces this sense of vitality. A Proustian view of lover creating the beloved dominates, and, with action proscribed, the emphasis falls on waiting. Labove waits from the time Eula is eight years old, seeing a miracle of "puberty in the foetus." After he leaves, everybody must wait a year until Eula develops. In the "tomcatting" time, waiting breaks into fighting. And the reader, who has been kept waiting too, never finds out how things went after the horse stopped to drink in the creek.

Eula herself merely sits and eats cold sweet potatoes. Over half the fifty pages or so of her story show the "virile anchorite" schoolteacher, football player, and unpracticing attorney restraining himself. Dramatically, the proof of Eula's power comes in her drawing back the proverbial hill boy possessed by the dream of vocation achieved through study. Her brother's angry protectiveness, certain of defeat and determined to postpone it indefinitely, unites with

Labove's fierce repression to heighten the value of the property. The boys in church waiting for her to come of age and the whip fighting still later add the final dramatic increments.

But the Faulknerian poetry expressing what the inarticulate cannot say does most. Metaphors of abundance and deprivation control, alternate, and combine. Labove's masochistic vision of her future works in all three:

> He could almost see the husband which she would someday have. He would be a dwarf, a gnome, without glands or desire, who would be no more a physical factor in her life than the owner's name on the fly-leaf of a book. There it was again, out of the books again, the dead defacement of type which had already betrayed him: the crippled Vulcan to that Venus, who would not possess her but merely own her by the single strength which power gave, the dead power of money, wealth, gewgaws, baubles, as he might own, not a picture, statue: a field, say. He saw it: the fine land rich and fecund and foul and eternal and impervious to him who claimed title to it, oblivious, drawing to itself tenfold the quantity of living seed its owner's whole life could have secreted and compounded, producing a thousandfold the harvest he could ever hope to gather and save.

These combine with the prime mover unmoved:

> He took one look at her and saw what her brother would doubtless be the last to discern. He saw that she not only was not going to study, but there was nothing in books here or anywhere else that she would ever need to know, who had been born already completely equipped not only to face and combat but to overcome anything the future could invent to meet her with. He saw a child whom for the next two years he was to watch with what he thought at first was only rage, already grown at eight, who apparently had reached and passed puberty in the foetus, who, tranquil bemused and not even sullen, obedient to whatever outside compulsion it had been had merely transferred from one set of walls to another that quality of static waiting through and beneath the accumulating days of burgeoning and unhurryable time until whatever man it was to be whose name and face she probably had neither seen nor heard yet, would break into and disperse it. For five years he was to watch her, fetched each morning by the brother and remain just as he had left her, in the same place and almost in the same position, her hands lying motionless for hours on her lap like two separate slumbering bodies. She would answer "I don't know" when her atten-

tion was finally attracted at last, or, pressed, "I never got that far." It was as if her muscles and flesh too were even impervious to fatigue and boredom or as if, the drowsing maidenhead symbol's self, she possessed life but not sentience and merely waited until the brother came, the jealous seething eunuch priest, and removed her.

And Faulkner regularly calls in the mixture of myth and reality:

Even with that already forty miles of start toward freedom and (he knew it, said it) dignity and self-respect, he could not do it. He must return, drawn back into the radius and impact of an eleven-year-old girl who, even while sitting with veiled eyes against the sun like a cat on the schoolhouse steps at recess and eating a cold potato, postulated that ungirdled quality of the very goddesses in his Homer and Thucydides: of being at once corrupt and immaculate, at once virgins and the mothers of warriors and of grown men.

This use of myth, though, emphasizes not the 1920's distance but Eula's closeness to Olympus. Myth enlarges rather than degrades—she *is* at the source of fertility and power. And when all this turns out wasted on Flem, the earth laments:

If he had lived in Frenchman's Bend itself during that spring and summer, he would have known no more—a little lost village, nameless, without grace, forsaken, yet which wombed once by chance and accident one blind seed of the spendthrift Olympian ejaculation and did not even know it, without tumescence conceived, and bore—one bright brief summer, concentric, during which three fairly well-horsed buggies stood in steady rotation along a picket fence or spun along adjacent roads between the homes and the crossroads stores and the schoolhouses and churches where people gathered for pleasure or at least for escape, and then overnight and simultaneously were seen no more; then eccentric: buggies gone, vanished—a lean, loose-jointed, cotton-socked, shrewd, ruthless old man, the splendid girl with her beautiful masklike face, the froglike creature which barely reached her shoulder, cashing a check, buying a license, taking a train—a word, a single will to believe born of envy and old deathless regret, murmured from cabin to cabin above the washing pots and the sewing, from wagon to horseman in roads and lanes or from rider to halted plow in field furrows; the word, the dream and wish of all male under sun capable of harm—the young who only dreamed yet of the ruins they were still incapable of; the sick and the maimed sweating in sleepless beds, impotent for the harm they willed to do; the old, now-glandless earth-creeping, the very buds

> and blossoms, the garlands of whose yellowed triumphs had long fallen into the profitless dust, embalmed now and no more dead to the living world if they were sealed in buried vaults, behind the impregnable matronly calico of others' grandchildren's grandmothers—the word, with its implications of lost triumphs and defeats of unimaginable splendor—and which best: to have that word, that dream and hope for future, or to have had need to flee that word and dream, for past.

Faulkner keeps his heightening credible by a double technique: letting the Mississippi Thais draw her anchorite back from the desert; and mixing the intense and high-flown with the country comedy of dog packs, tomcatting, and "Stop pawing me, you old headless horseman Ichabod Crane."

The Hamlet moves closer than any of Faulkner's other major works toward a casual, "natural" structure—away from the machine ideal implicit in earlier experimental literature. Still, a visible line of progress appears. Until the last section the novel makes increasingly wry jokes about people who try to control themselves and whatever part of the environment they take an interest in. A variety of characters and circumstances demonstrate the tricks the irrational plays on "rational" aims. Such opposition occurs, of course, in Faulkner's other work, but here he gives his characters more hope of making their limited aims work. The comic tone derives from having so many at heaven's gate—and letting only other people and a few internal contradictions stand in the way. (The simpler, more definable ambitions of Faulkner's characters take them closer to self-realization than Warren's characters come in the novel which actually uses this phrase as title.) *The Hamlet* with its country segregation of goals looks forward to the "piecemeal technology" of the fifties.

Thus, from the gamesmanship which works after a fashion for Ratliff and sours Ab, the novel moves to the intenser, more painful joke of sexual anticipation, disregarding all personal qualities but one. The famous pastoral about the idiot in love with his cow broadens as it summarizes the paradigm. Word beauty celebrates a transforming tenderness in sex, absurdity underlines the Proustian point that object matters little. With these two areas of bearable losses staked and measured, Faulkner moves to the question of how much can be borne.

Mink meets the wryest joke of all. For him Faulkner gets in almost every range possible to the mixture of comedy and intensity. More than any other character, Mink tests the limits of mind as an agent for planning and controlling the future. How much unexpected emotion and obstacle can a man tolerate and still function effectively? (The answer is, A great deal, but not enough to win.) Mink represents in its purest form the impulse to be a force rather than a consciousness, to oppose a sea of troubles by direct, violent act. Donald Kartiganer calls him a heroic rebel, humanly preferable to the accommodating and resilient Ratliff. Though Faulkner's perspective can include both characters, Mink unquestionably calls up the greatest dramatic writing in the novel. By the test of productive sympathy, he ranks as the central figure. For his unsuccessful handling of aggression tests the sincerity and staying power of every socially acceptable mode of channeling. He sets the basic equation. If every frustration produces a corresponding aggressive impulse, as modern psychology argues, and every mode of sublimating brings its percentage of defeats, can enough pent-up energy be dissipated? Society has a method, of course, for ultimately controlling Mink: it puts him in the penitentiary. But what about the short run?

Though Mink seems heroic, he is not finally a hero of the definitive act. Faulkner, like the law, assumes that outbreaks will occur from time to time. Channeling aggression will never work perfectly. Mink is the hero of living with consequences, a hero of strain. To a degree he understands this himself. When he murders his neighbor, he may be acting irrationally but not without a plan. Events are still following it when satisfaction ends and the first obstacle appears. Mink realizes that he has killed an enemy and acquired a corpse. Faulkner's mixture of fear, foresight, and fact conveys the felt life of Mink's first reality problem, disposing of the body:

He must rise and quit the thicket and do what he had next to do, not to finish it but merely to complete the first step of what he had started, put into motion, who realised now that he had known already, before he heard the horse and raised the gun, that that would happen which had happened: that he had pulled trigger on an enemy but had only slain a corpse to be hidden. So he sat up behind the log and shut his eyes and counted slowly until the shaking stopped and the sound of the galloping horse and even the outrageous and incredible shot had died out of his ears and he could rise, carrying the slanted gun still loaded with the shell which had failed to explode, and emerge from the thicket, already hurrying. But even then it would be dusk before he reached home.

The elements in this combination for evoking strain give the section its force. Mink keeps reacting "rationally" to the unexpected event. When the corpse develops a soul, in the howling hound, Mink puts in nights trying to silence it with shotgun and ax. He accepts the chance of money for escape, and rejects the offer when it offends his idea of honor. When Lump Snopes attempts to go shares on Houston's money without having suffered for it, Mink defends principle by cunning delay and finally with a club. Only the hound can make him panic.

But Faulkner mixes this cerebral element with emotion and comedy in extraordinarily skillful ways. Everything that interferes with Mink's schemes seem to him—and the reader—absurd. When the obstacle is primarily external, comedy dominates. Lump's playing checkers to win and chasing Mink across the cornfield breathing adenoidal pleas for reason play broad humor against Mink's intense purpose. On the other hand, his daytime stupor stands with some of Faulkner's best horror writing about the feeling of powerlessness. Mink's hearing sounds, knowing that someone is watching from the door, and yet being unable to pull himself from sleep recreates nightmare. His hour-by-hour terror at too little time as he tries to find the ax, get rid of Lump, and locate the tree with the body conveys a great strain still compatible with coordinated activity. His desperate swings at the hound show this tensely held organization breaking down. And, in a great twist of crime-and-punishment absurdity, his determination to silence the dog lets the sheriff capture him effortlessly. Mink's suicide leap from the buggy shows him straining to the end, after effort has no hope beyond inflicting pain on the self. And Faulkner's final still shot totals the cyclical result of all this struggle. Mink hears the chain gang coming in and clamors for his right to food—frustrated and discriminated against again.

With Eula gone, the final section looks toward finding common ground for the Ratliff and Mink spirits. Faulkner forecasts developments in the novel by beginning an interchange between his compartments. Earlier episodes hint at connections. Ratliff's skill in bargaining about sewing machines and promissory notes produces a sample of Mink's frustrations. The cosmic joke carried through Ike and the cow echoes in the murder story. Mrs. Mink's entrapment of the lonely young fugitive has led to multiple angers; her leaving him after the crime heightens his aloneness. And Mink's vengefulness over his inability to deal with all these devils around him gives depth to Ratliff's insulated but straightforward story.

In the last section the Mink spirit appears in Armstid, another tenant farmer. He too believes in direct dominance. His delusion that he can tame wild ponies to the plow leads him, however, into partnership with Ratliff, the devotee of applied mind. They come together through a common dream of achieving immediately a wealth that will enable them to tower over daily circumstance. But Flem tricks Ratliff about gold at the Frenchman's Place by the simple ploy of planting some while Ratliff, overusing his head and overestimating Will Varner, is looking for a second convolution. Too much intelligence overplays itself in practical dealings. Faulkner leaves the problem by recording the different responses. Ratliff can live with a wry recognition of his own limits. Armstid goes mad and keeps on digging. The contents of the compartments do not integrate, but they edge the fictional center away from contemplation toward dealing with the available. The moral value of the flexible and the dogged remains after the overwhelming victory of the efficient producer.

In sum, *The Hamlet* sees the comic scene as a *preparation* for present struggles and develops a maneuver for making competitive games half acceptable because they enrich a dreary life and channel "natural" anger. Frenchman's Bend is the training camp for Jefferson, the center of adult reality for Faulkner, and, significantly, both Ratliff and Flem continue there in the succeeding volumes of the trilogy. The action makes a doubted way of life familiar and deep rooted enough to be lived with; scene and a style exist for this drama, and for some people a wry conciliation may be possible. But it remains contradictory. Angers will still get out of hand and lead to overreaching or outbreak, but they are humanizing and give intensity to life. Schemes may lead to the sterility of Flem, but they enliven things for Ratliff and he lives to scheme again. At best the supposedly rational goals of society barely channel the aggressions—and when they do, the tone is comic—but Mink's anger cannot be channeled. The wavering tone of the novel, which has aroused so much controversy about whether it has a direction at all, reflects Faulkner's sense of a precarious traditional balance always threatened by the uncontainable.

Faulkner shows the fractured self trying to respond to the pressure of the times by pulling itself together to act toward defined objectives. But Faulkner retains a loyalty to the fracturing pressure. He likes a self kept loose at the plate, alert to many impulses. The tension between the possibility of prevailing—by defining purpose more precisely—and the appeal of the fracturing self, rich at least in intensity of feeling, produces his compartmental structures. Faulkner thus avoids the exclusions which Warren has to make; he does not want finally to sacrifice any part of the self for the sake of control. He is willing to live with the diffuse.

However much *The Hamlet* may be a probing advance for Faulkner, younger writers have found its scene and maneuver unsatisfying. Not only does the city represent adult reality to them, but the consolation that things have always been this way conveys little meaning. (If so, they ought to be better.) But the younger writers see play as a right and training, the push of society to pass on its wisdom of experience, as the critical locale. The hero can resist, adapt, or run from its impact—but not avoid exposure. Their increased sense of personal vulnerability—and opportunity—makes them write not geographies, but autobiographies. An "I" with all its disunities upon it must confront the necessary and available. In place of Faulkner's overview, where protagonists can be sacrificed to understanding of the total situation, a hero with an uncertain mixture of strength and weakness and an inadequate chart of reality must confront point-by-point issues. First person technique for the newer novelists coincides with first person thinking. And first person sacrifice always comes harder than third person.

So, for all Faulkner's immediacy, he is more detached and analytic than his successors. Where he is broadly genetic, they are direct, personal, familial. Their heroes have only an occasional moment to imagine what the large social past may have been. For generic purposes, nothing yet written surpasses *The Catcher in the Rye* as American Angry. In fact, anger *at* the book has matched that in it. Readers resent being drawn so sympathetically into a fairly congenial illness, and Ratliff after Ratliff has had a try at downing it. The defects are all there—endless self-pity, Sherwood Anderson "Gee whiz" naïveté—but a novel that can keep getting denounced for more than a decade must have at least three lives, if not nine, and another besides the illness seems probable.

Salinger sensed even earlier than the young men in England a rebellion against opportunity. He became the first to find a scene, language, and action for impatience with the more rigorous adolescence which postwar hopes demanded. The first drive in *The Catcher in the Rye* is the hero's to achieve *at once* adulthood as he imagines it to be. He does not want to spend years learning how to write English, get along with girls, or be liked by his associates, but his only answer comes from an inherited idea of adult play, followed by retreat to a childhood ideal of it. The response of wounded idealism is American Standard with a twist.

A similar rebellion of the young after World War I succeeded, but then the older generation had lost its nerve and did not fully oppose bright youth announcing that everything in the past had been done wrong. After World War II, though, veterans of the depression as well as an expected war showed more fight: adults were willing to see young personality distorted quite a bit from its natural bent in the interest of controlling the environment. When Sputnik went up, parents promptly agreed that the Russians had done it first, not because they had concentrated on doing it, but because high school kids were not studying algebra hard enough.

Salinger's scene of the private school, like the pastoral in *The Hamlet,* contains in itself a widely trusted ideal. Holden can have the rewards if he only works within its rules. And the rules *are* the ideals: get an expensive education, compete for marks but learn living with others, do what you are told is good for you and the group. The novel has been popular with intelligent young people because, for lack of a better, they believe in and do these things, yet want to rebel against them without seeing how.

The Catcher in the Rye is pivotal in this discussion because Holden actually experiences a *how* with some tradition and hope behind it. He sets out to oppose complete play to what he thinks of as complete coercion—either/or. His start looks 1920-ish, but the young in the twenties could join a party of party-going to outrage the stuffy. Holden knows of no such group; so his rebellious play must be solitary. In an irony that Salinger understands well, Holden becomes the greatest phony of them all. By trying at sixteen to act like a midwestern businessman on a binge—renting a hotel room, ordering drinks, getting a call girl, spending to impress the bellhop—he distorts his real self far more than the school means to.

His next move, the retreat toward childhood, intends both to intensify play and purify it. "Phony" means to him doing things he cannot believe in and thinks that others cannot. But Old Phoebe going round and round on that carousel is real—and the favorite scene in the book for Salinger enthusiasts. The ideal figure of Catcher in the Rye wants to protect children so cheerful at play that they are likely to fall over cliffs. A similarly clean, intense pleasure comes from the ice skating. Holden does not, of course, and does not want to wholly escape sex and the equivocal. In courting his sister, he finds a safe situation which happily suggests a telling violation of the mores. His demand, though, that play be innocent is exactly what was to be proved—that school is not virtue and play not guilt. However, his ultimate rationale for his hopes and behavior is highly traditional. The lessons which the school offers are perhaps civilizing, but certainly man-made, and his justification for his distaste invokes the natural—in his case, the childlike.

Salinger leaves it at almost that, but not quite. The framework of illness puts a different perspective, regretful but realistic, on the soft interior of the novel. Salinger knows that to act so radically on an ideal of childhood play in the 1950's is to be judged ill—in fact, to be ill—and this sickness of the sensitive becomes the subject of his later work. In his novel, society does not create the disease, at most it aggravates it. We do not see enough of society to establish an adequate cause. We do see the illness that has been the century's signature for sensitivity interacting with an ideal of play more overt and more doubtfully held than any in Faulkner.

The Catcher in the Rye expresses a lyric insight. Its twin success of the same year, *The Adventures of Augie March*, deals with play, competition, and cost in breadth and depth. One logic would recommend proceeding directly to it, but in the interest of polarizing a change of heart we have already skipped several intervening steps. Faulkner and Elizabeth Bowen forecast the end of pastoral hopes gone sour in a commercial society. Robert Penn Warren is the last major novelist to *feel* the present as a direct evolution from an agrarian economy and agrarian values.

Novels of Forces

FOUR

The Poet Turned First-Degree Murderer: Robert Penn Warren

While Faulkner dips through light swells toward posterity, the small craft warnings are flying for Warren. His failure to produce a major novel in eighteen years fosters disappointment, common as such cases are in the history of literature. His paperbacks are becoming harder to depend on. They go out, come back in smaller print, go out again. Young people revive the suspicion of academic conspiracy that political opponents raised a generation ago.

Yet none of these flags signals weather as surely as the doubt within. Some of us who cheered Warren as the voice of the age when the good novels came out now find ourselves quick to honor and reluctant to reread. And when we do, uncertainty sets in at points that once seemed exciting. The intricate cross-symbolism looks too right. Mother is a thrice-kept woman, the upright judge is the real father, but the Scholarly Attorney is another father and so is Willie, and a complex of murders, suicides, insanities, and cries of "oh, oh" must occur to reconcile Jack and us to them all. The pure girl must take a mud bath to become marriageable, and an ancestor had it worked out the whole time. No one questions the logic of all this—that causes the trouble. As discovery broadens into "wisdom" and mannerism in fiction shifts from management to style, gratitude for the superb diagnostician recedes and the harsh issue becomes what, if anything, Warren does better than others who agree with him.

The current question does not outdate existing answers. From the first, Warren has had good luck in his interpreters. He had helped teach hundreds, and many of the best minds reciprocated by giving him as accurate a reading as we have for any contemporary except Eliot and Faulkner. Skillful critics mapped the conflict between the need to kill father and be reconciled with him, the power of self-recognition, the significance of narrators, the intricacies of structure, the relationship to Faulkner, the meaning of violence, and the reasons for style. Good craftsmen put mortar between these bricks. Less generous interpreters performed their service for truth by naming the vulnerable points—"drug store gothic" and the like.

Yet, though Warren has won a place in history, these concerns may not prove enough to keep him alive. They may help to bury him. For a philosophical novelist benefits immensely at first from the time spirit. Literary historians have explained the effects of the first World War on literature and said much less about the second. The earlier case was dramatic, the later revolutionary at a more sophisticated level. The first completed a revolt against simpler souls, vaporized any surviving faith in commercial industrial civilization as a value in itself. The discipline of the second war drove home to rebels that this kind of society remained an ineluctable modality of the visible, but revolt came against an élite committed to sensitivity—not by denying its worth, but by making it seem less satisfying than an earlier generation had hoped.

The short-run literary effect of the second war was thus exactly opposite from that of the first: to parallel rather than fight the imperatives of war. War, after all, gives purpose to the random acts and thoughts of individuals. More than that, it makes naval lieutenants out of automobile salesmen and price control administrators out of academics. The diversity of wartime needs liberated the pent-up energy of the thirties by giving even sensitives a chance to try running the world—or some well marked-off corner of it. The novelists of the forties, formed on the frustrated purposefulness of the preceding decade, transferred their feelings to the new universal need for power and direction. In wartime, communication media drive the idea of organized force into the safest noncombatant consciousness; only an insane detachment could have prevented novelists from taking an interest in self-expression through channeled effort and applied thought.

Moreover, the world suddenly needed its imaginative men. With the depression over and situations everywhere fluid—particularly with the pressure for results making questions public service rather than sedition—novelists as well as scientists found themselves speaking like authorities. In the vacuum of diminished public confidence, imaginative men found their charts, pieced together mostly for fun by their predecessors, more accurate for locating and navigating than popular tradition. After being disregarded for so long, writers naturally turned garrulous and a bit arrogant. Jack Burden's wise-guy voice, an invention not yet obsoleted out of the American novel, speaks for a new man suddenly even prouder of his knowledgeability than of his tender toughness. He can influence events, defy authority with the backing of authority, and intimidate policemen. All by talking.

Unfortunately, though, the valuable charts were scattered—in novels, poetry, psychology, philosophy, anthropology, history, the *New Republic*. Everybody had been so busy sawing lumber that no one had designed a house. Under the shotgun pressure to codify knowledge in order to apply it and assuage anxiety, existentialism caught on as a sort of Everyman's blueprint; but in countries less given to naming, each novelist had to make his own. At a minimum he had to reproduce the supercharged sense of crisis and examine a kind of knowledge that could conceivably prove helpful. The threats of anonymity and narrowed personal purpose thus developed toward the contemporary passion for *identity*. The word, of course, usually means something generous, large in inner turmoil if not in effect on the environment. The first generation, which provided size at the risk of being unable to integrate the fractured self, was an age of pure science—knowledge for its own sake and its shock effect on ignorance. Its successor has been an age of applied science. The 1930's already had a great impulse to *do* something, but all the talk faltered at the difficulty of making a start. Levers existed for moving the world, but no platform. The bottled-up anger produced Faulkner's long waits followed by sporadic violence rather than Warren's planned use of force.

So the novelists of the forties, inheritors and discoverers at once, are militants with feelings—and morality. The second war *was* more obviously moral than the first: the enemy of civilized arrangements defined himself more clearly and desperately. In any great national conflict people have to believe in power—more than that, take an interest in it. Only winning guarantees the bad old world they didn't like. But the second war showed power, hitherto more or less disreputable, as the public defender. Without its use the situation, however mixed and bad, would become unmistakably worse. This shocking new worth activated imaginations to the testing of hopes that constitutes the novelist's most utilitarian contribution to society. During the thirties moral power had remained a perpetual possibility. The forties brought it into real life, forced people to live with its effects, gave them a taste and distaste for it.

If Warren is a first-rank novelist, it is not because he is "wise"; he simply brings the most energy and knowledge to bear imaginatively on this point of collision. No other novelist so committed to modernism—with its devotion to truth of the inner life, its alliance with a presumably superior past, its confidence in its vision of something better than commercial industrial society—so powerfully conveys the surprise at being given world enough and time to try translating arrogance into actuality. In all of his best novels, this pent-up anger finds itself freer than it had dreamed possible to press upon living flesh. Where in Faulkner violence counterattacks against unbearable stasis, violence in Warren acts calculatingly in the name of concretely envisaged freedom. Warren is a true shock novelist—not in his plots or his embarrassed sexuality, but in his focus on the tender, murderous imagination of the twentieth century suddenly authorized to practice control upon events. He shows more forcefully than any of his rivals what enthusiasm for control is and where it hurts most. He writes the emerging novel of forces with a more violent drive than Snow or Greene or Sartre or Camus.

My case for Warren thus rests upon his militant imaginative energy warring with his cultural inheritance. The social and self diagnoses are parts of this, though not necessarily the most lasting ones. The clash within the Puritan ethic—maintaining high motives while getting what you want—has diminished. The sense of a locatable crisis has spread out in search of an object. The once central issue of self-knowledge has moved on to, After self-knowledge, what? Acceptance transforms insight into one element in a new equation. And in the hard realities of time, critical emphasis on self-knowledge now threatens Warren's continuance as a live figure. True, the idea of such questing, with its tendency to transform the novels into cautionary tales, can turn into self-recognition forced on a protagonist who can *never* know enough soon enough. But the limits of Warren's explanations appear more starkly now than they did fifteen or twenty years ago. Essentially, he depends upon a commonwealth of guilt grounded in the family romance. Though fewer people now question this chart, more recognize its crudity. Such sophistication can make the wish behind the cross-referencing drama seem too tensely held. Straightening everything into a tight pattern may be impossible and undesirable—may be, as Herzog's psychiatrist says, a dangerous inability to tolerate ambiguous situations.

In the novel of forces scene must carry a good deal of the weight once assigned to fluid consciousness. Though the drive in writers who came to maturity in the forties resembles that generated by wartime necessities, the best instinctively shift the milieu to civilian situations which parallel the feelings of the time but not the prime circumstances. What looks like genius in retrospect may have been nearer to *Irma La Douce's* "simple economics." In Mailer and Jones, who do not shift, emotions become futile expressions against irresistible authority. Greene's, Warren's, and Snow's transferring militancy to civil life allows feelings to return as real forces in decision and consequence.

Warren's first two novels led to his breakthrough in *All the King's Men*. In *Night Rider* the fundamental drive is for definiteness. Kenneth Burke first recognized the importance of its division into day and night worlds, and one point should be added. The day world is radically indefinite. It consists of claustrophobia in the train, the miscellaneous crowd, release and exhilaration in Munn's speech followed by letdown and question, victory in Trevelyan's trial succeeded by doubts as to justice. But the night world makes definiteness seem a possibility. In the dark the great fantasies can be acted out. Munn can lead a search of the negro cabin and terrorize its inhabitants; can retry Trevelyan and exact punishment in the lynching; can recreate Confederate myth in the Morgan raid and ambush at the ford; can try Senator Tolliver, the avatar of the day world, in his own mind and set out to destroy him. This militant search for definitions grand enough to encompass all complexities is basic to Warren's best work. And he represents the resistance thoroughly, ranges all over for every complication that might thwart definition.

In *At Heaven's Gate* the former All-American is the official militant myth-hero and the financier the myth-villain. But these explain too much and too little. The two dynamic characters are Sue Murdoch, whose anger defines her, and Slim Sarrett, the poet as theatrical man. Sue looks forward to Warren's militant heroes. Slim has found the combination for both enlarging his estimate of himself and keeping it enough within bounds to skid by. He has created the self which he chooses to present to the world. He does it by absorbing literature, learning to box with safe ferocity, and replacing his respectable Baptist parents with a romantic story about a prostitute mother.

If Warren is to remain among the major novelists, though, *All the King's Men* must stand as more than a monument to some minor Muse like the American Political Novel. Warren makes this rereading hard to do. Unlike most contemporaries, he does not automatically enlist the reader's collaboration. His drive for definiteness leads him to finish sentences that his fellow novelists like to leave dangling. Above everything else, he is an anxious writer. At the end of *All the King's Men*, his fear of the ferocity within leads him to tie up loose ends in a frenzy of reconciliations—with Jack's mother, Judge Irwin, the Scholarly Attorney, Anne, and Cass Mastern. He has to protect the new life at every point from the threat of emotional kickback. So he returns to that fountain of modern renewal, youthful hopes, and tries to carry them intact across the barrier of adult years.

But up to that point he had been doing better than most novelists. He writes powerful dramatic scenes. He brings together militant energy and a theatrical imagination at a time when theatricality carried man's hope; and he fixes these upon a double locale admirably suited to testing their range. Even in 1945 no one needed a philosophical fictionist to discover some discrepancy between ends and means; the easier universals get established in the consciousness of the race earlier than that. Warren's theatricality sets up a conflict between subtler ambivalent feelings—a love-fear for the integrity of anger, a love-hatred for slyness, and an impossible yearning for personal force.

Unity of being through anger appears in its pure form in Willie's speech after he finds the city machine has tricked him. Willie is completely himself, the farmers are completely themselves; yet they are all in the betrayal together. The pros, Jack and Sadie, hitherto cut off by their knowledgeability, unite with the One and the Many. Willie taps their animosity toward the process they have devoted their lives to. Though Willie later increases his power to mould the crowd, this unity never reoccurs. Jack and Sadie become themselves again. While the speech lasts, though, it achieves the wanted transcendance: it makes anger and love, public and private, identical. A vindicating unity closes the space between hero and populace, good and mixture, anger and effectiveness. In Warren, as in Elizabeth Bowen, desire for this kind of leap is absolute. Characters come to terms with not getting, but cannot stop wanting.

Yet, for all its satisfying power, spontaneously expressed anger accomplishes little more than the impassive anger of the rednecks. Change and control require mind, applied knowledge, method. The shadow falls between these and pure inspiration. The critical conflict in *All the King's Men* occurs not between ends and means, but between spontaneity and technique. More than anything else, Jack Burden expresses distrust for the use of mind divorced from the integrity of anger. Loss of an exciting, unifying vision determines the opening attitude toward Willie. The means he uses in the drug store speech at Mason City are not immoral in the sense that his coercing Judge Irwin is. They are not even seriously false. They amount to little more than what courses in public speaking inculcate daily in respectable universities—adapting the material to the audience. Willie tells the farm town crowd that he has slopped hogs and got manure on his shoes. He does not need votes just now. He has acted for these people in building highways and schools despite the Establishment's opposition. Everything he says is so.

At the bottom of Jack's resentment lies not untruth but a concept of Nature. He dislikes in Willie what he dislikes in himself—the self-conscious use of mind and knowledge. In so far as the farmers and townspeople represent an untutored self, any intellectualized means of dealing with them becomes by definition unnatural, since it destroys the wanted unity between complex and simple. Willie's skill at reducing distance and getting the rustics to share the glory of the governorship offends Jack because it is technique and not impulse. Jack admires from the heart Willie's ability to impose personal force on other people. He admires Judge Irwin's power to resist. But these are rare gifts. A man of Jack's sensitivity cannot hope to match them. Given a generalized sense of grievance equal to Willie's and the folk's, he must depend upon indirection—talent and acquired skills. So he hates the part of his hero that must also utilize these civilized stratagems. The bedrock ideal remains, as in *Night Rider*, the defining act of imposing will.

The traditional case for Warren rests on his "wise" perception of conflicts between means and ends plus his understanding the self in relation to them. But his great claim to endurance rests on his "immoral" impulse, his secret sharing with the enemy. No other contemporary touches Warren's powerful identification with energetic intelligence—his enthusiasm for the efficient producer. In dramatizing the drive that Snow only suggests, he expresses better than anyone else the spirit of the forties. Politics in Warren appeals through its ruthlessness, its ethic of the imposed will, its by-passing the claims of decency and the civilian rules for muffling conflict. It allies with war and hero worship rather than democratic referral to committee. Only because Warren feels this drive in his bones can he raise the serious moral issue for an organizing society—the question of *degrees* of flexibility.

The power of the novel comes from imposing two forms of energy, embodied in Willie and Jack, on the permanent scene of state politics. The driving use of personal force and charisma plus applied intelligence brings on the threat inherent in anger itself, but the chances for men sensitive to suffering as deprivation to take over and hold the machinery of control have become real enough to power a full-scale imaginative test. That the effort could be made at all reflects an enormous shift in the sense of felt life. For Faulkner that collective dream did not die with Sutpen in the nineteenth century; it never existed.

It is important to be clear on the nature of the action in *All the King's Men*. Vulnerability to the threat of anger within and without makes the structure concentrate on staying power. Summaries credit Willie with accomplishments—roads, schools, even the hospital contract—but the three main actions after his quick rise to office are all defensive. He defeats the impeachment threat. The purifying hospital plan arises from guilt dramatized by the attack. The last political program fends off MacMurfee's blackmail attempt. (Judge Irwin dies almost accidentally during this episode—

a pedestrian who does not get out of the crosswalk fast enough.) Warren has a theatrical mind—loving to elevate forces and bring them to moments of truth—and his political drama poses a single large question: can men sensitive to pain, endowed with anger beyond the pragmatic but clear only on short-run purposes, *retain* any control on the direction life takes? Does enthusiasm have staying power?

So in the over-all action the proponents of directed aggressiveness fight a defensive battle for control and good repute against the reaction of self-interest and earlier styles. The "directed" in their program handicaps the rebels. Both sides use aggressive means, but the new men waver because their use of technique is in its nature "insincere." Keeping in touch with their rural justification forces them into a frantic side-race. Warren records better than anyone else so far the grinding mesh of energy, sensitivity, and applied knowledge. After twenty years the settings, scenes, and language that do this retain their power. And the effect depends upon a plausible but magnificent distortion, inherent in the scene—that government runs mainly by deploying shameful knowledge.

But who is Willie Stark? He is the ideal figure the age had been working toward ever since it had decided to discard the artist's passivity. The New Man, simultaneously effective and sensitive. He embodies the triumph, and strain, of the Energy Principle. His "greatness" means his ability to team hitherto antagonistic forces in the name of righteous anger. As noted before, the novel of forces depends heavily on scene for emotional effects that earlier appeared through fluid consciousness; one of Warren's greatest superiorities to writers who agree with him lies in making a dual scene multiply the vitality of his ideal tragic figure.

For Warren redoubles the energy of his already energetic hero by making him the one and only master of two naturally hostile locales, the soured pastoral of the rednecks and the predictability-loving political machine. These two huge metaphors extend outward from central cores. The pastoral furnishes suppressed anger given, in a state of nature, to sporadic outbreak. Faulkner had already discovered that rhythm. The machine supplies a perfected technique for fighting without being destroyed. The one wants to kill its masters, the other to make them prevail smoothly. Only the Hero can combine these contradictory drives into purposeful force. And only Warren has been able to combine them with theatrical character into the hero that the age demanded and did not like.

Our tolerant present favors mass forgiveness for the Fugitives; their good deeds since have made up for their foolishness about forty acres and a mule. But with Warren we shall be forgiving too much. The same analogical sympathy, along with the same remoteness from the farmers' actual lives and hopes, permeates *All the King's Men.* In other novels the mixture creates the falsest notes in his work. When Warren tries to come close to the folk, he gets corny, but in his masterpiece he holds Mason City and the campaign trail at a photographer's distance that is exactly right for him.

Willie is *of* the soured pastoral world—and he can manage it. Moreover, his discovered talent for dramatizing himself as the voice of its will not only works, but enables him to live with the discrepancy between *of* and *for* in a comfort that the "sincere" sensitive man, Jack Burden, finds impossible. The protagonists' effort to base the complex upon the simple resembles the impulse that Empson describes for the Elizabethans*, but Warren's being the heir to fifty years' increase in range and depth of consciousness expands the gap—quantitatively if not qualitatively. Also, instead of using clownish contentment to contrast with urban whatever, Warren makes clownish frustration and aggressiveness a correlative for a universal sense of being deprived. So the farmers provide the visible moral base—and the only one—for the sophisticates' acts. Even more important, their inexpressible anger steps up the horsepower that drives, enlarges, and justifies the application of mind and technique.

The first peasant to appear embodies this combination superbly:

> Somebody back in the crowd yelled, "Hi, Willie!" The Boss lifted his right hand and waved in acknowledgment to the unknown admirer. Then the Boss spied a fellow at the far end of the soda fountain, a tall, gaunt-shanked, malarial, leather-faced side of jerked venison, wearing

* *Some Versions of Pastoral.* London, 1935.

jean pants and a brace of mustaches hanging off the kind of face you see in photographs of General Forrest's cavalrymen, and the Boss started toward him and put out his hand. Old Leather-Face didn't show. Maybe he shuffled one of his broken brogans on the tiles, and his Adam's apple jerked once or twice, and the eyes were watchful out of that face which resembled the seat of an old saddle left out in the weather, but when the Boss got close, his hand came up from the elbow, as though it didn't belong to Old Leather-Face but was operating on its own, and the Boss took it.

Ritualized instinct may not be solving many contemporary problems, but it has one in common with the sophisticates—the consequences of aggression.

"How you making it, Malaciah?" the Boss asked.

The Adam's apple worked a couple of times, and the Boss shook the hand which was hanging out there in the air as if it didn't belong to anybody, and Old Leather-Face said, "We're grabblen."

"How's your boy?" the Boss asked.

"Ain't doen so good," Old Leather-Face allowed.

"Sick?"

"Naw," Old Leather-Face allowed, "jail."

"My God," the Boss said, "What they doing round here, putting good boys in jail?"

"He's a good boy," Old Leather-Face allowed. "Hit wuz a fahr fight, but he had a leetle bad luck."

"Huh?"

"Hit was fahr and squahr, but he had a leetle bad luck. He stobbed the feller and he died."

Warren does more than make the scene represent; his gratuitous affection shows through. For this old leech-gatherer muddies his role as justifier of his betters' anger. Willie's providing a lawyer for the son goes beyond getting schools and roads for the deserving. What Warren likes about his dismounted cavalryman is ferocity muffled by a learned, emotion-concealing style of response. Soured pastoral incarnates the fighting spirit, however limited its techniques.

But the rural can no longer serve so unequivocally to represent the counter-ideal of community. The eros of Warren's countryside is individual and not powerful. Lucy Stark does represent love as nurturing and nursing, but she makes her stands for the integrity of anger. Her teaching job, the politicians believe, causes Willie to fight for sound school construction—and get his start. She leaves him when he refuses to fire the corrupt state auditor. Her scene is the porch at the Stark farm, her sister's chicken ranch—and the hospital. She comments on political life chiefly by her absences and serves as the measure of Willie's distance from angry pastoral.

Militant individualism has killed the tribal ideal of community. In one of the best early scenes, public taste for the lost image inspires a newsman to photograph Willie patting the aged farm dog on the porch of the old home.

"Here, Buck," the Boss called.

Tom Stark prodded the dog with his toe for a little encouragement, but he might just as well have been prodding a bolster.

"Buck is gitten on," Old Man Stark said. "He ain't right spry any more." Then the old man went to the steps and stooped down with a motion which made you expect to hear the sound of old rusty hinges on a barn door. "Hi, Buck, hi, Buck," the old man wheedled without optimism. He gave up, and lifted his gaze to the Boss. "If he was hongry now," he said, and shook his head. "If he was hongry we could guile him. But he ain't hongry. His teeth gone bad."

The Boss looked at me, and I knew what I was paid to do.

"Jack," the Boss said, "get the hairy bastard up here and make him look like he was glad to see me."

I was supposed to do a lot of different things, and one of them was to lift up fifteen-year-old, hundred-and-thirty-five-pound hairy white dogs on summer afternoons and paint an expression of unutterable bliss upon their faithful features as they gaze deep, deep into the Boss's eyes. I got hold of Buck's forelegs, as though I were girding myself to shove a wheelbarrow, and heaved. It didn't work. I got his front end up for a second, but just as I got him up, he breathed out and I breathed in. One gust of Buck was enough. It was like a gust from a buzzard's nest. I was paralyzed. Buck hit the porch boards and lay there like the old polar-bear rug he resembled.

Then Tom Stark and one of the reporters shoved on the tail end and I heaved on the front end and held my breath and we got Buck the seven feet to the Boss. The Boss braced himself, and we heaved up the front end, and the Boss got a gust of Buck.

That gust was enough.

"God's sake, Pappy," the Boss demanded as soon as he had mastered his spasm, "what you been feeding this dog?"

"He ain't got any appetite," Old Man Stark said.

"He ain't got any appetite for violets," the Boss said, and spat on the ground.

"The reason he fell," the photographer observed, "was because his hind legs gave down. Once we get him propped we got to work fast."

"We?" the Boss said. "We! What the hell you mean *we*. You come kiss him. One whiff would curdle milk and strip a pine tree. *We*, hell!"

The Boss took a deep breath, and we heaved again. It didn't work. Buck didn't have any starch in him. We tried six or seven times, but it was no sale. Finally the Boss had to sit down on the steps, and we dragged Buck up and laid the faithful head on the Boss's knee. The Boss put his hand on Buck's head and looked at the photographer's birdie. The photographer shot it, and said, "It is the nuts," and the Boss said, "Yeah, the nuts."

The Boss sat there a few seconds with his hand on Buck's head. "A dog," the Boss said, "is man's best friend. Old Buck, he's the best friend I ever had." He scratched the brute's head. "Yeah, good old Buck," the Boss said, "the best friend I ever had. But God damn it," he said, and stood up so quick that Buck's head slid off his knee, "he don't smell a bit better'n the rest of 'em."

The Capitol and the dog smell alike from being used to sell rural inspiration.

Nevertheless, energized by this soured pastoral, Willie is the man who can heal the Faulknerian fracture. He can harness applied knowledge to the anger arising from deprivation. He has the force and the technique to master the political machine. Warren's keeping this side of his scene omnipresent shows great skill. Some critics complain that Tiny Duffy, its center, is not much of a character. True. The real force is the machinery itself. It does not involve persons in any complex sense, but understandings, chains-of-command, needs, common embarrassments, and agreed-upon rewards. Without the professionals, government will not run; axiomatically, "good people" will not do the daily work or take the daily blows. Though these uncivil servants levy a tax on all transactions, some business does get through. The machinery has no direction, only a will to survive. Tiny Duffy was a power in state politics when Willie was a county treasurer and he succeeds Willie as governor. City or country makes little difference. Professionalism binds courthouse, city hall, and capital.

Since anyone who wants to direct society must use the machinery, Willie's argument to Hugh Miller, the upright young man who resigns, gets no answer in the novel. Warren represents this permanent force not by showing character in depth—depth is not the politician's dimension—but by turning on lights now and then in dark rooms. Jack's early visit to the Mason County Courthouse sets the basic scene and the tone of contempt mixed with acceptance:

"It ain't any of my bizness. I'm the Sheriff."

"Well, Sheriff," I said, "Whose business is it?"

"Them as is tending to it. If folks would quit messen and let 'em."

"Who is *them?*"

"Commissioners," the Sheriff said. "The County Commissioners, the voters of Mason County done elected to tend to their bizness and not take no butten-in from nobody."

"Yeah, sure—the Commissioners. But who are they?"

The Sheriff's little wise eyes blinked at me a couple of times, then he said, "The constable ought to lock you up fer vagruncy."

"Suits me," I said. "And the *Chronicle* would send up another boy to cover my case, and when the constable pinched him the *Chronicle* would send up another one to cover that case, and after a while you'd get us all locked up. But it might get in the papers."

The Sheriff just lay there, and out of his big round face his little eyes blinked. Maybe I hadn't said anything. Maybe I wasn't there.

"Who are the Commissioners?" I said. "Or maybe they are hiding out?"

"One of 'em is setten right there," the Sheriff said, and rolled his big round head on his shoulders to indicate one of the other fellows. When the head had fallen back into place, and his fingers had let go my card, which wafted down to the floor in the gentle breeze from the fan, the little eyes blinked again and he seemed to sink below the surface of the roiled waters. He had done his best, and now he had passed the ball.

"Are you a Commissioner?" I asked the fellow just indicated. He was just another fellow, made in God's image and wearing a white shirt with a ready-tied black bow tie and jean pants held up with web galluses. Town from the waist up, country from the waist down. Get both votes.

"Yeah," he said.

"He's the head man," another fellow said, reverently, a little old squirt of a fellow with a bald knotty old head and a face he himself couldn't recollect from one time he looked in the mirror to the next, the sort of a fellow who hangs around and sits in a chair when the big boys leave one vacant and tries to buy his way into the game with a remark like the one he had just made.

"You the Chairman?" I asked the other fellow.

"Yeah," he said.

"You mind telling me your name?"

"It ain't no secret," he said. "It is Dolph Pillsbury."

"Glad to know you, Mr. Pillsbury," I said and held out my hand. Not getting up, he took it as though I had offered him the business end of a cottonmouth moccasin in shedding time.

"Mr. Pillsbury," I said, "you are in a position to know the situation in regard to the schoolhouse contract. No doubt you are interested in having the truth of that situation made public."

"There ain't any situation," Mr. Pillsbury said.

"Maybe there isn't any situation," I said, "but there's been a right smart racket."

"Ain't any situation. Board meets and takes a bid what's been offered. J. H. Moore's the fellow's name."

"Was that fellow Moore's bid low?"

"Not egg-zackly."

"You mean it wasn't low?"

"Well–" Mr. Pillsbury said, and his face was shadowed by an expression which might have been caused by a gas pain, "well if'n you want to put it that a-way."

"All right," I said, "let's put it that way."

"Now look a-here–" and the shadow passed from Mr. Pillsbury's face and he sat up in his chair as suddenly as though he had been stuck by a pin–"You talk like that, and ain't nuthen done but legal. Ain't nobody can tell the Board what bid to take. Anybody can come along and put in a little piss-ant bid, but the Board doan have to take it. Naw-sir-ee. The Board takes somebody kin do the work right."

"Who was it put the little piss-ant bid in?"

"Name of Jeffers," Mr. Pillsbury said peevishly, as at an unpleasant recollection.

"Jeffers Construction?" I asked.

"Yeah."

"What's wrong with Jeffers Construction?"

"The Board picks the fellow kin do the work right, and it ain't nobody's bizness."

This is business as usual, Before Willie. Afterwards, things move. The great scene showing Willie's mastery of the machinery comes with the state auditor.

I saw the Boss in shirt sleeves, cocked back in an easy chair with his sock-feet propped on a straight chair in front of him, and his tie askew, and his eyes bugging out and a forefinger out in the air in front of him as though it were the stock of a bull whip. Then I saw what the snapper of the bull whip would have been flicking the flies off of if that forefinger of the Boss had been the stock of a bull whip: it was Mr. Byram B. White, State Auditor, and his long bony paraffin-colored face was oozing a few painful drops of moisture and his eyes reached out and grabbed me like the last hope.

I took in the fact that I was intruding.

"Excuse me," I said, and started to back out of the door.

"Shut the door and sit down," the Boss said, and his voice moved right on without any punctuation to something it had been saying before my entrance, and the forefinger snapped. "–and you can just damned well remember you aren't supposed to get rich. A fellow like you, fifty years old and gut-shot and teeth gone and never had a dime, if God-Almighty had ever intended you to be rich he'd done it long back. Look at yourself, damn it! You to figure you're supposed to be rich, it is plain blasphemy. Look at yourself. Ain't it a fact?" And the forefinger leveled at Mr. Byram B. White.

But Mr. White did not answer. He just stood there in his unhappiness and looked at the finger.

"God damn it, has the cat got your tongue?" the Boss demanded. "Can't you answer a civil question?"

"Yes," Mr. White managed with gray lips that scarcely moved.

"Speak up, don't mumble, say, 'It's a fact, it's a blasphemous fact,' " the Boss insisted, still pointing the finger.

Mr. White's lips went grayer, and the voice was less than loud and clear, but he said it. Every word.

"All right, that's better," the Boss said. "Now you know what you're supposed to do. You're supposed to stay pore and take orders. I don't care about your chastity, which from the looks of you you don't have any trouble keeping plenty of, but I mean it's poverty and obedience and don't you forget it. Especially the last. There'll be a little something coming to you now and then in the way of sweetening, but Duffy'll tend to that. Don't you go setting up on your own any more. There just aren't going to be any one-man bonanzas. You got that? Speak up!"

"Yes," Mr. White said.

"Louder! And say, 'I got that.' "
He said it. Louder.

Warren is not a cheerful novelist, but this overpowering surprise attack comes near being a hymn to pure Joy. The personal energy to impose force in this degree inspires Jack's admiration and discipleship. The exhibition of command is perfect—and perfectly tempered. Willie gets his man back into line, yet preserves the machine principle by not firing him. Substitution of another auditor would solve nothing; putting the fear of God into Byram White does tune the instrument.

The quality of the Boss's associates and enemies—aside from Judge Irwin—allows the reader to join in the pleasures of inflicting surprise. Their being less apt practioners of the same game insulates them from sympathy. Furthermore, the attack is usually against pretensions. Both Jack and Willie show some respect for Gummy Larson, who has none, but Jack is hostile to Duffy's clothing—his "rig"—legislators' dressing robes, and the Judge's living room. He wants his antagonists to discard decoration and face life in its functional bareness, as a continuous conflict of interests. And, despite all the qualifying, fun in inflicting pain on the deserving represents for Jack and Willie a true bent that the moral framework of the novel never encompasses.

So Willie ends as a not-quite-successful shepherd king, yoking a double sense of the self as at once simple and complex, basic feeling and sophisticated intellect. Some critics have disliked Warren's failing to show his "corruption" as a straight-line descent, but the genius of Willie's story comes from his waverings. The *eros* of the countryside, Lucy Stark, serves as a gauge of his motion toward and away from his soured pastoral base.

But who is Jack Burden? Several answers are possible. Obviously, the second major energy in the novel. For Willie, the most useful part of the machine. For himself at the end, the grown-up boy from Burden's Landing. For a majority of critics, the passive man caught in a moral muddle, expressing the doubt that attends action. This last view could not have survived so well without having some truth, but it lacks precision. If the active man means solely the leader, then Willie becomes the only candidate in the novel, but few citizens would deny the Secretary of Defense or even the Secretary of State some credit as men of action. And in the progress of the story, as distinct from the retrospective philosophical view, Jack does a good deal. Even as a doubter about the value of activity he falls below almost any average hero of the preceding generation. He is simply the best doubter who is also heavily committed to action.

Actually, during Willie's time in power, Jack is another effective sensitive man. He downgrades himself, of course, for not being an All-American tough guy—envies and hates Tom Stark, the analogue for the purely forceful part of Willie. Lacking this direct strength, he has substituted intelligence and technique. He meets reversals by thinking about them—trying to put them into some acceptable larger perspective—but he has also developed his own method of imposing force. He ambushes potentially stronger opponents by holding the hidden ace. The recurrence of these surprise attacks in Warren suggests how powerful their appeal to him is. In *Night Rider*, Mr. Munn, echoing a legendary Confederate ambush, returns to bushwhack his thwarted pursuers. Slim Sarrett slips in to strangle Sue in *At Heaven's Gate*. Jeremiah Beaumont creeps up in the dark and in stocking feet to stab Colonel Fort in *World Enough and Time*. And in *All the King's Men* itself Adam Stanton appears from behind a pillar to shoot Willie.

Ambush is Warren's figure for the thinking man's mode of attack. And in the modern world this systematic mode of administering shocks can win as many battles as show of force can. Despite disclaimers, Jack likes the game of surprise as much as Willie does. Willie means his "Gimme that meat ax!" but the telling political action involves no axes. The application of hidden knowledge that the legislators want to keep hidden prevents the impeachment, and Jack executes the plan. Discomfiting the leader of the MacMurfee faction unquestionably elates him:

> He opened the door, a big jovial-looking man with a fine manner, in a flowered dressing gown. He didn't recognize me at first, just seeing a big brown envelope and some sort of face above it. But I withdrew the brown envelope just as his hand reached for it, and stepped over the sill.

Then he must have looked at the face. "Why, howdy-do, Mr. Burden," he said, "they say you've been right busy lately."

"Loafing," I said, "just plain loafing. And I was just loafing by and thought I'd stop and show you something a fellow gave me." I took the long sheet out of the envelope, and held it up for him to look at. "No, don't touch, burn-y, burn-y," I said.

He didn't touch but he looked, hard. I saw his Adam's apple jerk a couple of times; then he removed his cigar from his mouth (a good cigar, two-bit at least, by the smell) and said, "Fake."

"The signatures are supposed to be genuine," I said, "but if you aren't sure you might ring up one of your boys whose name you see on here and ask him man to man."

He pondered that thought a moment, and the Adam's apple worked again, harder now, but he was taking it like a soldier. Or he still thought it was a fake. Then he said, "I'll call your bluff on that," and walked over to the telephone.

Waiting for his number, he looked up and said, "Have a seat, won't you?"

"No, thanks," I said, for I didn't regard the event as social.

Then he had the number.

"Monty," he said into the phone, "I've got a statement here to the effect that the undersigned hold that the impeachment proceedings are unjustified and will vote against them despite all pressure. That's what it says—'all pressure.' Your name's on the list. How about it?"

There was a long wait, then Mr. Lowdan said, "For God's sake, quit mumbling and blubbering and speak up!"

There was another wait, then Mr. Lowdan yelled, "You—you—" But words failed him, and he slammed the telephone to the cradle, and swung the big, recently jovial-looking face toward me. He was making a gasping motion with his mouth, but no sound.

This strategy of the hidden ace is instinctive with Jack. He brings it out instantly to humiliate the policeman—the mock tough guy—who stops him and Anne.

He was just talking. I knew he was just talking to hear himself, for it was late and he was bored and dull. I knew that, and should have said, respectfully, that I would be careful, or have said, laughing and perhaps winking, that sure, Captain, I'd get her home. But I didn't say either thing. I was all keyed up, and she was swaying in my clutch, making a kind of sharp, broken noise with her breathing, and his God-damned beefy, black-jowled face was there in front of me. So I said, "The hell you will."

His eyes bugged out a little at that, and the jowls swelled with black blood, and he lunged one step closer, fingering his stick, saying, "The hell I won't, I'm gonna right now, both of you, by God!"

Then he said, "Come on," prodded me with the stick, and repeated, "Come on," herding me toward the end of the pier, where, no doubt, the box was he would use to call.

I took two or three steps forward, feeling the prod of the stick in the small of my back, dragging Anne, who hadn't said a word. Then I remembered, "Listen here, if you want to be on the force in the morning, you better listen to me."

"Listen, hell," he rejoined and jabbed my kidney a little harder.

"If it weren't for the lady," I said, "I'd let you go on and bust yourself. I don't mind a ride to headquarters. But I'll give you a chance."

"Chance," he echoed, and spat from the side of his mouth, and jabbed again.

"I'm going to reach into my pocket," I said, "not for a gun, just for my wallet, so I can show you something. Did you ever hear of Willie Stark?"

"Sure," he said. And jabbed.

"You ever hear of Jack Burden," I asked, "that newspaper fellow who is a sort of secretary to Willie?"

He reflected a moment, still prodding me on. "Yeah," he said then, grudgingly.

"Then maybe you'd like my card," I said, and reached for the wallet.

"Naw, you don't," he said, and let the weight of the stick lie across my lifted forearm, "naw, you don't, I'm gitten it myself."

He reached in for the wallet, took it, and started to open it. As a matter of principle.

"You open that," I said, "and I'll bust you anyway, call the wagon or not. Give it here."

He passed it over to me. I drew out a card, and handed it to him.

He studied it in the bad light. "Jeez," he said, with a slight hissing sound like the air escaping from a child's balloon, "how wuz I to know you wuz on the payroll?"

"You damned well better find out next time," I said, "before you get gay. Now call me a cab."

"Yes, sir," he said, hating me with the pig's eyes out of the swollen face. "Yes, sir," he said, and went to the box.

Willie and Jack like to punish the pride by destroying the dignity of their objects. Enemies who sin by believing themselves more intelligent and knowledgeable bring special pleasure. Judge Irwin has sinned further by thinking himself morally better, but Jack plays at surprise even in their final scene, dramatizing the effect by holding back his evidence until the last moment:

"I'm asking you, Judge, as a favor to me. Wait till tomorrow to make up your mind."

"You talk like I didn't know my own mind, Jack. That's about the only thing I've learned out of my three score and ten. That I know when I know my own mind. But you come back tomorrow, anyway. And we won't talk politics." He made a sudden gesture as though sweeping off the the top of a table with his arm. "Damn politics anyway!" he exclaimed humorously.

I looked at him and even with the wry, humorous expression on his face and the arm flung out at the end of its gesture, knew that this was it. It wasn't the dabble of the foot in the water, or even the steady deep pull of the undertow or the peripheral drag of the whirlpool. It was the heady race and plunge of the vortex. I ought to have known it would be this way.

Looking at him, I said, almost whispering, "I asked you, Judge. I near begged you, Judge."

A mild question came on his face.

"I tried," I said. "I begged you."

"What?" he demanded.

"Did you ever hear," I asked, my voice still not much more than a whisper," of a man named Littlepaugh?"

"Littlepaugh?" he queried, and his brow wrinkled in the effort of memory.

"Mortimer L. Littlepaugh," I said, "don't you remember?"

The flesh of the forehead drew more positively together to make the deep vertical mark like a cranky exclamation point between the heavy, rust-colored eyebrows. "No," he said, and shook his head, "I don't remember."

And he didn't. I was sure he didn't. He didn't even remember Mortimer L. Littlepaugh.

"Well, I questioned, "do you remember the American Electric Power Company?"

"Of course. Why wouldn't I? I was their counsel for ten years." There wasn't a flicker.

"Do you remember how you got the job?"

"Let me see–" he began, and I knew that he didn't for the moment remember, that he was in truth reaching back into the past, trying to remember. Then, straightening himself, he said, "Yes, of course, *I* remember. It was through a Mr. Satterfield."

But there had been the flicker. The barb had found meat, and I knew it.

I waited a long minute, looking at him, and he looked straight back at me, very straight in his chair.

"Judge," I asked softly, "you won't change your mind? About MacMurfee?"

"I told you," he said.

Then I could hear his breathing, and I wanted more than anything to know what was in his head, why he was sitting there straight and looking at me, while the barb bled into him.

I stepped to the chair which I had occupied and leaned down to pick up the manila envelope on the floor beside it. Then I moved to his chair, and laid the envelope in his lap.

And Jack's excitement in quietly accumulating this evidence makes the search one of the best chapters in the novel. Whatever his second thoughts, Jack likes using technique.

And of course he hates it too. As indicated earlier, his hostility to it appears regularly in his disgust with Willie. The same repulsion forms the overt basis for his disgust with himself as executive officer. But Warren uses telling lyric scenes to show the fear of vacancy that makes Jack run.

It looked like those farmhouses you ride by in the country in the middle of the afternoon, with the chickens under the trees and the dog asleep, and you know the only person in the house is the woman who has finished washing up the dishes and has swept the kitchen and has gone upstairs to lie down for half an hour and has pulled off her dress and kicked off her shoes and is lying there on her back on the bed in the shadowy room with her eyes closed and a strand of her hair still matted down on her forehead with the perspiration. She listens to the flies cruising around the room, then she listens to your motor getting big out on the road, then it shrinks off into the distance and she listens to the flies. That was the kind of house it was.

Jack, not the imaginary farm woman, is listening to the flies, and he hears them immediately after Willie's speech in the drugstore. The simultaneous appeal and horror of simplicity have already struck him on the campaign trail:

But as the train pulls away, a woman comes to the back door of one of the houses—just the figure of a woman, for you cannot make out the face—and she has a pan in her hand and she flings the water out of the pan to make a sudden tattered flash of silver in the light. She goes back into the house. To what is in the house. The floor of the house is thin against the bare ground and the walls and the roof are thin against all of everything which is outside, but you cannot see through the walls to the secret to which the woman has gone in.

The train pulls away, faster now, and the woman is back there in the house, where she is going to stay. She'll stay there. And all at once, you think that you are the one who is running away, and who had better run fast to wherever you are going because it will be dark soon. The train is going pretty fast now, but its effort seems to be through a stubborn cloying density of air as though an eel tried to swim in syrup, or the effort seems to be against an increasing and implacable magnetism of earth. You think that if the earth should twitch once, as the hide of a sleeping dog twitches, the train would be jerked over and piled up and the engine would spew and gasp while somewhere a canted-up wheel would revolve once with a massive and dreamlike deliberation.

But nothing happens, and you remember that the woman had not even looked up at the train. You forget her, and the train goes fast, and is going fast when it crosses a little trestle. You catch the sober, metallic, pure, late-light, unriffled glint of the water between the little banks, under the sky, and see the cow standing in the water upstream near the single leaning willow. And all at once you feel like crying. But the train is going fast, and almost immediately whatever you feel is taken away from you, too.

You bloody fool, do you think that you want to milk a cow?

You do not want to milk a cow.

Politics has a more positive appeal, though, than escape from vacancy. For all the pride of ancestry, the machine is Jack's native habitat—not where he was born, but where he chooses to spend his adulthood. He has lived at its edge for years as reporter and columnist before he meets Willie. It offers some of the sureties of home. There he knows where he is, what everybody will do if somebody else does this or that. There his talent for using knowledge brings the highest price and gains the greatest respect. There, too, he can attach his native disgust to a suitable object. His scorn for legislators and officeholders is, he comes to see, also a form of self-disgust, but he habitually takes pride in his scientific understanding: he can predict exactly how these manlike machines will work. Tiny will cheat within prescribed limits and flatter beyond limit; MacMurfee will back off the impeachment or try to bluff, but hesitate to force a showdown; Gummy Larson will stay bought. By thinking of himself as consciousness and most of his associates as behavior, he satisfyingly simplifies daily life. He has to consider only Willie and Sadie as people.

Over-all, then, Warren shows far more militancy in Jack and more flair for his chosen field than criticism usually admits. Against these qualities the novel sets his saving instinct for seeing all around a problem and avoiding irretrievable outbreak, but Jack does not fit the pattern of the sensitive man leaning totally on the strong one. He and Willie are a team rather than player and pawn, and the combination's formidableness comes in good part from Jack.

Judge Irwin, the third major force, is a masterpiece of dramatic economy. He appears in only three scenes, yet everybody remembers him. The usual view sees him as the upright father who made one mistake—a kind of walking religious ethic secularized into the give-and-take of politics. Much as this view leaves out, he is not even quite so reliable as all that. He refuses the chance to avoid degradation because, he says, he has pledged his word. Still, the impetus for Willie's midnight ride early in the novel comes from Judge Irwin's having gone back on his word—for a reason, of course. Even his final show of reliability leaves him an accessory to MacMurfee's blackmail attempt. (In Snow's *The Masters,* an established scientist acts at once to stop a partisan from threatening a non-tenure fellow; politics in Warren includes no such idea of *noblesse oblige.*) Moreover, though Judge Irwin twice shows the power to make Jack feel guilty, this conscience never inhibits him in day-to-day conflicts. In the capital Jack never thinks of it and even at Burden's Landing finds its disapproval bearable.

The Judge takes his real memorableness from his theatricality—from being the Worthy Antagonist that the Hero must have. He is the counter-personal force. Right or wrong, he cannot be imposed upon. His strength comes from not wanting anything; he is the man of satisfied energies. And as such he is a Hector armored in nostalgia. The one symbol regularly associated with him—his pre-gunpowder artillery model—calls up for Jack memory of boyhood games. The Judge is archaic and likes the archaic. Self-interested individualism has replaced government by a coterie of friends, but Governor Stanton once stopped scandal at a price to anonymous sufferers because Judge Irwin was his friend. Despite his present alliance with the modern rascal MacMurfee, he presumably acts in a class interest, visualized in actual neighbors, rather than an immediately selfish one.

In his greatest appeal, though, he expresses personal force in the *style* of Victorian nobility. Just as his living room draws Willie's scorn for its graciousness, his talk conveys better than Willie's an aspiration to heroism. He can speak tolerantly about new men meeting new demands on state government and he can still believe in grand gesture. Withholding the secret that he is Jack's father just as he is about to commit suicide gives him a theatrical exit, which sums up his aim and Jack's longing for nobility in a self-interested world.

"I wouldn't hurt you," he said. Then, reflectively, added. "But I could stop you."

"By stopping MacMurfee," I said.

"A lot easier than that."

"How?"

"A lot easier than that," he repeated.

"How?"

"I could just—" he began, "I could just say to you—I could just tell you something—" He stopped, then suddenly rose to his feet, spilling the papers off his knees. "But I won't," he said cheerfully, and smiled directly at me.

"Won't tell me what?"

"Forget it," he said, still smiling, and waved his hand in a gay dismissal of the subject.

I stood there irresolutely for a moment. Things were not making sense. He was not supposed to be standing there, brisk and confident and cheerful, with the incriminating papers at his feet. But he was.

I stooped to pick up the papers, and he watched me from his height.

"Judge," I said, "I'll be back tomorrow. You think it over, and make up your mind tomorrow."

"Why, it's made up."

"You'll—"

"No, Jack."

I went to the hall door. "I'll be back tomorrow," I said.

"Sure, sure. You come back. But my mind is made up."

I walked down the hall without saying good-bye. I had my hand lifted to the front door when I heard his voice calling my name. I turned and took a few steps toward him. He had come out into the hall. "I just wanted to tell you," he said, "that I did learn something new from those interesting documents. I learned that my old friend Governor Stanton impaired his honor to protect me. I do not know whether to be more glad or sorry, at the fact. At the knowledge of his attachment or the knowledge of the pain it cost him. He had never told me. That was the pitch of his generosity. Wasn't it? Not ever telling me."

I mumbled something to the effect that I supposed it was.

"I just wanted you to know about the Governor. That his failing was a defect of his virtue. The virtuc of affection for a friend."

I didn't mumble anything to that.

"I just wanted you to know that about the Governor," he said.

"All right," I said, and went to the front door, feeling his yellow gaze and calm smile upon me, and out into the blaze of light.

But if the novel retains its power until Willie's death, the ending does not. It may well be plausible for Jack Burden. The divisions between self-consciousness and simplicity, betrayal and just revenge, action and withdrawal fade off into all-passion-spent, awareness-is-all. Sad Cass Mastern does not answer Willie much more than Ike McCaslin answers Sutpen or Ratliff does Mink. Jack is far from being the most distanced character in the history of fiction, and his weariness implicates the author.

Jack and, to a degree, Warren try to restore and reorder the adolescent past without integrating adult life into it. This falling back on the modern literary hope gives the appearance of applying psychoanalytic thought—straightening out the misunderstood family relationships, searching for renewal of interest in abandoned projects. But neither in psychoanalysis or real life can anyone sustain shutting out the intervening experience. As an interim solution, Jack's return may be plausible; as the redemption which some critics take it to be, it looks shaky. For it does not say what will happen when new problems revive Jack's assertive disgust. Warren does not believe that anything so endemic goes away. He simply leaves its recurrence and the acceptance of adult experience to Jeremiah Beaumont and the next novel.

For the time being everything hangs on Anne Stanton. The fiction falters at the point of resurrecting her. She is the objective guarantee of success in Jack's turn to seeking likeness instead of difference, harmony instead of conflict. The claim of the Stantons on Jack is their seeming integrated:

> I ought to have guessed that a person like [Anne]—a person who you could tell had a deep inner certitude of self which comes from being all of one piece, of not being shreds and patches and old cogwheels held together with pieces of rusty barbed wire and spit and bits of string, like most of us—I ought to have guessed that that kind of person would not be surprised into answering a question she didn't want to answer.

Anne refused to marry Jack earlier because he was not integrated:

> "Darling," she said tiredly. "I'm not trying to make you come here. Or get a job with Patton. Or anybody. I want you to do what you want. Just so it is something. Even if you don't make money. I told you I'd live in a shack."
>
> So I went back to the Law School and by dint of consistent effort succeeded in busting out before the end of the year.

The talent and weakness in drawing Anne makes her a metaphor rather than a personality. Possible complexities appear in summary. In youth she amounts to a series of play scenes—beach, roadster, tennis court. Concerning other people's ideal woman, *non disputandum est:* Jack likes the child in the budding girl. He comes to see a picnic episode as embodying the whole story:

> All at once she dropped his arm and laughed and began to run toward the water, but up the beach, toward a little spit, with her bobbed hair back loose on the air. I watched her run. She ran with her arms not quite outspread, crooked at the elbows, and with a motion of her legs which was graceful and free, and somehow awkward at the same time, as though she hadn't quite forgotten one kind of running, the child's

running, and hadn't quite learned another kind of running, the woman's running. The legs seemed to be hung too loose, somewhat uncertainly, from the little hips, which weren't quite rounded yet. I watched her and noticed that her legs were long. Which I had never noticed before.

The same combination occurs just before the attempt at consummation.

We ran up the right-hand sweep of the twin flight of steps leading to the gallery, then safe under the gallery roof began to stamp and shake the water from us like dogs. The running and stamping and the wet had made Anne's hair come loose. It was hanging down her back, with some odd wet strands plastered across her brow and one over her cheek to make her look like a child coming out of a bath.

Her finest moments come when she is stretched out, quiescent, receptive, but untouched:

We sat there in the car, arguing about the movie we had just seen and looking up the swath of light. Then the talking died away. She had slid down a little in the seat, with her head lying on the top of the back cushion so that now she wasn't looking out toward the horizon but up at the sky—for the top of the roadster was down—with the moonlight pouring down on her face to make it look smooth as marble. I slid down a little, too, and looked up at the sky, and the moonlight poured down over my face, such as it was. I kept thinking that now in a minute I would reach over and take hold.

And she proves untouchable—Jack's little sister, perfect playmate, sexually taboo. Too much alike.

"We oughtn't," I began, "we oughtn't—it wouldn't—it wouldn't be—it wouldn't be right." So I used the word *right*, which came to my lips to surprise me, for I hadn't ever thought of anything I had done with Anne Stanton or with any other woman or girl as being right or wrong, but as just something that happened, and hadn't ever thought about right or wrong very much in connection with anything but had simply done the things people do and not done the things people don't do. Which are the things people do and don't do. And I remember now the surprise I felt when I heard that word there in the air, like the echo of a word spoken by somebody else God knows how many years before, and now unfrozen like a word in Baron Munchausen's tale. I couldn't any more have touched her then than if she had been my little sister.

The return of Jack's mother, his image of woman as shameless sexual object, completes the taboo.

Jack's vision of fingertips touching—excitement and peace yoked perfectly—carries some power as selective memory. Anne's reappearance has logic, if less vitality. Her affair with Willie removes the taboo. And, while maintaining her celebrated "integrity," she reappears passive, receptive, guidable. In the later stages she always materializes in need of help and protection—telephoning, waiting in the hall, asking understanding about Willie or comfort about Adam or aid in finding him. This change from teacher to suppliant removes a barrier. And she has lost her childhood playfulness enough to be the perfect companion in the higher play of comprehending dead Cass Mastern. As with Cass, she is enough like Jack to create harmony and just enough unlike him to assure him that he is not looking at his mirror image.

The final rush of conciliations shows how much author shares character's anxiety to have all the pieces fit together perfectly. Jack's trying to make all events and people mesh asserts a form of control over the uncontrollable parts of experience. If they work into the web, they make sense, become a part of the necessity that anyone can live with. The number and complexity of the conciliations guarantee that they have harmonized *all* the dissonances. The princely father nobly dead, the repentant mother, and the dying saintly father fulfill a lot of wishes quickly. And telling the Cass Mastern story will add a warrior saint to the canon. No matter that Jack seems to have to write the Willie Stark story first. The falling off at the end of the novel does not destroy it.

FIVE

Efficient Saints and Civilians: Graham Greene

Warren arouses admiration, Graham Greene love. Warren is forever forcing us to share his embarrassed aggressiveness and then saying *beware*. His detractors become angry, while from time to time someone notes mildly that Greene's symbolism is too right or his Catholicism too tricky. Though the entertainments help create warmth and give Greene a sort of king's-x, his best novels transform benignly a problem at the center of our inheritance. Surrounded by novelists eager to convict us of bad faith, we like a good-hearted man.

No writer shows more clearly the assimilating force of the generation after 1930. In the nineteenth-century, resistance to the commercial drive for efficiency found one set of defenses in medievalism, conceived in both religious and heroic terms. But in

Greene the old opposites coalesce into a common pressure. The combination appears in his work not as idea, but experienced, lived through intensely, and absorbed. Efficiency and heroism, method and religion become meshed ideals. So while Greene moves to symbolize these newer standards of conduct, he wants simultaneously to know whether mere human weakness will destroy the precarious conciliation.

Of all the charges against modern literature, self-pity is the hardest to answer. Even the defense that it appears more strongly in second- than in first-rank novelists does not deny its omnipresence. Need has kept it a persistent if inadequate response that outlives circumstance. Hostility to the demands of urban civilization gives it a renewable base. It may debilitate effectiveness, but nothing else so readily supplies a pleasant view of the self. Surrealism for the world, sur-tenderness for the person—the formula creaks but survives.

If self-pity were actually so isolatable a flaw, the ringing words spoken against it ought by now to have eradicated it. But a crowd of relatives stands so close that shooting it down always looks dangerous. The long struggle in this century between inherited conscience and a tolerant view of biological human nature is a cousin. Projection into humane act has produced some of the glories of the age, giving it a claim to moral superiority over Elizabethans, Augustans, and Greeks. Even with individuals a ruthless separation of self-pity from sympathetic understanding for others may prove neither practical nor especially useful. An age which so thoroughly *feels* personality as dynamic rather than an aggregate of qualities cannot readily divide its moral defect from its hope of virtue. Yet even these kindly relatives might not have protected self-pity but for one invulnerable auxiliary—the self-kicking even more pervasive in our literature. The ever-ready proofs of personal inadequacy, colliding with the increased value put on sentient, vulnerable imagination and flesh, create a pressure, and the moral sternness of preachers like Warren will not be available to all the laity. Novelists have been more and more searching for sophisticated forms of relief, but the "natural" one is self-pity. Modern literature has found no alternative to going through this stage before getting beyond it.

And what causes the self-kicking? We do not need to guess. The great literature is explicit: gaps between the medieval heroic ideal, the modern ideal of piecemeal efficiency applied to unappealing problems, and a view of the self as passive, perceiving sensitivity. As we have seen, the earlier generation preserved itself by willingness to live with a vast space between Ulysses and Bloom, Pecival and the gashouse. It concentrated its hopes on an infinitely expandable inner world. At a time when this belief has lost force, Greene responds to depression-bred frustrations for which imaginative perception no longer provides a sufficient outlet. For all his smoothness, he restates the human problem.

His claim to significance begins from recognizing the gradual coalescence of feudal and industrial ideals. But since mythic heroes did not have to prove perennially efficient—they had only to rise to occasions—merging aristocratic and bourgeois ideals of excellence sharply increases pressure. To set up the problem, Greene searches the world for the warlike situations from which heroism has traditionally appeared. (These parallel, in the oblique way of literature, the conflicts which everybody sees and participates in.) His complexity of action reflects the new demand for not a one-shot, but a persisting heroism which can survive even anonymity. And these central concerns bring him to questions of overreaching, possible human effectiveness, reluctance to sacrifice sensitivity, and strategies of limiting the area of hope, gaining approbation, and renewing the battered will.

Looked at coolly, the deepest aim of novelists formed in the thirties seems mad. The frustrations of personal history from which literature derives came to grips with one of history's more enclosing situations. The two forms of claustrophobia reenforced each other to demand a breakthrough. So novelists set the available tools to work at producing a miracle. They want Bloom, with his particularized sins and stratagems upon him, to *become* Ulysses—in circumstances which make that unlikely if not impossible. They remove the escape clause from the first generation's melancholy; the leisure to live with that Shadow between the desire and the act no longer exists. And when they come up against the impracticality of this dream, they try to transcend the whole problem by transferring it to some invisible sphere of value. (That effort is the motive behind the strivings which R. W. B. Lewis describes in *The Picaresque Saint.*) But no first-rank novelist has been able to rest in the approbation of a boy, an ineffective priest, or even a Faulkner. For these novelists are also practical men. Having coalesced the dream of saintly heroism with the other of bourgeois effectiveness, they cannot satisfy themselves with one-shot transubstantiations and must continue chasing a persistent heroism under those unlikely, continuing, and anonymous conditions.

Yet this logically mad effort does not sound futile in Greene or Warren or their contemporaries abroad. If the dream does not succeed in practice, it comes close enough to almost inspire confidence in man's capacity for survival. These novelists bring an amazing ingenuity and intelligence to assessing human resources, analyzing problems into components, and choosing some areas for conflict while conceding others as lost. Their insistence on putting the best vision derivable from family, school, and imagination to the test of practice creates a greater tension between possible and needed than their predecessors had cared to live with. So they have replaced a lyric of dissatisfaction with a drama of forces.

The exotic scenes which Greene's heroes choose provide symbolism, and, as Lewis has shown, connect the primitive with childhood, but most importantly they limit even the possibility of establishing effective control. They clear away the childhood wish for omnipotence by putting it obviously out of reach from the start. The man who wants to be responsible and humane must resign himself quickly to establishing a little order in a big chaos. He will fight and, in *The Quiet American,* kill to maintain this sense of limited objective. And, despite the outrage in this country, Greene chooses his American antagonist accurately. The double hero in *All the King's Men* envisions total control of the clashing wills about him. Bellow's Herzog asks no more or less of himself than synthesis of everything in sight over the past two hundred years.

The intense pursuit of aims limited in advance parallels Greene's

British love for institutions. The Church embodies a fixed conscience, rules that may have some flexibility; colonial government provides an area of action with a built-in resilience, derived from experience of the possible. Scobie can consistently be a Catholic police administrator; the foreign correspondent can consistently support the French holding operation in Indo-China. And both can instinctively oppose the younger brother type who comes to activate some "logical" schema for total effectiveness. Greene combines the puritan conscience and work drive with an English taste for institutions and continuity, and, like the nineteenth-century Oxfordians, finds in Catholicism the best modern representative of this sense of reality. (There are many Anglo-Catholics, few Americo-Catholics. American puritanism retains its skepticism about institutions.)

So where Warren portrays the harsh thrust of a reviving will to control the environment, Greene balances. He too stands at the point where the new drive and the inherited ideal of sensitive intensity collide, but he weights the values more evenly. And this indecisiveness in turn leads to a different rhythm of action. The Warren hero cuts through his sensitivities to act, regrets having done so, and tries to reconcile afterward. The Greene hero never gets away from struggling with both/and. His will to effectiveness contends steadily with the kind of sensitivity that leads to drunkenness, self-pity, opium, and suicide. But even gone sour, the inherited "weakness" remains a value. Greene's immunity to the usual literary ill-feeling comes to a great degree from his making the struggle not between good and bad, but between goods. There are few bad impulses—many bad consequences.

Greene's immediacy disguises the fact that he writes a barer novel of forces than Warren, depending even more heavily on scene for emotion and sketching in already acceptable character types to represent the contending drives. His mastery of threatening tone further obscures his skeletons, but *Brighton Rock* is laid out with a ruler. It too intends to strip away defenses and get to the heart of the matter. Like the bigger Greene novels, *Brighton Rock* depicts honest tries to assert the best self in a world where it cannot prevail. Pinky, an odd best self, at heart is a streamlined, grotesque

Everyman. He wants to achieve total control of the environment by direct act; later, he becomes a miniature Macbeth trying to forestall the future. Throughout he is an organizer, whose need for ascendancy makes him prefer small and conceivably manageable groups, and his antagonist logically should be the pleasure principle. It is, of course: Ida identifies self-assertive hedonism with sloppiness in conduct and figure, turning to aggressive "nosiness" when frustrated of even passing satisfaction. While these opponents contend and institutionalized crime gives Pinky a lesson in the obsolescence of individual enterprise, Greene subjects his Everyman to a bewildering vision of self-sacrificing love in the ingenue. If high energy is the disrespectable ideal of the age, omnipresent in its novels and masked in its philosophy, the overmatched Pinky and his two women represent an anatomy of the contemporary sense of situation. Greene counts on the reader to identify with both Ida and Pinky—righteous pleasure and criminal force—and to hope for such a selfless heroine. As the novel progresses he builds up Pinky as energetic victim of his own rationalism by downgrading Ida's form of assertion.

The Power and the Glory stands at the center of the emerging sensibility of the period. The title announces a theatrical opposition. Remarkably economical and effective scene carries much of the inner life once conveyed by consciousness. Where Warren's tone slips and slides, Greene's never misses. And beyond this sure management, Greene himself typifies the emerging conflict, a temperamental activist whose heart is with the preceding generation's preferences in personality. In bringing extreme sensitivity over into story—purposeful activity—he parallels other novelists' revival of picaresque and Victorian forms. But again he balances. Unlike Warren, he does not bring a complex problem-solving pressure into his narrative. The antagonists operate on a simple contract—the chaser chases and the runner runs.

The ideal of efficiency crosses party lines—and makes the antagonists worthy of each other. The lieutenant yearns for effective government based on the farmers—the *All the King's Men* ideal. The whiskey priest wants to be an efficient Christian machine, bringing at least the mechanical forms of religion to the peons in the absence of anything better to offer. He hopes thus to maintain his own and his parishioners' sense of continuity. And his only protection lies in the inefficiency of the revolutionary government. His internal conflict comes, of course, from the difficulty in living up to his ideal; his "sins" amount mostly to having normal human feeling. They are either loving or narcotic. He has loved a woman, still loves his child, was once indifferent to suffering, and he drinks. These make up the sum of his failings, and all accumulate from the past. (Past sexual attractions frequently cause trouble in Greene.)

The drive behind the character of the priest is to normalize obsessive, heroic purpose—to make it compatible with the softer qualities of human nature. He has faced major problems—finding a cause, relieving anxiety and increasing happiness, taking great risks, refusing to quit—and most of his sins have proved life-sustaining at the time and under the circumstances. Heroism and "weakness" complement each other. But drunkenness, the sign of despair, does oppose and threaten effectiveness, though it also works as disguise in the jail scene. In the reconciling terms of the novel, it is the other side of the heroic coin. "Despair is the price one pays for setting oneself an impossible aim." Here it becomes the price of wanting to be an efficient Catholic under peculiarly unpromising circumstances.

For Greene's Catholicism is obviously moral, action-centered, rather than contemplative or mystic. The Church institutionalizes conscience, which for a Greene hero would be exacerbating in any case. It avoids the chaos of relativity and fulfills the human demand that there be some standard a man can measure himself by. (A side effect of the twentieth-century effort to reduce pain by reducing conscience threatens sense of purpose.) Accepting the Church's law as absolute establishes *agenbite of inwit* as in the nature of the moral world rather than a mere human misjudgment. Men choose to set up impossible aims for themselves. In sum and after all the anti-heroes and all the diagnoses of bourgeois civilization, men childishly still want to be heroes.

The power to choose one condition over another makes it possible at least to raise a question. Since a business civilization does not let individual grandeur come easily, Greene and the priest welcome the breakdown of institutions after the revolution. Opportunity arises from chaos—as many believed during the depression. The situation objectifies what Greene takes as an irreducible modern problem: the desire to assert individual heroism after the institution which rationalized the ideal has become an echo. The whiskey priest strives to be a useful man of God, maintaining people's hope and continuity, after every logical reason for doing so has gone. (Hence the many opportunities for escape and return to the debased institution still existing outside.) *Greene's central vision is the simultaneous existence and irrationality of the honest try.*

This brilliant stratagem of allying heroism with irrationality is the secret of its appeal. People will believe in the irrational. They have heard little else convincing for seventy-five years. But Greene sees what was also there to be seen, submerged underground and disguised in the myth literature of the first generation: that modern man has not abandoned his determination to be a hero just because it is hard and he is one among many. The threat of anonymity has only fixed him the more desperately on his goal. By making the priest concentrate on efficiency and denigrate himself for inefficiency, Greene performs another needed miracle. What intellectual, living comfortably and using *middle class* as a a faint swear word, can possibly fail to feel an occasional contradiction? Uniting the bourgeois aim of effectiveness with the aristocratic ideal of heroism creates a union that makes potential critics of Greene's esthetic talents hold back their hands.

Greene's faith is thus a desperate measure, taken because, beyond a certain point, self-interest fails to interest human beings. His sense of the remote source of the ideal goes beyond Warren's—he makes it invisible. Warren can see his peasants and judges, however inadequately they may represent their perfect forms. But the whiskey priest cannot see any representative of the Church, Scobie cannot see the England which once provided the ideal of good colonial administration. Even this echo of a direction, though, provides some rationale beyond narrow self-interest for the honest try. Selfishness is not imaginative enough to give range to the "outsize will." Faulkner's Jason Compson locates the end of that track: an anti-hero applies heroic energy to unappetizing tasks. And the only scope Faulkner sees to oppose Jason is Caddy's sexuality, Quentin's labyrinthine ways, and Benjy's bewilderment. (Sutpen's time offered more.) Faulkner sets up the vacuum which Greene tries to fill.

The whiskey priest indulges in more self-kicking than self-pity; he gains his claim to nobility from shifting his pity toward others. This transforming of the malign into the benign, taken almost for granted in *The Power and the Glory*, becomes the central exploration in *The Heart of the Matter*. Scobie's sense of life as "unalleviatable misery" determines his choice of the colonial Coast as his theater of action. It seems not only to objectify, but to prove beyond reasonable doubt the validity of his diagnosis. Yet, in a maneuver characteristic of the depression-bred mentality, he hopes not merely to reduce a little the misery of others, but to make them positively happy. His inherited self-pity embarrasses him and he turns it outward onto the world. The riddle of the end—Was he weakling or martyr?—means, Isn't this transformation worth something?

Still, while believing that this world and its conflicts give man reason to pity himself and hence others, Scobie faces far more directly than the priest the contradiction between his sensibility and the ideal of efficiency. By making Scobie's identification with other sufferers limitless, Greene brings his protagonist up against both the impossibility of universal benevolence and its betrayal of the work role. Scobie's inability to work out the degrees of responsibility which Bellow's more or less contemporary Leventhal finally understands leads to the desire for rest symbolized in pillows and nursing —and finally to suicide.

The conflict between life as sensibility and as effective action determines the supporting roles. Scobie's wife Louise and her admirer Wilson, sent from London to spy on Scobie, are sensibility people. They read poetry together; Wilson writes it. Scobie fears the expression of feeling, hates poetry. Louise, all self-sympathy, emphasizes both Scobie's refusal to express his, and his effort to play a supportive and conceivably noble role. Wilson's unabashed spying underlines Scobie's attempts at faithfulness. In the end Scobie wishes that feelings could be eliminated altogether so that peace of mind might prevail. His diary makes a kind of ideal statement. It shows no stress, is all activity and indisputable fact (temperature, 90 degrees).

Moreover, Louise from the beginning eliminates the traditional British hope for the good life through personal relations. She cannot love, and no one could love her combination of self-pity and nagging. With this possibility removed, Scobie has to depend on his concept of himself as a reliable organization man. As assistant superintendent of police, he has performed flexibly and effectively. But he has a strong backward pull. He thinks of all experience in terms of loss. His wife, his mistress, and his dead daughter all become children whose strength has not proved adequate to adult demands—children confused and exhausted. He sees the phenomenon repeated everywhere—in Louise's lost looks; his mistress' lost husband and childhood netball game; her lost mother; Scobie's lost young love; his fear of losing integrity, respect, and self-respect.

The childlike natives, living "where human nature hasn't had time to disguise itself," survive by lying, and their pervasive presence questions the possibility of good faith. Since deception inheres in the ideal of action as it does not in the ideal of expanding consciousness, it inevitably becomes a major concern of the contemporary novel. The demands of public role never coincide perfectly with the private view of the self. Instead of joking and muddling through, like some tragicomic novelists, Greene lays out the dilemma. His hero's ideal is uprightness; his conviction, that only lies make life bearable. In open alliance, "kindness and lies are worth a thousand truths in human relations." With Scobie's idea of public duty as responsibility for others' happiness and his private summary of experience as universal misery, he cannot think otherwise. He gives up only when so many responsibilities to so many people involve him in total contradiction. In this progressive action, religion functions as an ultimate barrier beyond which benevolent deceptions cannot go. To keep on helping his mistress, he deceives his wife. To deceive his wife, he takes communion without absolution or intent to give up the sin. What some critics consider the tricky religious ending is Greene's metaphor for the impossibility of either ducking or deciding Scobie's issue.

To go on as a novelist, Greene had to get beyond the logic of Scobie's suicide. Irreconcilable competing values made its rationale impeccable. In moving on, Greene chooses the direction which the age had been taking and which he had previously rejected. In *Brighton Rock*, *The Power and the Glory*, and *The Heart of the Matter* he glorifies the idealism of impossible aims and accepts the price of despair. In the name of maintaining sense of purpose, the novels counterattack the great modern movement to reduce conscience to humanly manageable proportions. Over the long run, though, Greene has proved unable to ignore the important fact that he had to obscure in achieving his effects—that life goes on beyond its great moments of crisis. Canonizing his heroes allows them to pick their finest hours—epiphanies of their careers—and suddenly demand a public reckoning of the over-all performance. This traditional deception of tragedy has had trouble sounding real to the modern world, strong as the appetite for it is. When so much changes so rapidly and demands response, *what next?* rings on the nerves more than *what was the final score?* Particularly when the answer is, a tie.

The End of the Affair has good scenes, but does not succeed. When *The Quiet American* bogged down in public over the question of whether Pyle was really like an American, Green's reputation began to depend more and more on the entertainments and the two earlier novels. Still, *The Quiet American* locates a new scene and a new direction. Most critics have taken Indo-China as merely another of Greene's primitive locales, analogous to Mexico and Africa. Again only a little order amid a big chaos seems possible. But the new scene differs in a crucial respect: the forces come nearer balancing. An arrangement exists. The French hold the towns and, in daylight, the roads. At night they may or may not hold a few scattered guard towers. They send out bombers and infantry sweeps. The rebels shoot back, die, disappear, return. Nothing decisive happens in this agreed-upon rhythm. Chaos threatens, but does not pervade as in *The Heart of the Matter*. The careless man may get killed or wounded in a guard tower, the unlucky may number among the moderate casualties. An effective organization hangs on in dispiriting but not totally defeating circumstances. Victory is ruled out from the start—an admittedly impossible aim.

For the first time in Greene, the action moves to reject such aims. He gains in reducing, though not eliminating, the self-kicking and self-pity inherent in an overreaching idealism, but sacrifies complexity and even credibility in his antagonist for the sake of clarity —makes the American a simple force rather than a rounded character. Once the reader grants the possibility of this kind of novel, it does not matter so much whether Pyle sounds real to people who know a few Yale men. When he acts to disturb the precarious and precious balance, he fulfills his function as the loved ideal become threat of disaster. Pyle descends directly from the priest and Scobie, in so far as they assert private visions of human needs amid the worldly, all but ineffective arrangements of institutional order.

The novel comes to life in its strangely still action: the frightening night in the guard tower; the bombsight and canal level views of the absurdly stable war; the counterattack against Pyle's bomb plans. Opposite these scenes, Greene sets quiet vignettes of the energy and skill Frenchmen are putting into merely hanging on: the bedeviled briefing officer trying to put a good face on failure; the police officer manipulating and controlling within the all-but-besieged city. In the picture of the rival newspapermen, the old bugaboos of hedonism and incomprehension get another glancing blow. All this activity, however, almost obscures the real action. Nothing happens.

As in Henry Green, the actions carry an overwhelming threat which does not quite eventuate. The protagonist, a British reporter, serves to applaud the all-but-anonymous forces which prevent chaos from prevailing and to record the anxiety under which he and they live. His heroes are the French—collectively. In the climax he does his part to help them make sure that the idealism of impossible aims does not upset the dangerous balance of forces. *The*

Quiet American celebrates a new and conceivably achievable aim, not of striking a spectacular blow for lost causes, but of maintaining an inconspicuous effort to "keep on keeping on." Without abandoning the hope of heroism or benevolence, Greene makes a major shift in their definitions.

The best to be said about Greene's next novel, *A Burnt-Out Case*, is that it continues to explore. It faces the logic of its predecessor. The newspaperman in *The Quiet American* meets experience with general disgust and a little faith in stalemate. Such limited interests may lead to apathy and, in the successful architect of *A Burnt-Out Case*, do. Even there the way down proves the way up. And *The Comedians* shows with real energy the persistence of Greene's values at a time when crisis is no longer easy to locate. Both the dedicated vegetarian and the confidence man yearning for heroism are ridiculous, and ineffective. But they are interested in life, while the self-interested man is disgusted. However disregarded even in death, men eager to engage themselves find a sense of aliveness, a way of looking past the well-organized "multiplicity" of the present.

Over-all and so far, Greene elevates the puritan drive left after all creating anew of the conscience of the race; relates it to twentieth-century self-kicking, self-pity, and humaneness; and makes his mixture of formidable entry in the race to orient ourselves. Critics quarrel with Warren's view of life and now even with Faulkner's, but few argue with so desirable an outlook as Greene's. Who wants to fight even the possibility of benevolent effectiveness?

The End of Grand Gesture

SIX

Portrait of the Artist as a Self-Creating, Self-Vindicating, High Energy Man: Saul Bellow

Saul Bellow's heroes are walking syntheses of modernism—in American-cut clothes. They catch on so readily because they seem better pictures of ourselves than we have had taken before. But they are modern with a difference: they think themselves problem-solvers rather than illustrators of dilemma and are full of surprise and anger when "natural" solutions fail to work. Some critics take Bellow's tongue-in-cheek word for it that these heroes are passive. After all, they seek everybody's advice and follow almost anybody's lead. But this public meekness deceives; at home they are hurriers, worriers, and scramblers. Even when spinning their wheels, they are high-energy men.

Bellow's heroes incorporate layer upon layer of ideal human images from the past seventy-five years. At bottom is the portrait of the artist, hypersensitive, imaginative, and increasingly knowledgeable. The suffering candidate for sainthood whom Lewis finds in Faulkner, Greene, and Silone lies immediately atop. (These layers both carry residues of religious feeling into secular enterprise. Bellow drops that element.) Crisis as the test of the soul and dynamics opposed to essences come from the war period. Civilian reaching for imaginative play after the decline of militancy indicates a late accretion. And, running through all the layers, intensity remains as the mark of being alive. Bellow has done the most encyclopedic job in fiction so far of absorbing and redirecting the cultural inheritance. No wonder that, like the Fifth Symphony in *Howard's End*, he appeals to all conditions.

The thirties and forties, driving hard for control and leaving this legacy of energy, had to enforce austerity. Warren and Greene necessarily move away from the twin goals of the twenties—inward expansion and fun—toward bareness. They emphasize vulnerability to pain. Even as they were beginning to respond thus directly to changed conditions and feelings, though, a slightly younger generation was being educated in the richer hopes of the early twentieth century. (Warren himself participated heavily in the training.) For these younger men the depression appeared not so much as gigantic betrayal and mismanagement, but as a fact—lived with, if not accepted, almost from the birth of awareness. A potential visible in retrospect existed: remove the fact and the vision of richness would reappear as still the best image of man available. But at the time Bellow began, in 1944, no one had removed the restrictions; war had intensified them. He set out to assert the vision anyway. Under unfavorable circumstances, *Dangling Man* lays out his hero's career-long problem of living life to the hilt while ridding himself of an increasingly unfunctional aggressiveness.

Bellow's heroes are the heirs of modernism because they feel one of its major drives and problems: they want to be self-created, and fear that they may be. In contrast to Warren's main characters, Bellow's are accidental revolutionists. Merely following their own bents, trying energetically to give their lives the freedom and scope that modern literature suggests as possible, puts them out of touch with family and personal past. And the distance results only in part from any individual act; much comes automatically with time, rapid change, and wide choice of interests.

Thus Bellow is conspicuously selfish. As Snow shows, the going idea of "identity" involves a strong social component. The concept is radically functional: whatever alignment of personal history and impulse appears must work at least passably in the world. But Bellow shades identity nearer than any other contemporary novelist toward the logical meaning of the word. His brand exists more inside the skin. Though the hope of managing events or liking people never disappears, he aims primarily at getting emotions tuned. Results count and hurt, but so do simple feelings of stability or joy or control. Cary's Gulley Jimson knows that he is in a state of grace despite "anything on earth." Bellow's canny heroes do not go that far, but they understand what Gulley means. (As with Cary, this hope inside the self, projected outwards, makes other characters fabulous —quickly tagged and half-seen thereafter.) Yet Bellow's inner moments, unlike Virginia Woolf's, have the feel of persisting for a while. So he creates the strange sense at the end of *Seize the Day*, *Henderson*, and *Herzog* that some great portable revelation, just missed by the reader and unspecifiable by the researcher, has occurred. In Iris Murdoch's *The Unicorn* such an era of good feeling ushers in wide-scale catastrophe; in Bellow the hero can trust his pulse. Even *The Victim*, Bellow's only novel where disorder really threatens to triumph, depends on straightening out the inner tangle. Events serve chiefly to guarantee enough stability for the exciting tension to continue. The final test comes in the happy realization, "I am alive and free. Perhaps even inspired."

But this counterattack in behalf of self-centeredness retains the heroic impulse of the forties to thing big, to ask a great deal of the new self. Bellow, as much a high-energy man as Warren, transfers the theater of action back toward the soul and so has no politics, no vast acceptance of responsibility for other people, no concentration on soluble issues. And because no clear test of success can exist, there is even greater dissatisfaction, more self-pity, but also, by the very multiplying of perspectives, humor. The same instinct for applying knowledge appears, but this time with a pride in it for its own sake rather than for its provable results.

Bellow assumes conditions to be fairly favorable and thus puts even more pressure on the soul to live up to its heroic calling. At the same time the situation gives nothing automatically. Everything, even minimum security, has to be fought for, won, and defended. The hero never gains sure control of himself or his surroundings, but he does orient by putting his problem in every possible perspective. Like the British tragicomic heroes, he wears out more problems than he solves. And in *Augie March*, *Henderson*, and *Herzog* doing so provides an energtic form of pleasure and a sense of heroic superiority which need never test itself against equals. The Bellow system at its working best is self-justifying and self-regulating.

This native endowment for asserting "I am alive" presently combines, too, with a stance of hopefulness—self-conscious, morally correct in the same way that the despair of earlier novelists was. (Anti-despair resembles anti-Communism—it knows less what it is for than what it is against. So did anti-hope earlier.) Both stance and natural cheer base themselves on faith in a rich society's allowing considerable margin for error and a final confidence in high energy itself. All this twisting, swinging alertness must mean something—and somebody—good.

The Bellow vision of the self-creating, self-vindicating man thus has both size and appeal. It offers a way out of not alienation, as Marcus Klein says, but out of the rigid streamlining for action necessary in Warren and Snow. (They are not alienated.) However, the system operates at its working best only intermittently; its sputterings make the stories. Self-creation occurs mostly through the higher play—games which promise purposeful assertion. After *The Victim* Bellow's heroes never lack a vision of this or some capacity for practicing it. Augie ventures, Wilhelm speculates in lard, Henderson goes on safari, and Herzog writes letters correcting the world. Even in their deeper distresses, the protagonists can still draw on this attractive power. Though they often cannot use it in ways that will prove satisfying, they retain room for maneuver. They can be trapped, but not totally.

Self-justification comes harder. Against the flexible strength of the playing mind stands the far less malleable sense of grievance, already well identified by Faulkner and Warren. In Bellow grievance inheres in the vision. His hero regularly feels himself not loved and respected enough. He wants to do what he wants to do, but cannot have actual confidence in it and must seek outside support. Yet to him other people appear to have all followed the Warren and Snow prescriptions: they have narrowed themselves into forces rather than fluid personalities—and developed philosophies to justify their choices. Thus the maxims of the "reality instructors" always cut across the hero's vision of continuing self-creation. He becomes particularly vulnerable to characters like Tamkin and Gersbach who can make him feel better about himself.

Worse yet, the strategy available earlier does no good here. *The Hamlet*, *All the King's Men*, and *The Masters* see possibilities of channeling anger into contest, playful or otherwise, but the Bellow hero sees enough angry contest all about him; its existence makes him want to play. So he cannot try for the simple transformation of aggressiveness into productive force; he must exorcise. Failing that, he retains his flexibility by suspecting his sense of grievance.

Recent times, trying to love the reality principle, have characteristically seen life as a contest of wills rather than an ocean for imaginative exploration, but Bellow's popularity testifies to how partial an enthusiasm for this refurnished vision actually exists. The difficulties that novelists have noted about controlling the environment do not arise accidentally, but inhere in the attempt. An inevitably hostile view of the surroundings—or, rather, of obstructing parts—can be lessened by dominating them, but such superiority does not come cheaply and, when achieved as in *All the King's Men*, feels threatened by counterattacks. Too, errors in judgment become magnified in their effects. If a more tolerant view of the environment could be reached, some of these tensions would ease, but the price would be abandoning contest—and what could substitute? Bellow chooses to combine this question with another implicit in twentieth-century literature. Granting a stronger drive outward, perhaps tolerance can still begin at home.

One Bellow issue therefore becomes how to take a pleasant view of self—given its formation in early years, its resistance to change, its aggressiveness, its proneness to fit reality to obsession, its dependencies. Bellow appeared with an appetite for turning the official self-contempt into modest pride rather than heroic apotheosis. To satisfy that he has had to do much what the British comic novelists had already been doing—accept all the derogatory estimates of human nature and still find possibilities enlivening, enlarging, exciting enough to overbalance. But the unsoftened drive for control of the environment in America makes self-kicking more endemic in our fiction than in British—and harder to overcome convincingly.

Bellow thus has to express directly distaste for life as a series of crises, to be met by major dislocations and centering of forces on a single big objective. Aggressive temperaments like Warren, Snow, and Iris Murdoch take crisis as opportunity: it gives miscellaneous dissatisfaction a directed excitement. Big dramatic actions in *All the King's Men* characteristically begin with Sadie telephoning Jack: all hell has broken loose over here. A good thing—the world needs Jack. But other temperaments do not seize emergency as a chance to take positions, decide issues, do something, anything—break through the stasis of daily living. The more timid merely feel anxious.

So a saving respect for probability, event, other people, and ideas keeps Bellow from sounding like Thomas Wolfe. Bellow's awareness about the continuity of modernism accepts the facts, but its emphasis on intensity makes for a difficult balancing act. The realism of the age, beefing up hope, has to engage the evidence for despair. More than most, Bellow has shown himself able to teeter on these wide-apart rocks without falling into the creek. He can identify with pain almost as completely as Greene without making a full commitment to its value. His endless balancing depends on seeming to make author and suffering hero identical while actually establishing crucial differences; it suspends the inner story in awareness of other equally dynamic processes—motives, alternatives, highs, lows, and conflicts-to-come. Though Bellow can say, "I suffer; therefore I am," with the best moderns, he hates more to stop after having said it.

This demand for both feeling and perspective creates a continuing ambivalence toward that major hope of the inheritance for exorcizing anger, depth psychology. Like other contemporaries, Bellow does not dare break with the way of thinking, but often seems its resentful captive. Protagonists like Wilhelm and Herzog show anger at its authority and failure to repair all the damage done by experience. The satire on Tamkin and Dr. Edwig sounds from the heart. The hostility comes from treating psychoanalysis as a pejorative classifying system, with its own particularly frightening set of names—"depressive," "narcissistic," "hysterical." The hero assigns to himself the effort to have the individual assert his best possible self. (The soul seeks its own autonomy without footnoting sources of the concept.) The doctors thus become pure diagnosticians or, like Tamkin, false appliers of knowledge. But Bellow's generation has absorbed the psychiatry of upset where the first generation only knew about it and, like Sartre's prisoners in Hell, will not leave the well-furnished room yet.

Still, these known ways of managing the mind are normative. Trilling rightly says that Freud's vision is tragic—endless compromise with inevitable defeat. This view crosses the one right of man which the age since 1914 has insisted on—the right to intensity. Henderson's "I want—" has no limiting predicate. That side of the mind is totalitarian, whereas depth psychology tries to govern by a three-man committee, with the ego as chairman. The modern demand that everything be tested on the nerves—because no other value is sure—endorses a fullness of feeling that can threaten sanity, but can also seem preferable to norms and compromises. Bellow, though, is no old-fashioned all-for-intensity man; he shares the current passion for getting along. His strategy carries "I want—" as far as it can go without bringing catastrophic retaliation from the brutal norms. But how far is that? How far can even the most talented balancer crowd Freud, society, and necessity in the name of pleasing himself? Orienting ideas have become indispensable, but do not themselves produce feeling. So psychiatry, like history, provides a needed but inadequate tool. Fragments of both orient. A total scheme moves too far toward the dissociation of thought and sensibility.

Thus only a hyphenated word could describe Bellow's substitute for the immediately preceding militancy. *Stubborness* seems right when the reader disapproves the hero's course, *tenacity* when he approves. Warren's protagonists are often sprinters who wonder why they faded; Bellow's are all routers. Within a few pages the hero appears immersed in his problem and he works full time at it till the end. But the possessed hero is the less original side of the story. He possesses his problem too. He values it, turns it inside out, tosses it in the air to see how it looks revolving, and welcomes its return after threatened respites. Herzog's intense loves have turned into hand-to-hand combat, but he views all less intense ones as frivolous. Critics who emphasize passivity miss the main phenomenon: the tremendous energy the Bellow hero puts into even following other people's leads.

This sense of possibilities, obstacles, and misconceptions expresses itself in Bellow's developing forms of fiction. In the beginning, his hero is an exploring consciousness poking out from a stubbornly-held center. This core of conviction makes him much more a force than reflective characters like Hans Castorp and Marcel, but, aware as he is of an impinging larger situation in the war or possible new depression, his energy scatters itself. It heightens his anxiety over being able to manage the whole effort. He has the sense of being overextended, but even more of being unformed, unhardened into an effective personality. His flexibility is simultaneously his strength and weakness.

At first, other people seem dim; Joseph in *Dangling Man* seeks privacy. But with Allbee, in *The Victim*, Bellow discovers the part that other people play in his heroes' lives. Allbee is the father of all the later fabulous characters. Thereafter the protagonist recognizes certain other people as Forces—with special talents for at once attracting, repelling, promising, threatening. Only people who are themselves to the hilt can break though the hero's self-absorption. They alone seem interesting and real. The guides and "reality instructors" therefore show a larger-than-life definiteness. The hero, often at some cost in immediate pain, seeks out these apparently integrated forces as a complement to his own indefiniteness.

After *Dangling Man*, with its supernumeraries, the Bellow hero takes little interest in anyone who is not fabulous, who does not have his prime quality in excess. Even when characters appear not very remarkable, like Padilla or Clem Tambow, Augie declares them so by fiat. In modern British comic novels, eccentricity ordinarily marks individuality; in Bellow, it accentuates representativeness. Imaginative detail proliferates within a fixed stance and does not signal dynamic possibilities. These rest solely in the protagonist. His associates cannot change; they can only illustrate more of themselves. (He can, of course, change his mind about their meaning.)

Dangling Man introduces the basic problem: self-creation under bare circumstances. Bellow all but labels the novel a portrait of the artist as a young man. Not only is imaginative discovery the subject, but Joseph lends his mistress Joyce's book just before his wife mysteriously wants to read it. Presumably both might understand him better. And the ending parodies Stephen's ringing declaration:

> This is my last civilian day. Iva has packed my things. It is plain that she would like to see me show a little more grief at leaving. For her sake, I would like to. And I am sorry to leave her, but I am not at all sorry to part with the rest of it. I am no longer to be held accountable for myself; I am grateful for that. I am in other hands, relieved of self-determination, freedom canceled.
>
> Hurray for regular hours!
>
> And for the supervision of the spirit!
>
> Long live regimentation!

Parody as well as parallel shows how much *Dangling Man* respects Joyce's values. The short novel depends on a thickness of detail more common in the story and proceeds by a series of epiphanies rather than a developing narrative. Since the hero, called simply Joseph, has responded more to hopes generated by school reading than by family example, his initial values descend from the first-generation novelists—a civilized style, an expanding inner world. "He is a person greatly concerned with keeping intact and free from encumbrance a sense of his own being, its importance." He dresses well, wanting "to avoid small conflicts of nonconformity so that he can give all his attention to defending his inner differences, the ones that really matter." He scorns the theatricality defense, recognizes the ambivalence of good-and-evil, and ranks judgment second to wonder, since each person bears "the imprint of strangeness in the world."

The promise of *Dangling Man* comes from its mastery of tone and its early isolation of conflict. The hero is at home, literally, with his thoughts. Despite his feelings of malaise and self-division, the entries in his diary show an extraordinary consistency. He likes his unmade bed, identifies with his grubby neighborhood, takes naturally to his chosen work of finding himself. Being of two minds interests him more than it makes him unhappy; he embraces the spirit of alternatives. But he comes upon the built-in difficulty of a self-regulating system: it has no test of validity beyond the nerves and can win no undeniable victories. It cannot confer recognition on itself.

Joseph's quarrel with society thus comes not from its power to enforce conformity, but from its withholding forever vindication of the private personality's worth—thereby forcing the whole burden on the individual. The quiet dramatic action brings the finely tuned, internally consistent self against the Sartrean bugaboo, Other People. The normalizing, civilizing view practical in one room becomes impractical in a group. Others bring out—and show—the impulse to demand recognition. In the first dramatized scene Joseph shouts at an ex-comrade who refuses on party orders to acknowledge him. In the best scene he spanks his niece for trying to treat him as a nobody. At a party he deplores a man's cruelty to his ex-girl-friend under hypnosis. He comes to believe that his wife does not value him enough when she asks him to cash a check. (The bank manager already treats him as a non-person.) *Dangling Man* lets Bellows sum up at the beginning of his career the conflict of the preceding fifteen years. The ideal of the artist—imaginative, internally consistent, self-regulating, sensitive to his environment yet invulnerable to it—comes against feelings of deprivation and angry desires to impose on the surrounding world. His temporary solution lets the Army impose on him—"Long live Regimentation!"

Though Joseph has laid out a "plan" for self-development, the first-generation dream of expanding consciousness depended upon leisure, and war has removed that. The novel breaks up the inherited stance under the pressure of uncertainty: the most impressive occurrence is what does not happen. Given an indefinite number of months to "take stock," Joseph finds that the imaginative resources supposedly available on call do not exist in him. Entries in his diary for a whole day go like this:

> December 29
>
> Slept until one o'clock. Out at four for a walk, I lasted ten minutes and then retreated.

The actual episodes all illustrate the threat of losing control. Inherited faith that imagination and style will overbalance disturbances from the outer world fails, and unsuspected aggression takes over. Joseph, who has thought himself a "mild" man, has outbursts at friends, relatives, landlord, and neighbor. An unbuttoned, whiskey-drinking old man next door becomes his grotesque image of himself. Ambivalences between dependence and independence, approval and sought disapproval, deprivation and aid torment him. The novel which begins declaring faith in imagination and style ends looking forward to will imposed from outside.

Because culture as the wisdom of the race takes time to codify, it lags behind actual event and feeling. In *Dangling Man*, Bellow, brought up on Mann, Proust, Joyce, and, most notably, Thomas

Wolfe, sets his inheritance up against fresh circumstances and recoils. The journal form, with its appearance of reproducing reality exactly, free from tags and patterns, records each shift of perspective. Over and over the diary reports: everybody says it's there, but I don't feel it. Bellow begins with a "crater of the spirit" from which the teeter-totter motion toward a dynamic balance appears: touch bottom on one side and an opposing weight begins to push the board back up—as Allbee in *The Victim* puts it, "When people get tired enough of being the way they are, they'll change." Herzog's consolation about the stability of instability is present from the beginning in Bellow, though as hunch rather than theory. Joseph is willing to go to the edge of sacrificing control for the sake of possible richness; but in the unmanageable situation of wartime anxiety, living without recognition, he cannot find the promised imaginative resources. The rightful inheritance is somehow withheld.

Dangling Man stays with the reader more for its approach—the knowledgeable, thinking protagonist; the acquired faith and its failure to encompass enough reality—than for memorable scenes or characters. The promise appears in the poetry of shabby surroundings, loved for their stability and disliked for their too perfect coincidence with state of mind.

> I came down on the El, getting off at the Randolph and Wabash station. There were crooked streaks of red at one end of the street and, at the other, a band of black, soft as a stroke of charcoal; into it were hooked the tiny lights of the lake front. On the platform the rush-hour crowds were melting under the beams of oncoming trains. Each train was followed by an interval of darkness, when the twin colored lamps of the rear car hobbled around the curve. Sparks from the street below were caught and blanked in the heavy, flat ladder of ties. The pigeons under the sooty, sheet-iron eaves were already asleep; their wadded shadows fell on the billboards and, with every train, fluttered as though a prowler had sprung from the roof into their roost.

Bellow's next novel faces the problem of control, but characteristically he means self-control. *The Victim* presents his first stern test of self-vindication, under conditions that encourage little self-creation. The story begins from a memory of depression and wartime bareness and a fear of its return. What really returns is the nagging aggressiveness—monstrous in Albee, troublesome in the protagonist Leventhal. That ghost must be dealt with before even the outlines of an enriched life can appear. At the end the ghost is gone and a pale rainbow emerges.

A writer's total work colors feeling for any single novel. If Bellow had not gone on, *The Victim* would get more credit. It seems as well done as it could be. It combines short story suggestiveness with Bellow's best sustained narrative. Nothing should be done in any different way—and a great deal gets done. The only explanation for its receding among his works, praised and put down at once as his "most Jewish novel," must be that it is a defensive operation and people love Bellow for the forward energy he shows elsewhere. For most of *The Victim* the protagonist is underneath his problem; the public demands that a Bellow hero get moving.

Yet Leventhal represents Bellow's first discovery of how to make a facet of personality seem character in depth—by linking it to ambiguous situations in the environment. The job incidents sketch with magnificent selectiveness what hurts about working. In contrast to Warren's letting his hero accept blame for everything that goes wrong, Bellow shows an objective situation untailorable to many human needs. Personal fears and disappointments merge with the social problem of making necessary work satisfying. Leventhal, who has survived a period of rejection while getting established, from all evidence is doing a reasonably effective job, but he resents an office's not being a family. His fellow workers take no interest in his problems and offer minimal sympathy on even such a semi-public occasion as his nephew's illness; his boss concentrates on procedures and results. The only satisfaction available is, as Henry Green's butler hero would say, being "properly valued." Even this takes only negative form: no immediate threat of losing the job exists.

Bellow thus creates Leventhal—or at least his initial stance—out of the ambiguous security and insecurity of work. By Darwinian lights, Leventhal is too specialized an organism for maximum survival chances. He meets the critical demand for experience only in editing trade papers—and New York has a finite number of trade papers. Job-hunting memories keep the imponderables of "influence" and "blacklists" before him. Transferable loves and hates may or may not exist, but even their possibility looks formidable where the individual feels himself a replaceable part. When Leventhal takes an afternoon off to attend the sick child, no one objects. The only consequence is discomfort—a vague apprehension that some efficiency rater has entered this lapse and will add it to other equally insignificant ones to come out presently with an unfavorable balance.

Bellow's other step in creating Leventhal links him to domestic life in a brilliantly oblique way which removes almost all the pleasures of family and leaves only its anxieties. He and his sister-in-law Elena, both worriers, have married instinctively confident mates, but these are absent for half-plausible reasons. When Elena adopts Leventhal as responsible-party-in-residence, she asks him to reassure her, though no clear grounds for confidence exist, but will not trust his judgment. The boy's disease gets better and worse, the doctors do not know enough about its rare form, Elena's worries are contagious and mix with Leventhal's own. The immediate issue centers on "sensible," professional care in a hospital against loving, and dangerously ignorant, care at home. Elena's Italian ancestry makes it easier for Leventhal to project his own fear of emotional illness. Blame and suspicion, distaste and avoidance result, without mitigating the guilt of family obligation.

The combination of these two lines, job and domestic, charts Leventhal's orbit—reluctant, pushed, hurried, torn between conflicting obligations, doing nothing that he wants to do and resenting everything he has to do. His central sense of existence becomes doubt about being able to handle these two unrelated sets of problems. Hurry and irritability are his main symptoms of being himself. Yet he has proved able to live with these pressures. The dangerous confrontation with the submerged self involves the same fear as *Dangling Man*—of public outburst resulting from these barely penned angers.

Again Bellow makes brilliant use of the oblique angle. Instead of successive illustrations as in *Dangling Man*, the threat of outbreak here turns on a single historical episode, so far in the past as to be no more than a general contributor to Leventhal's anxieties. His telling off a prospective employer had no devastating effects at the time, but when Allbee, the down-and-out WASP, reappears and blames the outburst for losing him his job and causing his present condition, the whole issue of outbreak reopens. Allbee alternates between seeming a nightmare figure, unavoidable and endlessly reproachful, and a blusterer easily put down by firmness. Friends wonder why Leventhal encourages his intrusion, but Leventhal, who would like to think well of himself, wants to prove once and for all that the anger he feels at core is not so evil as to overwhelm his good qualities. Allbee's denunciations give him masochistic pleasure, but also excuse for outbursts of self-justifying that seem to have some chance of winning. Others' opinions differ on the case; Leventhal is on his own.

Allbee himself comes near to being the earlier twentieth-century hero turned inside out—eternally self-pitying but aggressive in identifying who's-to-blame. In so far as Leventhal accepts a secret sharer's terms for the conflict, Allbee is an effective monster—dangerous, monolithic, invincible. But Bellow has faith in a reservoir of sense if only the misapprehensions can be removed, and, in so far as Leventhal does not take the world as made up of friends and devils, sane and insane, he can see Allbee as sponger, sophist, whiner, and crawler. Allbee in actuality deflates readily:

He put the question with an unfinished flourish and Leventhal looked at his sweating face and only now realized how drunk he was.

"Who wants all these people to be here, especially forever? Where're you going to put them all? Who has any use for them all? Look at all the lousy *me's* the world was made for and I share it with. Love thy neighbor as thyself? Who the devil is my neighbor? I want to find out. Yes, sir, who and what? Even if I wanted to hate him as myself, who is he? Like myself? God help me if I'm like what I see around. And as for eternal life, I'm not letting you in on any secret when I say most people count on dying. . . ."

Leventhal had an impulse to laugh. "Don't be so noisy," he said.

"I can't help it if the world is too crowded for you, but pipe down."

Allbee also laughed, strenuously, with a staring expression; his entire face was distended. He cried out thickly, "Hot stars and cold hearts, that's your universe!"

"Stop yelling. That's plenty, now. You'd better go to sleep. Go and sleep it off."

"Oh, good old Leventhal! Kindhearted Leventhal, you deep Hebrew. . . ."

"Enough, stop it!" Leventhal interrupted.

Allbee obeyed, though he went on grinning. From time to time he released a pent-up breath and he sank deeper into the armchair.

In the end Leventhal's ambivalence, which causes his trouble, saves him. When he recognizes his own capacity for drunkenness, sponging, and resisting sensible help, he can see Allbee as human-size. Allbee's bringing the woman to the apartment—possibly a sign of improvement in diverting him from his mania—seems to Leventhal a betrayal of their compact to concentrate on the question of guilt. He can throw out a devil who is not tending to business. Allbee's whimper, "We all have needs," humanizes him at the expense of his image as monolith. When he tries murder-suicide as revenge, Leventhal can strike back for life on the best terms available. He has already decided to ask his wife back before everything is just right for either of them.

Drama in *The Victim* rests on the same inability to tolerate ambiguous situations that Herzog's psychiatrist diagnoses in him. Only when Allbee finally shows that his righteousness is for the most part plain hostility can Leventhal make out the proportions. But the novel deviates from the prejudices of modern literature toward extremes by turning on the question of degree. The two protagonists share a common illness, but Allbee's loyalty to his grievance is total, Leventhal's partial. When Leventhal can both accept the similarity and recognize the difference, he has moved from blockage to release. The difference defines his individuality. He has been able to function in spite of wanting not to; Allbee has chosen to twist his self-defeating feelings into a public show. Everybody turns out to be both self-pitier and aggressor in the name of his just deserts. When Allbee gets tired enough of futile revenge, he puts his sponging and talking talents to work. The most surprising reversal in the novel—and its ultimate cheer—comes in the discovery of Allbee successful as advertising man and gigolo. All-or-nothing, though the human tendency, may not be necessary.

The large movement of the novel obviously depends on setting Leventhal against a grotesque of his own fears and anger; moving him to a point where he identifies with the fear and where only its total removal promises relief; then bringing him, as much from exhaustion as wisdom, to distinguish between the extreme and his own actuality. The teeter-totter rhythm between self-debasement and self-acceptance works for both antagonist and protagonist. Moreover, Bellow gives the conflict movement by repeating this major rhythm of control and desperation in miniature throughout the novel. Allbee makes his most telling attack by adding wife to job problem and Leventhal gets ineffectively angry, but he keeps bringing mind and energy to the issue.

In a general way, anyone could see that there was great unfairness in one man's having all the comforts of life while another had nothing. But between man and man, how was this to be dealt with? Any derelict panhandler or bum might buttonhole you on the street and say, "The world wasn't made for you any more than it was for me, was it?" The error in this was to forget that neither man had made the arrangements, and so it was perfectly right to say, "Why pick on me? I didn't set this up any more than you did." Admittedly there was a wrong, a general wrong. Allbee, on the other hand, came along and said "*You!*" and that was what was so meaningless. For you might feel that something was owing to the panhandler, but to be directly blamed was entirely different.

People met you once or twice and they hated you. What was the reason; what inspired it? This Allbee illustrated it well because he was too degenerate a drunk to hide his feelings. You had only to be yourself to provoke them. Why? A sigh of helplessness escaped Leventhal. If they still believed it would work, they would make little dolls of wax and stick pins into them. And why do they pick out this, that, or the other person to hate—Tom, Dick or Harry? No one can say. They hate your smile or the way you blow your nose or use a napkin. Anything will do for an excuse. And meanwhile this Harry, the object of it, doesn't even suspect. How should he know someone is carrying around an image of him (just as a woman may paste a lover's picture on the mirror of her vanity case or a man his wife's snapshot in his wallet), carrying it around to look at and hate? It doesn't even have to be a reproduction of poor Harry. It might as well be the king of diamonds with his embroidery, his whiskers, his sword, and all. It doesn't make a bit of difference. Leventhal had to confess that he himself had occasionally sinned in this respect, and he was not ordinarily a malicious person. But certain people did call out this feeling. He saw Cohen, let us say, once or twice, and then, when his name was mentioned in company, let fall an uncomplimentary remark about him. Not that this Cohen had ever offended him. But what were all the codes and rules, Leventhal reflected, except an answer to our own nature. Would we have to be told "Love!" if we loved as we breathed? No, obviously. Which was not to say that we didn't love but had to be assisted whenever the motor started missing. The peculiar thing struck him that everything else in nature was bounded; trees, dogs, and ants didn't grow beyond a certain size. "But we," he thought, "we go in all directions without any limit."

Through most of the novel this defense seems not to work. Leventhal's confused excitement grows, the drama comes from the recurring defeat of "rational" by irrational. But, repeated often enough, this method of generalizing the problem, discussing it with friends, and defining differences gives the ending its credibility. Since the struggle is close all the way, the balance has only to tip a little to release Leventhal from his self-imprisonment. When he comes to see "insanity" as a matter of degree rather than either-or and when Allbee fails to keep on embodying his victim's fears perfectly, Leventhal can at least decide whether he is for continuing or not.

The Victim shows advances on both the two novels that obviously stand behind it—*The Trial* and *Ulysses*. For Kafka the charges conscience brings cannot be specified; hence his hero can use only the simplest functional intelligence and must operate on nerves. Bellow presses toward definition. In Allbee he embodies the accuser, identifies the charges, and makes it possible to question not only the right but the power to pass judgment. With the possible area of guilt limited, intelligence can try to assess degree. Leventhal does his work despite the crisis, thinks, consults, helps his sister-in-law, tries to create pleasant circumstances like taking Phil to the zoo, listens to wise old men, and goes to the Harkavy party. By accepting these diversions he keeps the conflict mobile and prevents the obsession from becoming his entire life. This drive to keep stirring the porridge forestalls the Kafka failure, and gives literary form to a new attitude toward conscience and fear.

Much of the novel's power depends on its making Leventhal a consciousness worth saving. Unlike most Bellow heroes, he has no charm. Whatever identification the reader makes with him must derive from his problem and his way of meeting it. The basic concept of mind remains the same as in *Ulysses:* absorbing encounters and events to a major obsession. But, where Joyce poses no overwhelming problem for Bloom's lyric improvising to solve, Bellow puts every hour under the Kafka pressure. In these circumstances Leventhal's consciousness shows the characteristic novel of forces impulse toward orientation—toward moving the conflict around, changing its terms, looking at it from other angles, mapping its course. The interest of Leventhal's mind comes not from its unexpected juxtapositions, though he has some, but from intellectualizing within tighter limits, arriving at unusual conclusions about human tendencies in general. (If quirkiness is universal, Leventhal stands even with everybody else and is no more lunatic than his contemporaries.) The impulse to think of himself as primarily sufferer and so to see suffering all around him comes out on the ferry ride:

After a hurried supper of a sandwich and a bottle of soda at a stand near the ferry, Leventhal crossed to Staten Island. He walked onto the deck with his hands in the pockets of his fully buttoned, wrinkled jacket. His white shoes were soiled. Posted beside a life ring, his dark forehead shining faintly under his ill-combed, thick hair, he gazed out on the water with an appearance of composure; he did not look as burdened as he felt. The formless, working, yellowish-green water was dull, the gulls steered back and forth, the boat crept forward into the glare. A barge was spraying orange paint over the hull of a freighter, which pointed high, lifting its bow out of the slow, thick cloud. Surely the sun was no hotter in any Singapore or Surabaya, on the chains, plates, and rails of ships anchored there. A tanker, seabound, went across the ferry's course, and Leventhal stared after it, picturing the engine room; it was terrible, he imagined, on a day like this, the men nearly naked in the shaft alley as the huge thing rolled in a sweat of oil, the engines laboring. Each turn must be like a repeated strain on the hearts and ribs of the wipers, there near the keel, beneath the water. The towers on the shore rose up in huge blocks, scorched, smoky, gray, and bare white where the sun was direct upon them. The notion brushed Leventhal's mind that the light over them and over the water was akin to the yellow revealed in the slit of the eye of a wild animal, say a lion, something inhuman that didn't care about anything human and yet was implanted in every human being too, one speck of it, and formed a part of him that responded to the heat and the glare, exhausting as these were, or even to freezing, salty things, harsh things, all things difficult to stand. The Jersey shore, yellow, tawny, and flat, appeared on the right. The Statue of Liberty rose and traveled backwards again; in the trembling air, it was black, a twist of black that stood up like smoke. Stray planks and waterlogged, foundering crates washed back in the boat's swell.

Conversely, though, after being angry at his former benefactor, he can try to assess the relationship fairly:

In all likelihood Williston had made up his mind that he was responsible for what had happened to Allbee and while he would listen—if Leventhal knew him—with an appearance of courtesy and willingness to suspend judgment, he would already be convinced. To imagine himself pleading with him filled Leventhal with shame. Didn't he know, he himself, that he had never consciously wanted to harm Allbee? Of course he did. It was for Williston, even if he was his benefactor, to explain why he was ready to believe such a thing. And when you said that someone was your benefactor, what did it actually mean? You might help a man because he was a bother to you and you wanted to get rid of him. You might do it because you disliked him unfairly and wanted to pay for your prejudice and then, feeling that you had paid, you were free and even entitled to detest him. He did not say that it was so in Williston's case, but in a question like this you couldn't be blamed for examining every possibility, or accused of being cold-blooded or heartless. It was better to think well of people—there was a kind of command that you should. And on the whole it was Leventhal's opinion that he had an unsuspicious character and preferred to be taken advantage of rather than regard everyone with distrust. It was better to be genuinely unsuspicious; it was what they called Christian. But it was foolish and miserable to refuse to acknowledge the suspicions that came into your mind in an affair like this. Because if you had them you should not put on an innocent front with yourself and deny that you did.

At the same time Leventhal was reasonable enough to admit that he might be trying to release himself from a sense of obligation to Williston by finding fault with him. He had never been able to repay him. Was he looking for a chance to cancel the debt? He did not think so. He wished he could be sure. Ah, he told himself, he was sure. He had never felt anything but gratitude. Again and again he had said—Mary could testify—that Williston had saved him.

And he can push the whole problem out into the world at large:

With everybody except Mary he was inclined to be short and neutral, outwardly a little like his father, and this shortness of his was, when you came right down to it, merely neglectfulness. When you didn't want to take trouble with people, you found the means to turn them aside. Well, the world was a busy place—he scanned the buildings, the banks and offices in their Saturday stillness, the pillars ribbed with soot, and the changeable color of the windows in which the more absolute color of the sky was darkened, dilated, and darkened again. You couldn't find a place in your feelings for everything, or give at every touch like a swinging door, the same for everyone, with people going in and out as they pleased. On the other hand, if you shut yourself up, not wanting to be bothered, then you were like a bear in a winter hole, or like a mirror wrapped in a piece of flannel. And like such a mirror you were in less danger of being broken, but you didn't flash, either. But you had to flash. That was the peculiar thing. Everybody wanted to be what he was to the limit. When you looked around, that was what you saw most distinctly. In great achievements as well as in crimes and vices. When that woman faced her husband this morning after he had most likely tracked her all night from joint to joint and finally caught her catting, too red-handed to defend herself; when she faced him, wasn't she saying, silently, "I'm being up to the limit just what I am"? In this case, a whore. She may have been mistaken in herself. You couldn't expect people to be right, but only try to do what they must. Therefore hideous things were done, cannibalistic things. Good things as well, of course. But even there, nothing really good was safe.

The reader keeps turning the pages of *The Victim* because it combines predictability at the national level with surprise at the local. The source of this unexpectedness is a refusal to lump, an insistence on discriminating. Leventhal has competences and incompetences, but neither extends across the whole range of his personality. He has a major conflict, happy moments, "irrelevant" experiences that presently relate to his cure, visions of conciliation with his wife, irritations, lapses, times of firmness, others of indecision, security with the apartment manager and his wife, insecurity with the Italian grandmother. His drive for mobility combines with these complexities to keep the reader unsure. Leventhal can almost manage his neurosis, but he threatens not to.

This way of putting the human problem represents a real shift of emphasis. Bellow is the first major American novelist since World War I not to begin from a sense of betrayal. Nothing in *The Victim* corresponds to Hemingway's abstract talk, Fitzgerald's big rich, or Warren's impressive fathers. Bellow starts from vulnerable imagination and sensitivity operating in a world not especially devoted to perpetuating either. To Leventhal the city as obstacle means crowds in the automat, job specialization, impersonality, long trips on the Staten Island ferry. The opening page sets up the basic irritation:

> On some nights, New York is as hot as Bangkok. The whole continent seems to have moved from its place and slid nearer the equator, the bitter gray Atlantic to have become green and tropical, and the people, thronging the streets, barbaric fellahin among the stupendous monuments of their mystery, the lights of which, a dazing profusion, climb upward endlessly into the heat of the sky.
>
> On such a night, Asa Leventhal alighted hurriedly from a Third Avenue train. In his preoccupation he had almost gone past his stop. When he recognized it, he jumped up, shouting to the conductor, "Hey, hold it, wait a minute!" The black door of the ancient car was already sliding shut; he struggled with it, forcing it back with his shoulder, and squeezed through. The train fled, and Leventhal, breathing hard, stared after it, cursing, and then turned and descended to the street.

The friendly city means homey objects, often dirty, and an occasional recognizable face appearing among the obstructors. Yet Leventhal has chosen this life in preference to his father's grocery store in Hartford, and no seer knows how to change radically its conditions. Leventhal takes interest in meeting even casual acquaintances—some slight meaning has appeared out of rush and the collision with the Others. He often blames his employer for not acting like a father, but only a mad selectivity like Allbee's can find a First Cause for New York.

Another originality of *The Victim* lies in its early recognition of change both in society and expectancies. However far from ideal these conditions are, they are better than Leventhal and his generation had feared. Wartime dangling has ended. The depression dread of no job at all has proved unreal. Though Leventhal had difficulty getting his first chance, he has now worked for six years and acquired the experience that presently gets him a better place. The ending may be an epitaph for a small winner, but Leventhal takes a good job, a coming baby, and an occasional night out with his wife as evidences of some success: he has evaded his more unbearable fears.

Yet the dynamic of Bellow's early work differs from Iris Murdoch's, though she too has been alert to such changes. "Normal" pessimism represents a more desperate condition to him than to her. Her heroines who defend the daily have a confidence about living with ordinary despair that his heroes do not. They must work out of it to survive. Bellow builds both continuity and a dynamic for change—the teeter-totter rhythm—into a single consciousness, while she usually splits the drive to regroup from the need to stabilize. But both differ from earlier novelists in making "motion sickness" a motive for cure instead of for a groan. *The Victim* accepts vulnerability as a starting point, but shows a new willingness to test whether inner dynamics may work toward integration of personality rather than toward catastrophe. Leventhal does end with a pleasanter view of himself than he had and in so doing feels less hostility to his world.

With the ghost of aggression temporarily pacified, Bellow was free to explore what enriching life and creating the self could mean. When the public at large speaks of him, it means *The Adventures of Augie March*. By now it must be unsure whether Bellow created Augie or Augie created Bellow. Certainly the book laid the foundation for his preeminence, and made him loved as few American novelists have been. Chester E. Eisinger concludes his book on dozens of angry novels in the forties with a cheer for the appearance of *Augie* early in the fifties. If the novel has an obligation to bring the news rather than reenforce the known, by 1953 the public had an unfed appetite for good news.

Bellow did not just stumble onto his triumph. From the beginning he had grasped a crucial dilemma—that circumstances change rapidly while feelings and cultural formulations resist change and attempt to assimilate indigestible matter. Tension between the two establishes the conflict in *Dangling Man* and *The Victim*. Both press to bring the hero into line with present reality and with his real, as opposed to his inherited, feelings about it. Bellow differs from Warren, who also tries, in his prejudices about a norm. Warren assumes it to be the past, with the present somehow to be fitted in. Bellow suspects that the present is the crucial reality and that the past may be related to it by tangents, mutations, and accidents more than by simple evolution. Where Warren's search for a tight logic ultimately bewilders him, Bellow's looser sense of connection enables him to pick up pieces here and there for whatever they may be worth.

At the extremes, of course, stand two possible attitudes toward change. The nineteenth century seized on evolution and wanted to believe that, with many exceptions, change worked for good. The twentieth got dramatic proofs that this was not necessarily so. But the modern cultural formulation developed its own inertia and, while urging ideal changes, fell into viewing most of those actually occurring as working for the worse. In the postwar period, however, this one-piece suit began to feel wrong, even though nobody could prove just where it failed to fit. But once novelists, like the physicists, began to break the problem up into smaller components, a new way of seeing the issue opened up. Bellow not only helped devise the strategy, but in *The Adventures of Augie March* found a form for exploring its possibilities.

The structure looks simple enough, and most critics take it as so. That capacious barrel for all episodic narrative, *picaresque*, seems to contain it nicely. But *picaresque* applied to this novel suggests only how it progresses, not what holds it together or makes it appeal. For the story means to do more than merely keep going; it wants to turn lead into gold. While seeming to ground itself in everyday city life, it aspires to a miracle.

Thomas Mann had done something like that in the thirties and again in the fifties with his Joseph novel and *Felix Krull*, and, though Bellow often seems closer to Kafka or Joyce in developing a narrative, his values are closer to Mann's. He too keeps battling the question of bourgeois and artist. He respects the bourgeois virtues of talent and drive while passively resisting them. Unlike most American novelists, he likes and uses learning, even if he suspects it to be only the imaginative form of acquisitiveness. He takes a similar joy in ironic ambivalences and alternative ideas.

The Adventures of Augie March appeals because it eats its cake and has it too. It celebrates the bourgeois virtues of talent and drive while diverting them to imaginative play. The indispensable step was to get around the culture's channeling of aggressiveness into competitiveness, but, with his questioning about cultural clichés, Bellow sensed what Salinger did not—that no time in American history had ever been so favorable for doing so. Paradoxically, the more business succeeds in its aims, the more it enhances the value of play. A luxury civilization looks for the enlivening. Moreover, as business approaches becoming a form of civil service, it loses the soaring appeal it still had for Dreiser. With that loss, it also loses its monstrousness and need not even be opposed in the encyclopedic style of the thirties.

As late as *At Heaven's Gate*, the omnipresence of business is assumed. Warren's rebels fight their way out of its appeal into a bewildered vacuum. Most of them have been too engaged to think, What next? Those who have faced the issue become either opposition specialists like the union organizer Sweetwater or mirror watchers like the poet Slim Sarrett. Dos Passos and Steinbeck had to create business villains, but Bellow need not show Augie's brother Simon as very bad to make the standard channel of aggression unappealing. As the rejected career—but rejected without too much of a struggle—it can even have its friendly side in Simon, as it does in Herzog's brother. A business civilization used to tolerate its intellectuals—part of the time, at least. Bellow is the first major American novelist to see that intellectuals can now afford to tolerate, if not actually condescend to, business. A solid public demand for imagination exists.

But this negative point does little more for the novel than provide a recurring, not too insistent, pressure on the hero. The first strategy for forward movement is the choice of the hero himself. This is still widely misunderstood. A psychiatrist has proved that no real person could continue reacting as Augie does. He is undoubtedly right, and, if more people believed him, questions about Augie's plausibility and shadowiness could not be put as they often are. For Augie is not a character in the ordinary fictional sense; he is more a stylized prime motive, the impulse necessary to keep the exploration going. He is also a voice, a commentator telling us how to take all this, and a master introducer of some fascinating people he thinks we ought to meet before deciding finally what the world is like.

In choosing Augie, Bellow operates within the postwar concept of character as force rather than full consciousness. Yet he retains enough of the first generation's values to give Augie's consciousness more range than most contemporary heroes' have. Its prime motive, to find giants in the earth if they still exist, in turn enlarges the characters he introduces. But as a force he opens up a new way of seeing personality. Augie's strategy to define himself satisfactorily—as a superior person, that is—means joining-and-rebelling at the same time. He shares imaginatively the energy of an Einhorn or a Thea and accepts readily the role of helper, but also sees all around them. He recognizes their heroism, absurdity, invincibility, and pathos. For himself he rejects the parts of their personalities which do not feel right to him. And he reserves the right to return if the merchandise does not prove as advertised.

Does this make *The Adventures of Augie March*, then, an education novel? Not really. The traditional novel of that genre shows the hero trying experiences and learning something from each to be stored up for future use. Presently he has a well-armed vision.

Though Augie may have learned a few things at the end—such as not to go hunting lizards with strong-willed girls—he primarily *experiences*. If he had not gone hunting, he would have been stealing books in Chicago and piecing the world together in his head. Thea's proposal is simply the most exciting—in anticipation—to turn up at a time when he is otherwise unengaged. Openness to experience plus willingness to turn in an honest report is his value in itself. For any real person, of course, this can be only a partial approach to life. As a force rather than a full consciousness, Augie represents that energetic and adventurous part. The novel tests how much confidence can be placed in it if pessimism does not foreclose the question in advance.

Augie March develops too in the postwar manner of combining atmosphere with forces representing other people. Like Iris Murdoch's, Bellow's scene specifies precisely, but it also depends on giving more than enough for the purpose. The principle for the supporting cast is the same as for the major figures and follows Leventhal's view of human nature:

> On the other hand, if you shut yourself up, not wanting to be bothered, you were like a bear in a winter hole, or like a mirror wrapped in a piece of flannel. And like such a mirror you were in less danger of being broken, but you didn't flash, either. But you had to flash. That was the peculiar thing. Everybody wanted to be what he was to the limit. When you looked around, that was what you saw most distinctly. In great achievements as well as in crimes and vices.

In Augie's selective memory everybody in northwest Chicago was engaged in being himself to the limit. Despite poverty, a wealth of feeling and planning existed.

The foremost talent in the novel shows how this youthful experience of abundance amid seediness—of down-to-earth excess—provides a critique of and spur to all later experience. And the seediness is important to this Garden of Eden: it guarantees the abundance and diversity of neighborhood, pool hall, and the fringes of the Einhorn family because nothing much is at stake and no one can impose finally on anyone else. Anarchic surroundings permit movement and choice. Orderly ones mean orders. When Augie later tries living in style with the Renlings and the Magnuses, he finds rules—and the power to make them stick.

The Chicago scenes are memorable more in their total force than separately, but the reader who does not recall Mrs. Kreindl as Mrs. Kreindl comes away with knowledge of a milieu where emotion gets itself expressed and overexpressed. Jimmy Klein's stealing may be more dramatic than his family's expensive tastes in furniture and clothes, but these too stay with Augie. Kreindl makes a life for himself with burlesque, dinners downtown, and narcissism. Five Properties lives for his joke, told over and over. Dingbat Einhorn, poorly equipped for the competitive life, lives for the pool hall and his prizefighter, who cannot fight. The virile old commissioner ignores his age. And Grandma Lausche, who exerts the greatest moral force, emphasizes that all things are possible for the sly and charming.

Bellow's comedy of manners here—for it is comedy of manners despite surface difference—reverses that of an English novelist like Anthony Powell. In Powell's *The Music of Time* the hero and his élite assume that all people with right of entry will be roughly alike. They will say the same things, order the same wines, play the going parlor games. Comedy develops when crudities like egotism and obsessiveness break through the expected manner. Powell starts with the human demand that everybody else be a mirror image of the self—and slowly turns it into assent to individual differences as giving vitality and variety, but also permanent disappointment.

Bellow's novel also sets up a conventional expectation—but, this time, instead of correctness, it is scheming. The community, from Grandma Lausche outward, values the *necessary* use of mind. Egotism shows itself on the surface, not bothering with concealment, and pleasure is a by-product of the ingenuity needed to get along. However, the characters who become more than community representatives and achieve individuality do it, not by breaking through the expected manner, but by exceeding it, carrying it beyond practical purpose. Einhorn's use of mind is outrageous and unnecessary

—except as play. Instead of dealing directly with their problems, which often cannot be dealt with, the comic individualists construct elaborate games on the pattern of old practicalities.

A second transformation of this pride in playfulness provides the force in Augie's personality, the core of his defense against the older community values. Critics who see him as simply resisting the rationales of commerce and specialization often find him shadowy—logically enough—but Augie's real existence lies less in his actions than in his voice, and the reader who has once heard it can never mistake it for someone else's. Not only the set pieces like introducing Einhorn in the company of Caesar, Machiavelli, and Ulysses, but any page describing people has this joy in excess, in superabundance of its kind. Simon arriving at the Michigan resort, for example:

> Taller than most, blond and brown, there was my Germanic-looking brother. He was dolled up like a Fourth of July sport, and a little like a smart gypsy, smiling, his chipped tooth foremost, his double-breasted plaid jacket open wide, knuckles down on the handles of two grips. He gave off his fairness with a kind of heat in the blue color of his eyes, terrifically; it was also in his cheeks, down into his neck, rich and animal.

The description of Simon's girl friend adds a characteristic downgrading:

> But she, although in a self-solicitous way, was a beautiful piece of tall work, on colossal but careful legs, hips forward; her mouth was big and would have been perfect if there hadn't been something self-tasting in it, eyes with complicated lids but magnificent in their heaviness, an erotic development. So that she had to cast down these eyes a little to be decent with her endowment, that height of the bosom and form of hips and other generic riches, smooth and soft, that may take the early person, the little girl, by surprise in their ampleness when they come on. She accused me of examining her too much, but could anybody help that? . . .
>
> But personally I didn't care too much for her. Partly because I was gone on Esther. But also because of what came across as her own, that is, apart from female brilliance, was slow. Maybe she herself was stupefied by what she had, her slaying weight. It must have pressed down on her thoughts, like any great vitality in nature. Like the aims that live

in the blood of grizzly or tiger, bearing down on the mind of such beasts with square weight, a manifestation of one thing carried out completely, to the very stripes and claws.

The analysis of Mrs. Renling moves with the same enthusiasm to the grimmer side of excess energy:

> There's one thing you couldn't easily find out from Mrs. Renling; I never knew what was her most deep desire, owing to her cranky manners and swift coversation. But she wanted to try being a mother. . . . But all the same I was not going to be built into Mrs. Renling's world, to consolidate what she affirmed she was. And it isn't only she but a class of people who trust they will be justified, that their thoughts will be as substantial as the seven hills to build on, and by spreading their power they will have an eternal city for vindication on the day when other founders have gone down, bricks and planks, whose thoughts were not real and who built on soft swamp. What this means is not a single Tower of Babel plotted in common, but hundreds of thousands of separate beginnings, the length and breadth of America. Energetic people who build against pains and uncertainties, as weaker ones merely hope against them. And, even literally, Mrs. Renling was very strong, and as she didn't do any visible work it must have come, the development in her muscles, from covert labor.

This voice brims with pride in a perceptiveness, breadth of knowledge, inventiveness, and largeness of view foreign to the person being described. Augie asserts a private joy at being a peak of sensitivity, intelligence, and fluency surrounded by foothill dopes. He expresses a sense of the self as playfully, loftily observing people living under the shadow of old necessities and making virtues of them—superior to events because of esthetic vitality and the recognition of room for maneuver. This idea of self gives him the con fidence to resist the commercially minded, and his talent for voicing a competitive society's doubts and incongruities enables him to survive pleasantly on its fringes. Even more important, beyond the dramatic effect, the tone does more than anything else in the novel to make the reader identify with Augie. No one has done more than Bellow to tell us that we are all cool and superior observers of our associates.

In terms of the action, this vision of endless play tests every later opportunity for Augie. Adult life tries to make him narrow this richness, but for Augie the job offers none of Conrad's feeling of union with the community. The Jewish background represents not merely the predicament of man in the city, as one critic has said, but a traditional way of taking comfort from and enlivening the scene. Augie's early life is not an experiment, as enlivening is in Waugh and Huxley, but a proved fact. His problem does not resolve itself entirely because Bellow does not see how the happy vision can be carried whole into adult life or how its criticism of the present can disappear.

Nevertheless, Bellow does see more sharply than Salinger how mixed society's mandate to the young man is—and how many opportunities the confusion opens up. Augie's conflict arises between familial and individualistic, but the problem will not factor into these opposites because the family has trained him to believe in both. The tradition itself is split and has never settled upon the means by which to sustain the two values together. At the same time that Grandma Lausche is congratulating herself on holding the family together, she is nagging the brothers to make something of themselves and not be like Mama. While Einhorn plays his games amid a tribe of Einhorns and retainers, he urges a sharp individualism on Augie, who he says is "in opposition." But in opposition to what? To the family—in so far as it represents an inherited purpose.

The family thus stands for both richness and narrowness—the early representatives for richness and the later ones for concentration, self-denial, and pretentiousness. But the family is merely the readiest sample of what Augie opposes. More generally, he opposes the single standard—Simon's, Mrs. Renling's and the Magnuses' ideal of competitiveness rewarded by pretentiousness. The panoramic scenes work to show that this standard exists primarily for those who believe in it. Those who do not and are willing to pay the price—and there is a price on the conformist's choice as well as on Mimi's—find all kinds of half-successful schemes for taking an interest in life, and feel little guilt. Compared to Faulkner, Bellow finds a multitude of enrichments and eccentricities open to the alert so long as they make bows to the social order. The very number of minor characters in the section about the university shows the prevalence of off-trail lives coming to no unbearable disasters. Mimi, Padilla, Clem, and Kayo are getting along. These otherwise superfluous characters reenforce Augie's discovery that society permits far more flexibility than the doctrine of a driver like Simon admits. Individuality in interests and acts can survive for those who want it to.

Instructive as these almost anonymous individualists are, they do not share Augie's secret sense of destiny. The ground he comes to occupy lies between them and the two memorable monomaniacs—Thea and the ship's carpenter. Both try desperately to find new ways alone, but Augie's relations with them bring out the contradiction in all efforts to make community and high individuality consort: disliking the obvious way is not the same as liking someone else's experiment.

Thea, the high-priced huntress, interests Augie and the reader because she offers an answer "of a certain magnitude" to observation and drift. She expresses her anger against the defeated promise of childhood by trying to dramatize pure destructiveness—eagle against iguana. (She takes no moral from the eagle's chicken-heartedness.) The very unlikeliness of her plan is the heart of its charm, the symptom of the congenial illness. But iguana-hunting turns out to be dangerous and exhausting—and so does Thea. Nevertheless, Thea and the lesser obsessives act on angers that Augie transmutes, and so great is their appeal that at the end no reader can quite trust him not to take up with others like them.

The mad carpenter, with his claim of creating life in the laboratory, jars Augie into compromise and gives whatever guarantee of continuance the ending can have. For the carpenter is Augie gigantified, without self-knowledge, destructive to himself and everyone around him. Inventive, he believes the world his room for maneuver and himself a Moses ready to lead—and sacrifice—the pygmies. He is of course the final powermad character, too, but in him differences merge, and Augie backs away from his strongest form of self-assertiveness for a half-business career, a part-time wife, and an acceptance of kinship with the housemaid walking off in the Normandy rain.

In sum, the novel glorifies the gifted amateur—looks for what can be loved in itself, tries to reduce the anger which attends discipline.

Aside from the hero, four presiding spirits dominate the novel—Grandma Lausche; Einhorn; Mimi, the all-for-love-knowing-the-price girl; and Thea. None of these are people the reader is likely to meet at work or dinner parties. Because Augie selects and reports them, they are themselves to the limit. Audacity is their trademark, not only in imagining but in acting out images of themselves that are beyond their powers. So they all suffer defeats and disappointments. But the images are *just* beyond their powers. The cheerful wonder is not that they lose, but that they come so close to winning—and, in the sense that heroic effort is better than apathy, do win. The novel honors these idealized figures. They are inseparably heroic, absurd, brilliant, and pathetic.

Three other characters provide the spirit of alternatives to this vision of life: Simon, who grows angry trying to follow the prescribed channel into business; Mrs. Renling, who gets only bitterness out of high style; and the ship's carpenter, who defines the borders of sanity and insanity in reaching beyond the achievable. On the fringes of the novel, the dependents suggest an alternative that creates a ground tone of anxiety. Mamma, Georgie, and, in the comic manifestation, Dingbat Einhorn, get pity, sympathy, and interest. Active as he is, Augie hears the sound of distress and wants to help.

Bellow's first three novels appeared within six years; he has taken twelve to publish the next three. There may or may not be a causal connection, but the second set comes into Iris Murdoch territory—regrouping after the first sense of life as illness-and-opportunity has spun itself out. *Seize the Day*, perfectly executed over a short distance, depends heavily upon its choice of moment—when a man realizes for sure that his grandly conceived rebellion against family is going to produce mixed results and that no armistice with family conscience will bring harmony. *Seize the Day* has none of the performance characteristics that determine tone in *Augie March, Herzog,* and *Henderson.* Voice, character, and act subordinate themselves to a situation. Tommy Wilhelm, failed actor, failed sales executive, and failing speculator, is less significant in himself than in the interplay between him and his two coaches.

In this kind of novel everything depends on execution—and it is perfect. The action twice moves through a rhythm of confrontation, collapsing resistance, and angry tears. Bellow's knack for reenforcing his tune with incremental repetition appears from the beginning, when Wilhelm tries to make his confidently prosperous business suit cover actually feeling punch-drunk. His tics give him away, but do not commute his sentence to keep on with the masquerade.

When it came to concealing his troubles, Tommy Wilhelm was not less capable than the next fellow. So at least he thought, and there was a certain amount of evidence to back him up. He had once been an actor—no, not quite, an extra—and he knew what acting should be. Also, he was smoking a cigar, and when a man is smoking a cigar, wearing a hat, he has an advantage; it is harder to find out how he feels. He came from the twenty-third floor down to the lobby on the mezzanine to collect his mail before breakfast, and he believed—he hoped—that he looked passably well: doing all right. It was a matter of sheer hope, because there was not much that he could add to his present effort. On the fourteenth floor he looked for his father to enter the elevator; they often met at this hour, on the way to breakfast. If he worried about his appearance it was mainly for his old father's sake. But there was no stop on the fourteenth, and the elevator sank and sank. Then the smooth door opened and the great dark red uneven carpet that covered the lobby billowed toward Wilhelm's feet. In the foreground the lobby was dark, sleepy. French drapes like sails kept out the sun, but three high, narrow windows were open, and in the blue air Wilhelm saw a pigeon about to light on the great chain that supported the marquee of the movie house directly underneath the lobby. For one moment he heard the wings beating strongly.

Bellow pinpoints Wilhelm's problem of reducing conscience to take account of frustration and failure by making the issue overt. Wilhelm confronts his actual father, still a guardian of the moral law at a vigorous seventy-eight, a doctor retired to community respect at a good hotel. No contemporary has produced a better comedy of the immovable object and the resistable force. (Father, wife, and friends find Wilhelm easy to withstand.) Henry Green writes superb comedy of misunderstanding, where a common language fails to communicate, but Bellow's is a comedy of perfect comprehension. Wilhelm and the doctor understand each other exactly. They are genuinely at cross-purposes and will remain so. Bellow heightens this kind of pained fun by skillful shifts in point of view:

> Dr. Adler thought that Wilhelm looked particularly untidy this morning—unrested, too, his eyes red-rimmed from excessive smoking. He was breathing through his mouth and he was evidently much distracted and rolled his red-shot eyes barbarously. As usual, his coat collar was turned up as though he had had to go out in the rain. When he went to business he pulled himself together a little; otherwise he let himself go and looked like hell.

As Wilhelm retreats, expectedly frustrated, he runs through the mental process that forms the crux of Bellow's doubts about biographical-psychological explanations. Wilhelm understands how his father became the way he is and why he cannot change, but the insight does not moderate at all wanting what he wants—the "blessing."

But if Wilhelm insists on being understood, Bellow is willing to let him be. So he puts him into the hands of a friend who understands all and mismanages everything. Tamkin is primarily a satire on the modern tendency, in the absence of any clear direction, to make depth psychology do the work of judgment. By his own account an inventor, psychiatrist, rich man, and scientific market manipulator, he blankets all human activity under the idea of guilt complex. As a comic figure he specializes in the plausible misapplication of knowledge:

> Dryly, as though he were dealing with a child, Tamkin told him in a tone of tiring patience, "Now listen, Tommy. I have it diagnosed right.

If you wish I should sell I can give the sell order. But this is the difference between healthiness and pathology. One is objective, doesn't change his mind every minute, enjoys the risk element. But that's not the neurotic character. The neurotic character—"

"Damn it, Tamkin!" said Wilhelm roughly. "Cut that out. I don't like it. Leave my character out of consideration. Don't pull any more of that stuff on me. I tell you I don't like it."

Tamkin therefore went no further; he backed down. "I meant," he said, softer, "that as a salesman you are basically an artist type. The seller is in the visionary sphere of the business function. And then you're an actor, too."

The comic interplay between Tamkin and Wilhelm proceeds again by making need overpower sense of probability. Wilhelm has only his last $700 to lose. He is going to have to find a job anyway.

The ending provides an excellent instance of Bellow's ability to live with his character's pained feelings while himself standing at a distance:

The great knot of ill and grief in his throat swelled upward and he gave in utterly and held his face and wept. He cried with all his heart.

He, alone of all the people in the chapel, was sobbing. No one knew who he was.

One woman said, "Is that perhaps the cousin from New Orleans they were expecting?"

"It must be somebody real close to carry on so."

"Oh my, oh my! To be mourned like that," said one man and looked at Wilhelm's heavy shaken shoulders, his clutched face and whitened fair hair, with wide, glinting, jealous eyes.

"The man's brother, maybe?"

"Oh, I doubt that very much," said another bystander. "They're not alike at all. Night and day."

The flowers and lights fused ecstatically in Wilhelm's blind, wet eyes; the heavy sea-like music came up to his ears. It poured into him where he had hidden himself in the center of a crowd by the great and happy oblivion of tears. He heard it and sank deeper than sorrow, through torn sobs and cries toward the consummation of his heart's ultimate need.

Seize the Day develops a paradigm, irreducible within its terms. Friends of mine who usually show good judgment think highly of *Henderson the Rain King,* but to me it seems a rather mechanical fantasy by an author who does better by intertwining fantasy and everyday. The initial stance devleops with Bellow's regular promise. Henderson on his wives and pigs is funny. So is he about blowing up the matriarchal water supply to kill frogs and grunting through his demonstration of strength in the arena. (This last scene takes on extra wit by its burlesque of the high value put on public performance in Bellow's other novels.) But the absence of a scene that takes hold enough to reenforce the action and the not overwhelmingly imaginative choice of lion-taming commits Bellow to spinning more than he can out of rough materials. The solidity of mind which he makes so much from elsewhere here becomes heaviness. The jokes lumber.

Yet to overemphasize these reservations would be unfair to the moral bounce of the book. This appears not only in the consistently live tone, but also in the willingness to hunt big game. The novel raises a major possibility for regrouping after a succession of defeats. It asks the kind of question that only a first-rate novelist would ask. Does there exist what Herzog calls "a primitive cure"? Is there some single big stance that can guide and hearten after people have failed to take their initial objectives? Can they *learn* to live instead of endlessly sobbing like Wilhelm? Henderson's conclusions reflect exactly my sense of the novel itself: the trip was worth taking, the results inconclusive.

Without *Henderson*, though, *Herzog* might have been impossible. *Henderson* removes itself from the fury and the mire to block out major issues. *Herzog* faces them with psychological realism about impediments, and comes up with a credible inspiration that men can learn. They can achieve a change of heart by a change of thinking. Even more important, Bellow proves that they have the most powerful motives for doing so. The prevalence of evil forces them to demand good.

The one problem in reading the novel is the temptation to let too much hang on the marital estrangement. Bellow needs it to upset Herzog and keep him upset long enough for his mind to work its problems over and over—worry them to death. So the divorce story is omnipresent without being especially fascinating.

Fortunately, *Herzog* is a big novel and can stand more mistakes than a small one. Judged by *Seize the Day*, where every gesture has expanding significance, its detail often means little more than it says. But *Herzog* tries for more. As I have said earlier, the hero often seems to be vanishing in recent literature because everyone agrees so thoroughly on what he should be like: imaginative, intelligent, self-centered, irritated, easily woundable, uncertain of what he should put his energies to. Sketching in these qualities spreads a wider net than risking individual traits which would almost surely prove more divisive between author and reader. In a fragmented culture which defends itself with "I'm all right, Jack," broad tone of feeling commands more adherents than case history. Herzog, however, undertakes the hard question: if this composite hero who attracts our sympathy easily is so valuable a personality, what's in him? What does this agreed-on consciousness amount to that makes it worth our continued loyalty? In his most developed, nearest-to-the-nerve hero Bellow offers a slightly disguised artist to a time no longer willing to recognize the transformed priest, the prophet, or the unacknowledged legislator.

One minimum requirement had to be met to make such a hero acceptable. This age has suffered enough reversals of expectation and outright disasters to demand that he operate under greater pressure than the protagonists of Lawrence, Joyce, Virginia Woolf, and Proust. Except for *The Victim* Bellow had got by until *Herzog* without having to sustain dramatic tension for a whole novel. A series of imaginative suggestions had worked. Here he chooses an action that does not have a guaranteed overlap with his readers' concerns. Divorce settlements may be common enough nowadays to make a fair-sized public from ex-participants, but Bellow's obvious aim for a major fiction goes beyond the specialized audience. The rest of the world, however, takes an interest in the more repeatable details, but defends itself against being drawn into the ferocity of the antagonists. Except where one party has achieved flagrant unpopularity, a few people side with one and a few with the other; most prefer to think that these two were not meant for each other and may not have been meant for anybody at all. A well-publicized divorce case cements marriages all around it.

Not even Bellow can escape this difficulty. His divorce story too comes out a twice-told tale, whose personal variants do not rescue it entirely from being somebody else's problem. Things are still tough all over, and, as Herzog sees, many of them tougher than his case. The wound is more to his middle-aged pride than to any particular need for his young wife. Bellow has all along been a novelist of endurable upsets, of things gone awry but not to smash with some "reasonable" plan for living. Something has to attack his off-balance, but scrambling, hero, and the divorce settlement here serves the purpose. It creates the uncontrollable situation which sets off Herzog's fantasies of impressing, imposing, and controlling. Bellow's decision to abandon the esthetic distance with which he had previously handled such estrangements and to go along with Herzog's ferocity ultimately creates its own angry humor as more and more conflicting details appear, but this retrospective gain does not entirely cancel out the tediousness of many details themselves. Yet in the end these variations carry an important point: Herzog cannot achieve self-justification in terms of so mixed-up an experience. And certain scenes do produce a fine comic mixture of self-pity and self-contradiction. In the best of all, Herzog glowers on the lawn in the Berkshires while Mady and Shapiro show off their knowledge about Slavic languages and history instead of bolstering his ego. Over-all, Herzog's continuing surprise at what-she-did-next makes the remote Mady into a comic figure, different from the Mady who actually appears at the police station.

Too, *Herzog* means to use the artistic personality without benefit of religion or saccharine, and for that the family background from which a poor boy becomes an arrogant, prosperous intellectual has to be included. But again the encyclopedic intention brings in a degree of flatness. Father could be a fabulous figure out of *Augie March,* but seems more clearly a construct—a gentle bootlegger with few memorable qualities. The various aunts and the loving brother consume pages without showing much more than that childhood is different from adulthood. Altogether, the family scenes make the common sociological point: that, in an age of mobility, many people feel a great distance between the two.

The divorce settlement story has more going for it sociologically speaking. Modern culture has undoubtedly intensified the antagonisms represented. The man expects pleasure and ego bolstering, the wife hopes for a career equaling her husband's in a traditionally male activity. Herzog sees Mady as aiming to become a "castiron bluestocking." The most perceptive action of the estrangement shows a profitless sibling rivalry. Herzog is shocked over and over that people obligated to be his partisans have defected to Mady's side—his psychiatrist, Dr. Edvig; his lawyer, Himmelstein; and, most important, Mady's lover, Gersbach. Herzog's dependence upon and hostility toward these betrayers is, if anything, greater than his feeling about Mady. Like most of Bellow's heroes, he is a born leaner. While he complains constantly of interference, his absorption in his own troubles makes them his only subject of conversation. (Bellow heroes do not ask about other people's interests or difficulties.) Even his daughter June seems more a counter in the rivalry than a member of the family.

Kenneth Burke's term* may suggest a reason for the limited interest of the divorce story. If symbolic action means bringing a wish not easily acted on in real life against the obstacles it would probably meet, questions of dividing up houses, insurance policies, cash, and even children do not represent wishes that society represses very strongly. Anyone who wants to can have a quarrel of this kind. Bellow recognizes the fact, of course; the pressure in the story is not to achieve the best possible settlement, but to escape entirely the upset and, without remarrying, get to the happier land presumably lying beyond. And some of the vitality in the novel novel does accumulate from the incidental obstacles. Herzog thinks of his own emotions as delicate and uncategorizable. Society's rough-and-ready way not only of cataloguing, but handling them repels him. His talks with the two lawyers, his kibitzing in the courtroom, and his detention in the police station expose him

* *The Philosophy of Literary Form* (Baton Rouge, La., 1941).

to the world's view of feelings. The Alexandrian style of cutting knots may not be tailored to the will or to sensibility, but, given its premises, even Herzog sees that it is not particularly unfair. The world has established rules for conducting a contest and does not mind seeing a few bruises.

If the divorce hostility seems to daze Herzog, it actually spurs him toward what he presently sees as the major human ideal. "The Dream of man's heart, however much we may distrust and resent it, in that life may complete itself in significant pattern. . . . Before death. Not irrationally but incomprehensibly fulfilled." The originality of the novel follows from its perception that prestigious cultural attitudes go far toward determining felt emotions. The emphasis of modernity on suffering, for example, encourages Herzog to prolong his sense of grievance. A change of heart must therefore mean a change of thought, and thinking becomes not rationalizing but a vital defense of the personality. The novel thus takes the form of a psychodrama about escaping dominance by "the murderous imagination" of the century.

Herzog's fondness for "expressive feeling" descends directly from Father Herzog and Aunt Zipporach—and ultimately from Russia. But the distance between this way of life and Herzog's gives this inherited tone no usable content. In adult life he has filled the vacuum with the Romantic inheritance as extended by the twentieth century's emphasis on aggression. For his great work he has been trying to order the history in terms of the later experience. There is so much to synthesize, though, that synthesis proves impossible, and, like Gulley Jimson, he is "stuck." This tension compounds his personal troubles. Both, however, suggest a humanly unsatisfactory key to motive: now that God is dead, men have made Death God.

The car stopped. As if he had come to police headquarters in a rocking boat, over the water, he wavered when he got out on the sidewalk. Proudhon says, "God is *the* evil." But after we search in the entrails of world revolution for *la foi nouvelle*, what happens? The victory of death, not of rationality, not of rational faith. Our own murdering imagination turns out to be the great power, our human imagination which starts by accusing God of murder. At the bottom of the whole disaster lies the human being's sense of a grievance, and with this I want nothing more to do. It's easier not to exist altogether than accuse God. Far more simple. Cleaner. But no more of that!

So to arrive at any "incomprehensible pattern" Herzog must not only understand how history has shaped the adulation and destruction extremes, but must find for himself some alternative—and convincing—way of thinking. He must find a Third Force to pit against the logic that, since we live amid exciting disasters, we may as well fall in love with their intensity. Given his own nature and personal history, he must do this without resort to Hulme's dry defense against expressive feeling. "The soul requires intensity. At the same time virtue bores mankind." How retain the intensity without embracing the self-pity and murderousness?

Herzog thus takes on the problem of continuity and rebellion in one of its most ambitious formulations. Despite all the talk about family feeling, Bellow follows Eliot in seeing cultural and institutional past as the crucial reality. The real movement in Herzog's story therefore occurs not outside Madeline's bathroom or in the police station, but in his head. The letters and the ideas undertake a guerilla warfare against the modernism that has shaped him. The early raids all fail and he finds himself back in the jungle of Gersbach, Mady, Himmelstein, and Aunt Zelda. In this period his mind produces mostly self-satire: intellectual pretensions take a beating from emotional incompetence and inability to fit the inherited pattern of personal relations. Herzog, making a cause of suffering, gives up his job and dwells on his most humiliating episodes. However, he does get in some superbly comic self-kicking:

Please, Ramona, Mose wanted to say—you're lovely, fragrant, sexual, good to touch—everything. But these lectures! For the love of God, Ramona, shut it up. But she went on. Herzog looked up at the ceiling. The spiders had the moldings under intensive cultivation, like the banks of the Rhine. Instead of grapes, encapsulated bugs hung in clusters.

I brought all this on myself by telling Ramona the story of my life—how I rose from humble origins to complete disaster. But a man who has made so many mistakes can't afford to ignore the corrections of his friends. Friends like Sandor, that humped rat. Or like Valentine, the moral megalomaniac and prophet in Israel. To all such, one is well advised to listen. Scolding is better than nothing. At least it's company.

Ramona paused, and Herzog said, "It's true—I have a lot to learn."

But I am diligent. I work at it and show steady improvement. I expect to be in great shape on my deathbed. The good die young, but I have been spared to build myself up so that I may end my life as good as gold. The senior dead will be proud of me. . . . I will join the Y.M.C.A. of the immortals. Only, in this very hour, I may be missing eternity.

Even at this stage, though, the novel does not say what Herzog says. Bellow unquestionably takes a risk in showing his hero's vindictiveness so unmitigated, since we follow the central consciousness throughout, but lays off that bet through recalled episodes. In these a whole series of witnesses for the defense appear. Aunt Zelda testifies to sexual incompatibility and selfishness. Phyllis Gersbach, the wronged wife, explains what a leaner Herzog was, demanding steady ego-bolstering from her husband. Gersbach, the betrayer, and Himmelstein, the chief "Reality-Instructor," deplore Herzog's luxuriating in the middling kinds of suffering. Simkin, the good lawyer, has no trouble baiting his friend into comic displays of anger and self-pity. Balanced against Herzog's convincing tales of Madeleine's antics and of his previous difficulties in personal relations, all these witnesses leave the reader feeling that the marriage problem had no desirable solution. With two people so committed to self-development, severe emotional illness in the wife, and a great deal of childishness on both sides, the case looks hopeless. About halfway through, the temptation to leave Herzog in his own problems becomes strong. After all, a solution already exists. Gersbach has Madeleine, quarrels and all; Herzog has Ramona, the goddess of sex and cooking. Madeleine has the daughter, Herzog cannot get her. Only financial details remain. But Bellow extricates himself from this incipient disaster, too. At the last possible moment, he makes Herzog see what the reader has been seeing for some time —but in a far more active recognition than the impulse to drop out.

Herzog's escape from his trauma and his momentum thereafter both depend upon the old virtue in Bellow's work—admiration for size in people and events. Herzog's imagination has awarded this value to his successor—made Gersbach a mysteriously effective Devil. Waiting to murder this created figure and instead finding a man in a sports shirt giving little June a bath dispels the dream. In one sentence Herzog recovers. These two "love-actors" are not big enough human beings to break his heart over. In the police station he is even confident that Madeleine will downgrade herself in the same way. When she curbs her desire to "vote for my non-existence," in order to keep the support money, she confirms his new view of her as a small-d devil. The capital-D one would have gone all-out.

But escape from mania alone does not make the novel, as it does *The Victim*. The over-all effect depends upon a double progression. One eventually decreases the size of the personal relations issue; the more significant one increases Herzog's own size. The novel is at the same time a performance, where the hero displays high intellectual skills for public approval, and a real search for an "incomprehensible pattern." At the beginning, Herzog has been conducting a single-minded assault on knowledge—an immense synthesis to explain how all the occurrences of the last two hundred years fit together after two wars and the bomb. His illness does not so much fragment this synthesis as bring out into the open his real feeling that things don't fit together now—or descend in evolutionary lines. Instead of producing a great book, his anger projects itself onto a series of essay topics. The letters are, from an ideal point of view, a bad symptom, threatening insanity; but they provide an outlet when he has no other and perhaps keep him from breaking. Some near the beginning express conventionally enlightened modern views: fall-out is not a good thing, the wishes of individuals indicate more about national aims than the Eisenhower committee report. But increasingly these truncated essays question the applicability of sophisticated modernism to Herzog's actual hurts and hopes.

One early letter calls for a moratorium on definitions of human nature. Those already existing and claiming comprehensiveness do not solve the worst problems. Neither pain nor excitement is equally distributed at all points, as a system implies. Unconsciously but thoroughly, Herzog is finding that some spots hurt a great deal and others not at all, that the known wonder drugs do not inhibit many present infections. The outlook in *Herzog* is still not a totally new one—still does not differ too greatly from that of the best contemporary British comic novelists in its balancing of pleasure and pain. Earnestness—American and individual at once—makes the difference. Herzog looks toward not merely expressing, but justifying a new set of attitudes, developed out of the stresses of daily life by a man who does not have margin to love the brutal "realities."

But if guilt and *angst* are not the natural form stress takes in daily life, what is? The failure of the broadest intellectual and cultural grasp to deal with major emotional upset—to help much with the "humiliating comedy of heartbreak"—stands out. Yet this kind of reaching and overreaching constitutes Herzog's main defense for considering himself a worth-while human being. At the age of forty-seven, he has been brought to wonder whether the "good in my heart" may be just a joke. "Awareness was his work; extended consciousness his line of business." But the generally failing dream of extending consciousness infinitely has affected Herzog's ability to order his materials and led him to remarks like "What this country needs is a good five-cent synthesis." Sheer increase of knowledge about human behavior becomes a burden rather than a brave new world. Moreover, competitiveness intrudes on the pure art of thought: professors at Berkeley and Wisconsin have already scooped him on some of his best ideas. Not just thinking, but fast thinking is required. The sincere questioner feels driven to be first as well as right.

Yet Herzog cannot swear off thinking. "His mind, immediately looking for formal stability"—the phrase describes the process that happens over and over when something painful arises. Even when his original dream of becoming "a marvelous Herzog" is most threatened, the abstract mode of converting emotion goes on of itself.

For example, throughout Herzog blames the population explosion for his own and the modern world's difficulties. Minds oriented to quality have not learned to deal with vastly increased quantities. Yet two or three people are actually causing most of his troubles.

Quantity has a secondary effect—it limits the counterattack of asserting a "marvelous" self. When in the letters he sets himself up as a straightener of the world's curves, the mere number of problems and weight of inert opposition make all "rational" answers seem absurd. They will not prevail and, given the complexity of the issues, might not work anyway. Twentieth-century doubt about motives gives them another blow. Knowing my own destructive impulses, would I trust myself with power? he asks. Numbers threaten the counterattacking self-assertion, too, through the increase of educated, probing minds at work on history. Others run the world, well or badly, and synthesize the past, often all too well, while Herzog is busy being upset. Numbers, in sum, reduce the margin available for private reverses. Society prizes the well-organized.

Under this logic, quantity and percentage prevail, and the individual can do nothing meaningful. The double wound to Herzog's pride—losing his wife and being unable to prevail intellectually—brings him close to accepting this conclusion. There seems no ground between self-satire and the near-megalomania which meant to conquer all history. But there is. In his characteristic way Herzog senses it, loses it, finds some more of it, backslides, and then recaptures it. His letter to Dr. Edwig does "tolerate ambiguities":

Dear Edvig, he noted quickly. *You gave me good value for my money when you explained that neuroses might be graded by the inability to tolerate ambiguous situations. I have just read a certain verdict in Madeleine's eyes, "For cowards, Not-being!" Her disorder is superclarity. Allow me modestly to claim that I am much better now at ambiguities. I think I can say, however, that I have been spared the chief ambiguity that afflicts intellectuals, and this is that civilized individuals hate and resent the civilization that makes their lives possible. What they love is an imaginary human situation invented by their own genius and which they believe is the only true and the only human reality. How odd! But the best-treated, most favored and intelligent part of any society is often the most ungrateful. Ingratitude, however, is its social function. Now there's an ambiguity for you! . . . Dear Ramona, I owe you a lot. I am fully aware of it. Though I may not be coming back to New York right away, I intend to keep in touch. Dear God! Mercy! My God! Rachaim olenu . . . melekh maimis. . . . Thou King of Death and Life. . . !*

A little farther on, being taped by another doctor, he sees the perspective cast on the intellectual life by his contractor brother.

Will is a quiet man of duty and routine, has his money, position, influence, and is just as glad to be rid of his private or "personal" side. Sees me spluttering fire in the wilderness of this world, and pities me no doubt for my temperament. Under the old dispensation, as the stumbling, ingenuous, burlap Moses, a heart without guile, in need of protection, a morbid phenomenon, a modern remnant of other-worldliness—under that former dispensation I would need protection. And it would be gladly offered by him—by the person who "knows-the-world-for-what-it-is." Whereas a man like me has shown the arbitrary withdrawal of proud subjectivity from the collective and historical progress of mankind. And that is true of lower-class emotional boys and girls who adopt the aesthetic mode, the mode of rich sensibility. Seeking to sutain their own version of existence under the crushing weight of *mass*. What Marx described as that "material weight." Turning this thing, "my personal life," into a circus, into gladiatorial combat. Or tamer forms of entertainment. To make a joke of your "shame," your ephemeral dimness, and show why you deserve your pain.

But what finally resurrects Herzog is his exhaustion. When he builds the excitement in his anger to the final stage, which in American novels means turning anger to violence, and finds himself incapable of it, he has worn out his own self-dramatization. Prolonged real trouble makes its owner tire of looking for trouble. It removes the margin which might otherwise make him take excitement on any terms rather than live with the boredom of virtue. So a series of psychological attacks on organized despair mark the forward-backward stages of his recovery. These take the form of answers to various existentialist writers, but, since the existentialists themselves codify fifty years of literature and thought, Herzog is laying the groundwork for a change of heart through a change of thinking. He is preparing to work forward cautiously under conditions that are not likely to get better. The heart of his position denies the value of building up despair in the absence of anything else exciting:

"Don't abuse yourself too much, Luke, and cook up these fantastic plots against your feelings. I know you're a good soul, with real heartaches. And you believe the world. And the world tells you to look for truth in grotesque combinations. It warns you also to stay away from consolation if you value your intellectual honor. On this theory truth is punishment, and you must take it like a man. It says truth will harrow your soul because your inclination as a poor human thing is to lie and to live by lies. So if you have anything else waiting in your soul to be revealed you'll never learn about it from these people. Do you have to think yourself into a coffin and perform these exercises with death?

Twenty-five pages further, he still has to keep convincing himself:

With the religious, the love of suffering is a form of gratitude to experience or an opportunity to experience evil and change it into good. They believe the spiritual cycle can and will be completed in a man's existence and he will somehow make use of his suffering, if only in the last moments of his life, when the mercy of God will reward him with a vision of the truth, and he will die transfigured. But this is a special exercise. More commonly suffering breaks people, crushes them, and is simply unilluminating. You see how gruesomely human beings are destroyed by pain, when they have the added torment of losing their humanity first, so that their death is a total defeat, and then you write about "modern forms of Orphism" and about "people who are not afraid of suffering" and throw in other such cocktail-party expressions. Why not say rather that people of powerful imagination, given to dreaming deeply and to raising up marvelous and self-sufficient fictions, turn to suffering sometimes to cut into their bliss, as people pinch themselves to feel awake. I know that my suffering, if I may speak of it, has often been like that, a more extended form of life, a striving for true wakefulness and an antidote to illusion, and therefore I can take no moral credit for it. I am willing without further exercise in pain to open my heart. And this needs no doctrine or theology of suffering. We love apocalypses too much, and crisis ethics and florid extremism with its thrilling language. Excuse me, no. I've had all the monstrosity I want.

But he is sure that the intellect must be used and assumes that by nature it is a problem-solving mechanism:

Unemployed consciousness, he wrote in the pantry. *I grew up in a time of widespread unemployment, and never believed there might be work for me. Finally, jobs appeared, but somehow my consciousness remained unemployed. And after all,* he continued beside the fire, *the human intellect is one of the great forces of the universe. It can't safely remain unused. You might almost conclude that the boredom of so many human arrangements (middle-class family life, for instance) has the historical aim of freeing the intellect of newer generations, sending them into science. But a terrible loneliness throughout life is simply the plankton on which Leviathan feeds. . . . Must reconsider. The soul requires intensity. At the same time virtue bores mankind. Read Confucius again. With vast populations, the world must prepare to turn Chinese.*

And toward the end he formulates his answer in dynamic terms:

That Will was studying him—Will who had become the most discreet and observant of the Herzogs—was transparently plain. Moses thought he could bear his scrutiny fairly well. His haggard, just-shaven cheeks were against him; as was the whole house (the skeletons in the toilet bowl, the owls in the fixtures, the half-painted piano, the remains of meals, the wife-deserted atmosphere); his "inspired" visit to Chicago was bad, too. Very bad. It must be noticeable, also, that he was in an extraordinary state, eyes dilated with excitement, the very speed of his pulses possibly visible in his large irises. *Why must I be such a throb-hearted character . . . But I am. I am, and you can't teach old dogs. Myself is thus and so, and will continue thus and so. And why fight it? My balance comes from instability. Not organization, or courage, as with other people. It's tough, but that's how it is. On these terms I, too—even I!—apprehend certain things. Perhaps the only way I'm able to do it. Must play the instrument I've got.*

His resolutions at the end recapitulate the powerful reasons against making Death God and express a determination:

Anyway, can I pretend I have much choice? I look at myself and see chest, thighs, feet—a head. This strange organization, I know it will die. And inside—something, something, happiness . . . "Thou movest me." That leaves no choice. Something produces intensity, a holy feeling, as oranges produce orange, as grass green, as birds heat. Some hearts put out more love and some less of it, presumably. Does it signify anything? There are those who say this product of hearts is knowledge. "Je sens mon coeur et je connais les hommes." But his mind now detached itself also from its French. *I couldn't say that, for sure. My face too blind, my mind too limited, my instincts too narrow. But this intensity, doesn't it mean anything? Is it an idiot joy that makes this animal, the most peculiar animal of all, exclaim something? And he thinks this reaction a sign, a proof, of eternity? And he has it in his breast? But I have no arguments to make about it. "Thou movest me." "But what do you want, Herzog?" "But that's just it—not a solitary thing. I am pretty well satisfied to be, just as it is willed, and for as long as I may remain in occupancy."*

The guarantee that all this is more than rhetoric rests in the drama of Herzog's own despair and recovery, in which the way down has proved the way up.

When Herzog finally emerges on the other side of upset, where is he? Unlike most contemporary writers, Bellow holds himself responsible for suggesting what a good state of mind would be. Order and warmth-at-a-distance provide the conditions. Herzog looks forward to a relationship with an attractive, mature woman interested only in sex and cooking—but not yet "the third Mrs. Herzog." Brothers and sisters-in-law will furnish a reserve of security without interference. The good life again resembles Gulley Jimson's answer, even more boldly adopted. Gulley's answer is the creative excitement he feels as he begins putting brush strokes on the church wall. Herzog's solution too involves the time of inspiration—but before it has to face the problems of direction or execution.* Not accomplishment, but the good feeling validates, and Herzog hopes to prolong it before having to find an outlet. Meanwhile he starts the water pump and begins to restore order around the house. He has escaped not only Mady, but the immediate obligation to synthesize. Creative excitement without the imperative to create is a kind of artist's nirvana. The novel ends in midair. The reader feels that something good, but baffling, has occurred, and looks back to see just how it came to happen.

In a sense it has no cause. It is a miracle. Obviously, though, it begins to happen in the police station. The estrangement has remained a relationship for Herzog, and the idea that Mady really wants to end it—"she wants to kill me"—helps to free him. But

* Frank Kermode's *The Romantic Image* shows how romantic agony and the ideal of inspired imagination intertwine. The artist suffers when he cannot produce a masterpiece a day.

actually Herzog works through his crisis just as Leventhal does in *The Victim:* he wears it out. He goes over it from every possible point of view, discovers the futility of direct action, and finally wearies himself and the reader so much that both are ready to believe in almost any new start. The novel follows the tendency of modern painful comedy to exhaust problems rather than solve them, but Herzog's highly analytical way is his own. When he absorbs his imperatives as part of cultural and personal history, they become familiars rather than demons. He does not *have to* finish the book just now. He does not have to bring up June to be a Herzog. Freedom is excitement poised for action—without the necessity of acting immediately. Again the sense of time to spare becomes the touchstone of removed anxiety.

Other twentieth-century novels show personality as ranging imagination, but no other one shows so powerfully the revolt of the mind against the imperatives of creative imagination while maintaining it as the only available value. Where the early moderns saw exploring consciousness as freeing man from the boring demands of society, *Herzog* sees the exploring as an inherited moral obligation, approved of and rewarded by society, but become a game where the easy victories have been won and where the hardest effort may produce only fragments. His Sisyphus staggers, too, under a heavy personal load and takes no particular joy in seeing the rock roll back down the hill. He is less confident than Camus' Sisyphus that he will have the strength to roll it back up again. But Herzog too ends in glorifying effort over paraphrasable discovery. If being relevant, exhaustive, and sincere have proved beyond him for the present, he has found a way of backing forward without backing down.

The sense of time validates the effect. Throughout his work Bellow shows degrees of anxiety through how much time the protagonist feels to be available—too much in *Dangling Man*, none at all in *The Victim*, a great deal in *The Adventures of Augie March*, a lessening amount in *Seize the Day*, leisure but fear of age in *Henderson the Rain King*, and both too much and too little in *Herzog*. Herzog feels his sanity restored when he regains the sense of time enough to work things out. He need not do anything about aggressors and rivals right now. One symptom of the good life is seeing a way open to a future beyond the immediate crisis. Happiness, such as can be, anyway, depends on having something exciting but not overwhelming to do and seeing time stretch out ahead, with no major change of course required.

But *Herzog* is not the full-scale attack on existentialism that many people believe it to be. It is a modification—under different circumstances. The Frenchmen who brought the concept into literature saw clear, universal dangers and did not believe that a choice of commitment would prove too difficult. In more civilian times, both Bellow and Iris Murdoch see that even formulating the issues requires more sophisticated instruments. Bellow does not deny the continuing presence of threats; but he attacks *dramatizing* them. He refuses to drape the world under any one blanket, whether it be *angst* or the Concrete Universal. He wants to know specifications and magnitudes. What dread? How much of it? Caused by what? Related to what also? *Herzog* is primarily a process of determining the right questions to ask and weighting these in the "incomprehensible pattern." When the hero finds how to put the questions, he all but has his answers. These refinements, though, build on the previous accomplishment as much as they oppose it. Bellow does not deny threat, much less want to abolish the will, but he does want to sophisticate it.

In fact, the deceptive part in Bellow is his keeping this crucial constant largely out of sight. Actually, his heroes are as strong-willed as Arnold Bennett's. This donné of their natures makes their frequent drift as frightening to them as to George Eliot's characters. They have the book written before they start, but their nervousness to push on in a pre-determined direction encounters their own dependencies as well as the world's resistance. So four of Bellow's six novels concentrate on blockades to the will. Surprise knocks the hero off balance and makes him question his human worth. The teeter-totter balancing follows. No systematic justification emerges, but qualities-in-motion carry him through: tenacity, knowledgeability, energy. Bellow's moral freshness derives from his faith in this Trinity.

But the public hero remains the author of *The Adventures of Augie March* and *Henderson the Rain King*. These two novels look beyond disgust and anxiety to a vision of creative play. They suggest that freedom may have a use. But they depend on the tests of soul in the other works and connect with them in their focus on the learned life. Not the learnéd one, but the life lived at great enough distance from childhood to demand acquired responses in place of many inherited ones. Together the six novels take the greatest surge of recent times in the endless, losing race to make cultural formulations fit experience. Bellow obviously expects the chase to go on forever.

In the end, an old esthetic division remains. Along with a liking for Bellow goes a dislike—or at least a discomfort at staying too long in his world. The "stability of instability" often creates the effect of living in a surreal melodrama. The people around the hero are so egregiously wrong. The sole guardian of unspecifiable faith, he keeps defining it so personally that potential allies have to drop out. Just below the charm, the Bellow hero, talking of *eros*, asserts a soaring, sensitive individualism over any possible ideal of community. He has the pride of his weaknesses. Suspicion occupies much of his time—in Leventhal, Joseph, Wilhelm, and Herzog, though not in Augie or Henderson—for he fears unjust and unqualified judgments accusing him of worthless or mad conduct. His nerves give him his claim to being of the saving remnant and involve him in constant diagnosis of a bad-faith, self-deceiving world. If Bellow has any one thing to say over and over, it is that his hero's drive creates a distorting lens, which he knows distorts but has no way of measuring how much. The knowledge distinguishes him—that and his hope of grinding a truer lens.

In restoring a high value to sensitivity and "flash," Bellow comes back to some of the old difficulties, leavened, of course, by comic self-awareness. Only occasionally does the hero meet his peers. If Bellow escapes alienation, he heightens aloneness. Perhaps no one can legitimately quarrel with that conclusion. Yet, if it does not make us nervous, it keeps us so. For no other contemporary touches Bellow in portraying Irritable Man, whose crossness is the converse of his aspiring to include so much life. Bellow is the poet of self-chosen discomfort.

SEVEN

Blurring the Will: Iris Murdoch

Bellow writes so persuasively that his hero's stance often seems the only possible one; his world of magnified phonies and self-deceivers with its few sane men appears to represent direct reality. Iris Murdoch is good for breaking through such enchantments. Perhaps even because she lacks Bellow's talent for giving size to personality, she excels in reminding of alternatives. Occasionally she seems concerned to do little else. More than any other novelist around, she brings to the surface the question raised in the first chapter—Can people who think as we have come to think write good novels? For she maintains a potentially reductive double reality—representative figures, revolving perspectives that bring the writer near to being a central character. She invites, and investigates, the question, Is it perceived order or performance? She responds naturally to the mind as force, but has to look for what it can apply itself to and wonder how it can maintain its humanity against its destructive tendency. So action and scene inevitably overshadow identification with character.

Unquestionably, defense by reduction hurts an expansive form like the novel. The unevenness of Miss Murdoch's work suggests how unsure anyone is what will help it. For Miss Murdoch is, in Waugh's phrase, a "good trier." (She would please some readers more if she were not always writing the novel she does not yet know how to write.) Her failures as much as her successes reflect a mind determined to find imaginative equivalents for a changing view of reality and wish. Her own work begins, in fact, from the dilemma she finds in Sartre:

> His inability to write a great novel is a tragic symptom of a situation which afflicts us all. We know that the real lesson to be taught is that the human person is precious and unique; but we seem unable to set it forth except in terms of ideology and abstraction.*

From the first, though, she realized how much better strikingly opposed forces work for drama than for the novel. The novel, in her words, gets its effect by blurring. While the abstract grounds for confidence in her as a first-class writer rest on an original play of forces blurred in behalf of "the absurd irreducible uniqueness of people and their relations to each other," what forces combined with what blurring has been her concrete problem.

Stages make the drama of her development, but one less abstract ground for confidence can be laid immediately. Miss Murdoch has by now progressed enough with her fictional world for it to have its own fable, told with increasing awareness and willingness to face new difficulties created by old solutions. The fable in its developed form goes like this. People of above-average competence, with no resources outside themselves, begin as egoists doing what comes naturally, and in the process injure and get injured. This first impulse exhausts itself in unsatisfying activism, which finally seems pointless. In this injury-inflicting world, eros is overmatched against aggressiveness. At some stage the individual naturally—not on existentialist principle—begins to think of regrouping, gathering his

* *Sartre, Romantic Rationalist* (Cambridge, 1953), p. 76.

scattered forces and centering on his best possibilities. The effort, because it is a counterattack, becomes a private attempt at rebirth, vulnerable because unsupported in the confusing social fabric.

At this point Miss Murdoch's most original insight appears. G. S. Fraser has noted her skill at giving solidity to the normal.* But normalcy is more than solid: it is the ultimate test of the unsupported will. Yet this norm, for which the personality is willing to fight so hard, seems in itself unattractive—amounts at bottom to an active, resentful, self-distrusting directionlessness. The characters who invoke this impulse against unconventional efforts to deal with defeat see in the attempted rebirths at best absurdity and at worst danger to sanity. The skill Miss Murdoch has developed in giving life to the struggle between these two claims is her own greatest claim to significance.

From the beginning Miss Murdoch had a feeling for the novel of forces, but did not know what forces really opposed each other. The assurance that she is a writer rather than the author of one good book comes from the steady growth in her sense of conflict. If fiction also grows out of our quarrels with ourselves, Miss Murdoch knew at first mainly that she felt quarrelsome. The professional philosopher came out not so much in the ideas, which other writers had also assimilated, as in the talent for puncturing other people's balloons. (British analytic philosophers are good at this.) Yet a forecast appears beneath the hyperactive surface of her first novel, *Under the Net*. The initial force she finds a character for is the practical joker—the enemy of grand gesture, the skeptical philosopher acting on the physical plane. Jake Donoghue does talk metaphysics during cold-cure experiments, but primarily he breaks and enters, tears down curtains, blows safes, steals movie-star dogs, spies from fire escapes, goes on binges, and uses judo on spiritual people. In fact, he does more outrageous tricks than most of the Angries' heroes put together and, significantly, damages even more property than Gulley Jimson.

Though this beginning in naïve egotism, confident in self-asser-

* "Iris Murdoch and the Solidity of the Normal," *International Literary Annual*, No. 2, 1959.

tiveness and adaptability, seems episodic in structure, two expanding metaphors control the actions. The metaphor for daily experience is, quite simply, property. Jake wants his property—manuscripts—protected by copyright; he regards other people's as in the public domain. He has thought of his affair with Madge as a simple property relationship, without upkeep costs. Unfortunately, Madge sees it in the same way, though with a sharper head for economics. When she replaces him with a bookmaker turned theatrical operator, she snubs Jake's appeal to feeling with concern for removing his belongings:

> "Now look, Jakie," she said, "you understand how it is. I want you to move your stuff out as soon as poss, today if you can. I've put all your things up in your room." She had, too. Various objects of mine which usually decorated the sitting room were missing. Already I felt I didn't live there any more.
>
> "I don't understand how it is," I said, "and I shall be interested to hear."
>
> "Yes, you must take *everything,*" said Magdalen. "I'll pay for the taxi if you like."

Love as transaction seems to Jake natural and unbearable. Much of the comedy arises from his view. The best sustained scene shows him and the bookmaker, his *alter ego* as operator, negotiating over damages for Madge with perfect understanding—the bookmaker buying off retaliation for invading a property right and Jake making what he can out of a deficit. When Madge finally gets her chance to star in a movie and her bookmaker has begun to conspire with her *alter ego,* she sees no reason not to buy Jake back as a gigolo. But this dream of interchangeable parts has its own negatives for everyone involved, and the natural response to frustration is an attack on property. When the most thoughtful character in the novel destroys his girl friend's furnishings, she hires Jake as watchman—and locks him in. When his spying suggests that the conspirators mean to steal his manuscript, he steals their dog star. He blows the safe of the friend who refuses to talk to him.

The competing metaphor in the back of the characters' minds is idyll—a dream of restful, harmonious communication between two soulful people in the Tuileries gardens—or the cold-cure station. For Jake this means Hugo, whose philosophical talk about the impossibility of communication fascinates him, and Anna, the pop singer whom he has discarded once but now sees expressing everything the daily deals cannot give. But this dream leads only to diverted searches and further destructiveness. The problem arises from Chekhov's formula—A loves B, B loves C, C loves A. (Since idyll operates through imagination rather than transaction, every character can yearn for the inaccessible.) But a greater difficulty, the desire for self-expression, also intervenes. Hugo, who talks about silence between people, devotes himself to big bangs: first armaments, then holiday rockets, leftist politics, and films about ancient Rome. His philosophy reflects his lack of interest in communication. When Jake throws Anna among the stage property nightgowns, her hurry to kiss and go expresses her absorption not only in another man, but in her conflict between pretentious drama and pop singing.

To meet these difficulties with the modern English novelist's hope in personal relations, the novel offers only regrouping—pulling back scattered forces and developing the best self. After the hospital scenes which underline the many injuries, Hugo turns to working with his hands as a watchmaker, Anna returns to singing. Jake retires from hack work to take a useful job—as hospital orderly—and write a good novel. The only property he has to show for all his dealings—Mars, the movie star—has ironically ideal qualities: though limited by age and dogdom, he is loving and totally obedient.

Of all the Angries with whom she began, Miss Murdoch alone shows from the first a radical dissatisfaction, and it makes her comedy less natural, more strained. She lacks her contemporaries' acceptance of rivalry and their awareness of benefits in a prospering society. *Under the Net* is a real farewell to the rat race. The business of her actresses, producers, writers, and gamblers is entertainment, but they do not produce pleasure. Jake does not, like Lucky Jim, enjoy denouncing his enemies; he wants to destroy them. He comes from nowhere, so far as the reader knows, and takes no satisfaction from better cars, clothes, paintings, or bathrooms. His hand-to-mouth living brings all the insecurities of the competitive world, but no image of a future through it. He can only lose the rat race or get diverted into meaningless politics.

Jake's childlike aggressiveness produces in the end that hard-to-create character, an unattractive rebel. Most recent angry comedy—Bellow, Amis, Salinger, Braine—has worked not through a plausible social voice in the narrator, but a private voice that strikes upon the reader's inarticulate sense of irritation. A childhood or adolescent sense of possibilities collides with the adult world's fixities. Though Jake Donoghue's voice also echoes, it seems to come from farther back in childhood than most contemporary protagonists'. The strained comedy follows from this early anger without the adult defenses of an Augie March. But, when Miss Murdoch later combines this restlessness and capacity for outrageous action with superior planning intelligence, she produces some of her best characters—Dora in *The Bell*, Randall in *An Unofficial Rose*, Marian in *The Unicorn*.

Aside from the sometimes strained comedy, the weakness in these early attacks is that they do not hit too much that Miss Murdoch really believed in. Commercialism, popular art, liberalism, and perfect love had already been pretty well deflated and were being deflated by other young writers. An educated young woman in the fifties might expect to satirize many of these. Nevertheless, Miss Murdoch began her definition of personality in an endless egotism worthy of characters in Ivy Compton-Burnett, and, unlike her contemporaries, had the drive to go on probing the hurt.

Under the Net already has the vision of living as a rhythm of expectation, reversal, disappointment, and reassertion of the will in some more promising direction. *Flight from an Enchanter* develops a second series of love skirmishes, this time with more serious concern for the central character. *The Sandcastle* begins her erratic series of discoveries.

The only way to reread it, though, is to discount in advance the barriers to interest. Roger Sale has pointed out in a lecture how much Miss Murdoch's best novels depend on complex plot and how little *The Sandcastle* has. A schoolteacher tempted to run off with a young artist stays with his family and goes into Parliament instead. The scene, too, echoes what makes the English novel what it often is—a public school where resisting change proceeds daily and confidence in continuity appears justified. Though the central character is convincing and likeable, the heroine is not, even though Miss Murdoch strains the old device of having other characters tell us how wonderful Rain Carter is. Prue, the daughter in love with her father, imagines too much. A resurrected dog follows her everywhere, a poltergeist named Angus appears from crowds and roadsides, a mole below the nipple convinces her that she is a witch with power to destroy her rival. And so on. Miss Murdoch's indulgence of these self-regarding, out-of-touch girls damages confidence in her own good sense.

Nevertheless, the novel takes a big step toward the later work. An original, if narrow, play of forces upon the central character directs the action. Need for orientation and desire for the lively oppose each other. A lyric of choice replaces the rationale of choice usual in the novel of forces. And these elements can move quickly into a comedy of awkwardness. They do not always coalesce happily in *The Sandcastle*, but they are there.

Camus' example in *The Plague* had shown how indispensable atmosphere is to the novel using characters as forces, but his atmosphere is dynamic—first dead rat, first case, first death, preliminary meeting, discounted statistics, many rats, desperate meetings, epidemic casualties. For Miss Murdoch, though, crisis, if present at all, exists behind apparent stasis. No decision seems called for. The marriage in *The Sandcastle* has been a struggle of wills with no saving warmth. Each conflict has been decided long ago—Nan can sulk for days—and the quarrels only repeat a necessary process. The fact neither reduces their intensity nor brings into the open the hidden dependencies and demands for change.

Where fictional atmosphere ordinarily implies mystery, even murkiness, the success of Miss Murdoch's comes from its precision. She writes as if she meant to subject all the symbols of stability in the English novel to an engineering survey. She builds St. Bride's

School of brick, to specifications. The reader can find his way from classroom to dormitory to bell tower to fence to tennis court to the retired master's house as easily as William Mor himself. Mor's responses to these checkpoints mark the choices of a lifetime. He takes the path to the retired master's house regularly, to the new one's only when summoned. He strides confidently into the classroom and braces himself before the studio, where the eccentric resident artist may arouse familiar irritations. Self-mastery and reasonable mastery of events come naturally inside the school fence. Easy success in public life and discontent in personal life outline the features of the Murdoch protagonist.

Against this solidity, the sandcastle offers an idyll separate from all the bricks that have built the life, but a skillful piece of management makes the idyll begin from the bricks—through the temptress' esthetic theories about them. Rain Carter believes that to paint a good portrait of the retired master she must get *inside* his way of life. In taking Mor as her guide to both school buildings and habits, she identifies their solidity with his solidity of character—and that with her father. But, to change Mor's loyalties and assert herself as a freeing spirit, she must lure him beyond fence and routine. The affair progresses by the increasing range of these lurings and Mor's increasing anxiety on unfamiliar, forbidden ground.

At this point Miss Murdoch begins to mix her lyric of choice with her engineering survey. The early energy of the novel comes from the awakening of love as anxious idyll; the family situation remains inert. (In the second half, idyll suspends itself in air and family reaction provides the energy.) The childlike spontaneity of the artist collides with the married man's worry that cutting too many flowers in the dark with an attractive young woman will anger his wife back in the living room. The same "innocent" anxiety arises when Rain impulsively includes a loft bedroom in the guided tour. The best lyric-of-choice scene develops directly as escape from St. Bride's—specifically, from lunch at the new master's. As usual with Miss Murdoch, the girl takes the initiative and when Rain goes swimming, presumably nude, Mor worries behind a few bushes on the bank. In haste to escape decently, he backs the car partly over the edge of the river bank. The following pages combine the most orderly planning for control with the anxiety, haste, and sense of impending discovery in an unlikely predicament that people think of as occurring mostly in dreams. Comedy, idyll, and worry mix in an original way. Grass and twigs under the wheel fail, a section of the bank gives away, the ground proves too soft for the jack, Rain looks still more appealing, digging out a rock topples the car on its back into the stream.

Against this episode, the wife's temptation is a burlesque lyric of choice. When she turns to an old family friend, her awkwardness and remoteness catch the decisive moments for a woman unaccustomed to being of two minds about anything. She lets him lead her in out of the rain and get on top of her in an old armchair in the backroom of his store without paying him any attention or ceasing to think about her problem. Before things have gone very far, she has worked it out. "Please call me a taxi, Tim."

On paper, the family reaction that dominates the last half of the novel ought to work better than it does. The same methods succeed brilliantly in Miss Murdoch's next novel. Even here, decisions do affect events—rapidly. The drama of Nan's speech announcing her husband's candidacy for Parliament—and with it his commitment to family—depends upon increasingly frenzied action preceding it. Every attempt at change sets off chaotic counteractions in behalf of normalcy.

Moreover, sharply conceived shifts in point of view play up the confusion. Miss Murdoch follows on principle the character who will take hardest what has just happened: the fantasiast daughter finding the note; the wife searching for consolation or revenge without knowing which she wants; the daughter burning a nylon stocking image of the rival; the mother puzzling over daughter's strangeness; the father desperately maneuvering a ladder from window to tower trying to save his son.

This complex management does not entirely rescue *The Sandcastle* from its softest characters, but does promise far more than Miss Murdoch's previous technique of parallel cases. Here the parallels integrate around an intensely felt puzzle: why a heroine keyed to dew, roses, art, father, river banks, and freedom cannot overcome a lazy and hostile wife. And the critical issue in the family quarrels—whether living means forward energy or stasis—does grind toward an adjustment. Nan knows what men want and, when she has to, can give it to her husband. The young artist can offer only herself. Rain, spontaneous, rebelling against all dullness, rigidly committed to her art and already competent at it, disregards everything in the daily world outside her own plans. If Mor leaves with her, she will continue painting on the Riviera while he will follow around without clear purpose. His desperate, unlikely scheme for a school of his own shows his need to recreate the conditions for his self-assertiveness; his traditional sense of masculinity demands a social framework. He wants most of all what he has been trying to do all along: define himself in work, be approved of by those he respects, help his children get on in life, advance to the larger field of politics, know where he is going. Nan's resistance in the name of "realism" can change with realities, but Rain, instead of seeing the vision of idyll as part of life, wants to embody and live it. She carries the sense of loss in the novel by ending a Cleopatra without an Antony.

Despite its weaknesses, *The Sandcastle* advances an individual sense of experience highly conscious of given conditions. The enthusiasm for mapping—not merely places, but procedures—represents the egocentric will in its daily activity. Behind this lies that vision of restful yet exciting communication between two soulful people on the river bank. At times of dissatisfaction, sympathy can throw off the mapmaking compasses and give the familiar a pleasant disquieting strangeness. But, when characters move to translate this lyrical impulse into activity, a comic awkwardness results as the vision, the life history, and the sheer intractableness of things collide. Automobiles, soft dirt, and big armchairs fit awkwardly into dream. All the elements for Miss Murdoch's success exist in *The Sandcastle;* she improves later at getting them together and exploring them more deeply and less conventionally.

The Bell does get them together. From the beginning the ground tone in Miss Murdoch's work has been a certain harshness. (Much of *Under the Net* shows author as well as character doing what comes naturally.) *The Sandcastle* tries to moderate this toughness with a "natural" tenderness based on idyllic vision. (Rain Carter is an effort to create a *feminine* career girl.) But Miss Murdoch's criticisms of Sartre for his neglect of the "precious and unique individual" suggest a feeling not given form in the early novels: a will to understand and ultimately like people on high principle. This more formidable assault on egocentric harshness—reminiscent of George Eliot—becomes one force in the real world with *The Bell*.

For *The Bell* begins from a man who has successfully regrouped his forces on just such high principle. The quasi-religious community Michael has founded after his homosexual difficulties is a going operation. The community itself superimposes nineteenth-century utopian hope onto the coterie defense—common in literature since Huxley—whereby a group of sensitive and oversensitive people support each other in roles more or less suited to their personalities. The characters' reactions to their religio-moral inheritance are as self-conscious as in *Antic Hay*, but this time they turn *against* militant atheism and a harsh assessment of human nature. Not in behalf of anything in particular, but generally in favor of goodness, friendliness, gardening, and tolerance. The members group to defend themselves against harsh judgments in a world ruled by standards of effectiveness.

The near-psychotic girl, the muscular Christian who suffers nervous collapses, and the homosexual hero have all failed by these standards. In their community Miss Murdoch finds her most effective counter-force to "natural" harshness. Nowadays pragmatic standards and acceptance of tension produce understanding for weakness, the need for mutual help, the general problem of a bearable "identity" which does not depend upon meeting every conflict successfully. Despite the bias of much modern literature, everyone who has faced difficult situations knows that human sympathy exists—and meaningfully. Just how meaningfully is the hard question. We do not have the full confidence in sympathy that we have in destructiveness, but no age has made greater efforts to shore up those who would otherwise fall out of the system nor shown more understanding for aberrant behavior.

So Miss Murdoch's religious community develops one of the most convincing correlatives so far for a force with which we actually do oppose destructiveness. For once everything seems to go right for her. Centering on a group makes her passion for flat characters to show every facet of a problem productive rather than diffusive. And, because the lesser characters are frankly and programmatically out of touch with everyday reality, she can handle their naïveté and illness matter-of-factly, free from the sentimental inflation of Prue and Rain Carter. Miss Murdoch still does not have the gift of making minor characters memorable, but she can make their group activities—sitting around the fireplace in the evening, fumbling through a business session, bird watching, gardening, gathering for a procession—both memorable and suggestive.

The Bell is another novel without a hero. Scene substitutes for one, and carries the vulnerable hope with its echo from the past. Self-conscious symbols have begun to exasperate the contemporary reader—not because, like his predecessors, he cannot understand them but because they often seem to stand between him and some simple meaning. The scene in *The Bell*, however, is so frankly representative as to disarm resistance. The converted eighteenth-century hall represents a middle ground between convent and city, a "rational" effort to do better by the sensitive than the world outside will. So an actual convent stands down the lake, and communication with the town for groceries and beer at the pub continues. The communicants neither defy the world nor retire from it completely.

The special distinction of the scene, though, is its physical existence. It is there, symbolically all right, but first and foremost there. (William Sansom, to take one among many, can effortlessly evaporate trees, tunnels, beaches, and automobiles into symbol.) This physical presence takes its force from being presented through the one character in the novel who has the Murdoch drive for orientation and a sense of the place as antagonist. The heroine's hostile survey of hall, grounds, lake, ferry, cabin across, nunnery at the end is at once emotional and so exact that a friend of mine has drawn from memory a map complete even to the room occupied by each character. (Miss Murdoch locates so well that she does not need to draw her own map, as Robbe-Grillet does for *Jealousy*.)

In terms of Frederick J. Hoffman's idea of space and the sense of self, where Dostoyevsky's rented room or Kafka's amazingly crowded village reflect the will in confinement,* the surprising aspect of this scene is its spaciousness. Here a few people inhabit acres, with big house, big rooms, well-kept grounds, woods, a pool, lake view, a ferry. Even the walls of the convent turn out to surround large gardens. The furnishings we see are rich and the cells, if any, represent promise and threat rather than a central idea of the self. This space and its attendant comforts reflect a more tolerant view won by a century of self-torturing confessionals. In such a scene the hero can plausibly recognize his wound as something less than monstrous and believe that he can live with it. (Dora, of course, brings to this self-consciously ordered setting the city's taste for downgrading icons.)

The hero's existence in the novel, as Dora recognizes, depends upon his identification with this scene—as its creator. Michael imagined it, chose the site, gathered the people, decided on gardening as the industry, wrote the constitution. Significantly, the heroine meets first the scene, then the leader. (In her later novels Miss Murdoch has become good at contrasting doer and deed.) Not only does Dora find the hall itself daunting, but the housewife-turned-colonist makes her feel an outsider subjected to the laws of a mad authoritarian society. Yet, when Michael appears, she thinks he looks weak, almost insignificant. She has not met before the paradox of weakness on one front subliminating itself into organizing power on another.

But in the novel itself, as opposed to his evident actions earlier, Michael does not act decisively; he works for maintenance and slow development. Many critics find him attractive, a near-saint defeated by trying for more than is possible, and the artist's-model, dumb-blonde, dissatisfied-wife heroine a nuisance. But Dora is just

* *Samuel Beckett: the Language of Self* (Carbondale, Ill., 1962).

the kind of nuisance who will always be there for the saint. Michael and his associates are trying to deaden pain by ritual, high sentiment, democratic process, and the regulated life. For such people the angry, skeptical, knowing mind represented by Dora will never go away—not only because it dramatizes the world's attitude toward their effort, but because it is the skeleton in their own closet. Dora's harshness speaks to both community and reader, not because it is as desirable as goodness but because it unquestionably exists. She speaks for one consensus of the modern mind and so makes the ideal discoverer of the little group long on good intentions and short on program. She brings one kind of reality principle to test hopes which may or may not pass.

Further, only such a hostile observer can establish the meaning of the experiment. The action of *The Bell* progresses like a medieval dream vision. It exposes the sinful, worldly character to a scene where presumably higher values reign, and, as in the medieval form, a double action occurs. The worldly character does come to recognize a higher possibility, but his very worldliness validates the vision. The dreamer begins where we are, thinks as we do, is no more likely to be fooled than we are. So the otherwise anticlimactic last chapter, where Dora stays platonically with Michael until they can regroup elsewhere, testifies for Michael's claim to a noble effort. Only the reformed heckler can give the benediction over such confused results.

As I have suggested, the ordinary miracle in Miss Murdoch's novels is how far she can get without characters. Creating memorable characters has usually depended in the past on looking at them from the outside, as completed objects, or looking at them so intensively from moment to moment that a sense of unity emerges. But Miss Murdoch's idea of the novel is primarily people-in-motion-toward-a-resolution. Dora alone in *The Bell* gives the sense of being a consciousness, a unit, and an actor. But consciousness and acting mingle so closely in her—she shares her creator's enthusiasm for having something happen—that she provides the dynamic for the novel. Like Jake Donoghue's, her activity takes the form of the big practical joke—grand gesture turned upside down in the name of an odd normality. Dora has mixed up her young life enough to be a candidate for the restricted environment and the regulated life, but she still holds the world's view of things. She blames her troubles not on society or the nature of human relationships, but on accidents—the wrong husband, the wrong friends. In coming to the colony she is exercising her feminine right to annoy the men in her life by shifting back and forth. Her complaint, like Jake's, is that no one pays her enough attention. Her husband prefers old manuscripts, her newspaper friend is as irresponsible as she and will not take her antics seriously. She returns to her husband because she can live only as a counterpuncher. His scholarly interests and bad temper provide a framework to fight; the amorphous bohemian world offers no striking point.

Petty issues spoil the fun in fighting with her husband, but Michael's bringing to the actual working stage so elaborate a vision as his community offers a worthy antagonist. If his way of reducing hostility is right, her love of chaos and identity-by-negative is wrong. Once she has oriented herself, the colony arouses her imagination. It offers a way to define herself through destructive action and to sustain her hold on resentful directionlessness. But the message she means to force on the visionary—you cannot divorce goodness from the old Adam—evolves into the education of Dora: you can't, but it means something to try.

(Much of what we think of as modern in the modern novel has, of course, been educational in the opposite direction. Writers demolish false hopes, presumably powerful in society, by the standards of the knowing mind. *The Bell*, however, sets up an image of hope as vague and vulnerable, nourished by people who have underestimated the destructive element and show only limited executive ability. The normal is no longer anybody's fool.)

Engineering survey and idyll turned utopian provide the base for *The Bell;* awkward comedy and a suspenseful play of forces make it go. The comedy fills the gap between Dora's defiant vision and her attempts to express it. At the simple level of discomfort, her disdain for the whole undertaking fails to deal with the housewife's sternness about how-we-do-things-here; her version of Rain's free and easy run through the grass as night ends in having to meet her sincere hosts barefoot. But the exciting awkward comedy grows directly out of the play of forces. The bell itself is a floating symbol like Henry Green's—it means what each character thinks it means and is of no "realistic" importance to anyone. The functioning of the colony depends upon its regular activities rather than donating a new bell to the convent. This sentimental gesture intends, though, to put a concrete bridge across a doubt—to ritualize continuity between the new group and the old faith. To Dora the medieval bell, which supposedly flew into the lake because of a nun's unfaithfulness, represents the continuity of rebellious human nature—its existence within the old faith even in its flowering. Her excitement about her practical joke, raising the old bell and substituting it for the new, grows as she sees a chance to join the issue squarely at the dedication. The battle of the bells then ties in with the battle over Toby, the idealistic young Christian. Michael unknowingly wants a homosexual relationship with him; Dora teases him with the possibility of a heterosexual one to gain his aid in raising the bell. Whoever can control him has won an umpire's decision. (Ultimately, neither side can; he fears dominance by both soft sin and wild impracticality.)

For Dora, the new bell must not get across the river because the lost faith and its echo cannot unite, the sensitive modern cannot boldly recreate meaning. The old bell, in her fundamentalist view, must remind the communicants of man's fallen state, the appeal of the illicit. (Back at the gatepost, too, a bit of illicitness has been going on.) Her attack intuitively hits on a central need. Seen from Michael's point of view, the attempt to organize wills toward kindliness seems a lost cause from the beginning. Seen from Dora's, only superhuman effort under all but impossible conditions can down this threat to rebelliousness. Actually, the members of the colony have a bond in disappointment and hope for renewal, but have different enough grounds for dissatisfaction to make the centrifugal forces very strong. Restoring the bell serves the religious function of uniting antitheses through a symbol which each can take in his own way.

Raising the medieval bell from the lake is an idyll in mechanics. The excitement of the project itself—search, tractoring, winching, hoisting the huge piece of metal into the shed—merges into the excitement of the approaching affair between the dissatisfied wife and the young idealist. But when the two, elated in the dark at their success, tumble together into the bell, the clapper clangs, awakening everybody and changing the cross-purposes idyll into awkward comedy. The same gap between Dora's vision of herself as worldly, superior spoiler and her actual feelings produces the comic, yet intense embarrassment as the newspapermen gather to report to the world how she has turned the solemn into the ridiculous.

So *The Bell* brings together Miss Murdoch's best talents. The highly structured actions mesh. The lesser characters do convey the problems of diversity-in-unity. Working on the well-mapped scene in the dark suggests at once knowing and not knowing where you are. The combative heroine's excitement makes both the mechanic idyll and the awkward comedy effective. If *The Bell* has a weakness, it comes from the hero's having to strike an attitude through the novel rather than participate interestingly. His one departure from this stance—the passing pass at Toby—is an uninspired way to break up the colony. There are conventions in wounds, of course, and homosexuality is a common one now, but its very conventionality makes it inadequate to the imaginative pitch of the novel as a whole. Yet even here Miss Murdoch saves some individuality in Michael's attempts at matter-of-fact acceptance—first of his past and himself, then of the discovery and breakup. In fact, though Dora has obviously been impressed by what success he has achieved with the group, her conciliation with him occurs as she sees him able to live with disappointment. Their last ride together is the orderly closing of the establishment. Her decision to give some purpose to her life is his victory.

But what can "victory" mean in this context of failure? At the minimum, it means a persuasive example of fighting against the will to directionlessness and its temptation to make a bad situation worse. At best, progress means expanding the sense of what is possible, for good or ill, and expanding sympathy for hopes and problems that are—and are not—our own. The initial impulse to widen the sense of self by increased understanding fulfills itself in the denouement.

In a word, *The Bell* sustains the kind of oblique imagination that the novel of forces requires. Inner complexity revolves around the strangeness which an "adjusted-to" scene takes on during excitement about a plan. Outer complexity means a multitude of planning intelligences bouncing off each other. Within the central project, these complexities unite. Dora proposes to interfere with the natural process of the absurd forcing itself upon the visionary—she means to act as its agent and speed up the revelation. Despite her genius for action, the absurd thwarts the destroyer as well as the idealist. Toby's unpredictability defeats her at the same moment that it defeats Michael. Reality refuses to conform to the will of either. With a crucial difference. However much Michael may be ashamed of the mildly homosexual episode, he is not ashamed of having founded the community. Dora, who suffers no guilt from greater sexual errors, does feel ashamed as she recognizes both her childishness and her identification with the group's hopes. Miss Murdoch differs most sharply from earlier novelists in her sense of what complications living gives rise to. In an eccentric coterie's to-do about a couple of bells, she isolates and gives warmth to what people do care enough about to fight over.

In sum, *The Bell* seems first-rate because, in a time when so many novels discover what we already know, it multiplies out to a bizarre symbol of confusions we have been feeling but did not have a name for. In making the party of hope chuckleheaded, Miss Murdoch embodies both our need and our suspicion. In the frenetic defense of "normal" egocentric pessimism, working hard and spinning wheels for no more than a cruel, contentious joke, she gets in a less acceptable suspicion about the meaning of our activism. Her paradox of impractical people working effectively for a time while "practical" ones play to defend going nowhere reverses a commonplace of modern fiction. Add the skillful management of growing resources—the property relation, engineering survey, idyll of mechanics eventuating into awkward comedy—and *The Bell* is strange enough to be striking, common enough to isolate the always-known-but-never-quite-put-together-before. By working out her own diagnosis of where things hurt most and by meeting imaginatively the problems the analytically-inclined novel of forces brings up, Miss Murdoch makes the reader share the excitement of discovery instead of nodding his acquiescence.

Despite some novelists' doubts, critics are in league with progress. Once their writer has found something, they like to see orderly development, promise fulfilled. So the pleasant step would be to record that Miss Murdoch's novels after *The Bell* expand its at-home strangeness and outrageous contest between grand schemers and practical jokers. But, instead of exploiting what she had presumably learned to do, Miss Murdoch chose next to risk more failures by returning to her most doubtful field—domestic relations. A Chaucerian would probably call *A Severed Head* and *An Unofficial Rose*, along with *The Sandcastle*, her Marriage Group.

But Miss Murdoch does not mean to re-approach personal relations in the spirit of "Housewives' Joyce," as Henry Reed once called Virginia Woolf's work. The new development has premises of its own. For one thing, the sense of confinement within previous choices becomes a greater pressure on hopes for renewal. Attempts at renewal themselves become more entwining. Most important, the dream of idyll, which had given rise to both the lyric of choice and the awkward comedy, disappears. Instead Miss Murdoch turns toward whatever excitement can arise from hard-headed appraisals and answers to problems normally treated with emotion. These later novels bring Dora's playful restlessness up against the "deepest wishes" which it resists—and which resist it.

A Severed Head tosses off a self-consciously flip answer to the kind of difficulty that people usually mull over without getting any answer. Again the confinement inherent in personal relationships opposes the possibilities of self-assertion within them. Pleasant stability versus imprisonment—can the good exist without the bad? Martin, the protagonist, believes that he wants a warm, compliant mistress and a friendly, tolerant wife. He assumes freedom for himself and confinement for his womenfolk as both desirable and possible. The action of the novel, though, shows this superficial egotism to be superficially egotistic—not what Martin really wants at all. Women actually engage his interest only when they fight back at him—the wife by demanding equal tolerance and the mistress by sending him her severed hair. But, since the personalities of both stay within the conventions of femininity, even these gestures become irritating complications rather than real renewals of interest in life. So in the end Miss Murdoch gives him as his Ideal Woman an ugly, middle-aged college instructor—a Medusa who likes to tell harsh truths, slice napkins in midair with a sword, and scuffle in the basement. Hints of meaning beyond meaning have tempted intelligent critics to see Honor Klein as some kind of primitive goddess—black, of course, not white—but her thin presence makes her more a figure for an Ugly Truth: beyond the pleasure principle, the desire to fight can be depended upon. She welcomes Martin to marriage as declared war with a worthy antagonist, free from the soft, the maternal, the self-sacrificing, the reproachful. May the best man-woman win.

A Severed Head carries to the extreme Miss Murdoch's love for cryptic suggestion at a fast pace. By this time, though, she had acquired a following. British critics were predicting that she would soon do the really big novel of the age. *An Unofficial Rose* seems to respond to this demand—and show how wrong it was. Not that the novel lacks quality, but the parts that make it big—realistic detail in static situations—get dull. *An Unofficial Rose* is sincere, ironic, and encyclopedic. And a serious issue is at stake: can people as they get older keep on making new personal arrangements once those arrived at "naturally" have spoiled? (The overall answer is: some can, some can't. It's a matter of personality.) The novel comes alive most in the character who can make his disgust, intelligence, and selfishness work together for regrouping.

So Randall, a fortyish grower of prize roses, appears first in a magnificent sulk calculated to frighten his wife, father, daughter, and anyone else who can be persuaded to take an interest. This time what his family mistakes for habitual moodiness turns into the sulk of decision. He will leave his wife, whose presence in the house reminds him of the ordinariness in life, for a slick-surfaced city girl. Miss Murdoch then skillfully plays off this abandoned stasis against a new one as the girl insists on having the means for the good life in hand before giving up her own prospects. At this point an evolution occurs. Randall changes from moody and mooning to a contemporary unconfident confidence man. He applies modern insight to his father's problems, and, playing upon past failure at romance and hopes for a renewal, persuades the old man to live through him—sell his "golden dream of another world," a Tintoretto nude, to finance the liaison. Against this psychology of transaction, Miss Murdoch sets her comic lyric description of the symbol for idyll:

> It lighted the room now, like a small sun. It was not a very large picture: it represented a naked woman and was almost certainly an earlier version of the figure of Susannah in the great "Susannah Bathing" in Vienna. Only it was no sketch, but a great picture in its own right and justly of some fame: a notable segment in the vast seemingly endless honcycomb of the master's genius; and well might a spectator think of honey, looking upon that plump, bent, delicious, golden form, one leg gilding the green water into which it was plunged. A heavy twining complication of golden hair crowned a face of radiant spiritual vagueness which could only have been imagined by Tintoretto. Golden bracelets composed her apparel, and a pearl whose watery whiteness both reflected and resisted the soft, honey-colored shades. It was a picture which might well enslave a man, a picture round which crimes might be committed. Mildred regarded it now as it glowed in the darkening room and recalled with indignation that Fanny had wanted to sell it. Small Fanny had feared it perhaps. . . .
>
> And still half amused at finding herself so elevated Mildred turned her gaze again to the worried preoccupied infinitely-to-be-looked-after bald-headed Hugh. Slow old Hugh, she thought, and her heart dissolved in tenderness. Mine.

Behind Randall's fixing on the city girl who represents his Tintoretto fantasy lies the wish for a love freed from emotionalism and based straightforwardly on possession. In Lindsay he has the right girl, the opposite of Rain Carter. No dew, roses, river banks, and sentiment over father or mother. Lindsay's furnishings are money, telephone, bed and tape recorder. Coldness itself supplies the thrill in this comedy-of-property romance:

"But you *will* come?" said Randall. . . . "You do love me, Lindsay, for heaven's sake?"

She looked at him sombrely, and as he gazed in supplication he seemed to see another symbol taking shape in her eyes, as if her beloved initial, on which he had used to meditate as upon one of the names of God, had transformed itself into the relevant question.

"Money," he said. "Yes."

Lindsay nodded.

"Yes," he said. "We must have money. That's the trouble, isn't it?" He did not insult her by saying, "I can earn money, if you help me." That was not a thing to say to a girl such as Lindsay. . . .

With a coldness which matched her own, and which he felt as deliciously provocative as the tenderest badinage of love, he said, "Will you get her dough?"

Lindsay smiled faintly and respondingly and her hand sought his. "Not unless I stay till the end."

"And how near is the end?"

Lindsay shrugged her shoulders.

"She pretends to be old, doesn't she," said Randall, "and she isn't really so old at all. Do you think she's ill?"

"She's not ill. She'll live forever."

"Hmm," said Randall. "Then we must think of something else."

"*You* must think of something else."

This conning comedy turns into a new comedy of awkwardness, though, when the chance for consummating the affair finally comes. Lindsay's absent employer, an older woman novelist, becomes a ghost for Randall's fears of impotence faced with so cool a young woman. Though the competent Lindsay takes the initiative, even she "looked like a poor condemned whore taken to execution in her shift." The gap between imagined beauty and cold character produces the best comedy in the novel. Buying his "little waif out to make her fortune, a Dick Whittington of the passions" seems to Randall natural. Taking possession becomes an emotional event, which presently turns out well enough.

Miss Murdoch seldom makes the common mistakes—only the uncommon ones. In *An Unofficial Rose* she handles convincingly the pathos of the rejected—and sentimentalizes the power of rejecting. The wife's indecisiveness about remarriage dramatizes an intense conflict in a woman unused to depending on herself. Juxtaposed to this, excess creates the feeling of refusals multiplying out to infinity. Long sections on the old writer rejecting Randall's father and his daughter teasing her playmate suggest a miraculous power that fascinates Miss Murdoch more than it can the reader. Randall rejects his wife, his girl holds him off until he can pay. Emma rejects his father, the father holds a neighbor in reserve, her husband neglects her for boys. The wife refuses, accepts, and refuses a new marriage, while at the end Randall prepares to slough off his prize for a dream of endless diversity. This concentration of refusals—some for interesting reasons, some not—reminds how much Miss Murdoch has been excited by them all along. Jake Donoghue simultaneously quits the rat race and the search for communication; the heroine of *Flight from an Enchanter* flees from one; Mor in *The Sandcastle* draws back from an "ideal" companionship.

An encyclopedia of attitudes toward love at midpoint and beyond may be a worthy aim, but what could Miss Murdoch have believed would hold the evidence together? (Most readers who like the novel do it by discarding the dull parts and looking back toward the good scenes.) The not quite successful glue is, like glue in general, a compound. It assumes that living is a dynamic process. People want it to be that way—and also want it perfectly stable and predictable. The characters who hold Miss Murdoch's loyalty know that personal relationships change. They choose to stand for no-nonsense about old emotions. Randall is a heel and Emma a witch, but their cool, aware competence expresses an ideal.

Emma expects change of secretaries so much that she can have Lindsay make her own arrangements. Randall at the end sees a vision of new and newer Lindsays. (The child witch, Miranda, demonstrates—at undue length—how natural and pleasurable this power of rejecting stable relationships can be, and how undirected it is without the adult intelligence of Emma and Randall.)

Though this wish controls the action and though Miss Murdoch, like Joyce Cary, may at times believe that directed restlessness is the hope of the world, she knows that people also cling, hesitate, mope, try to undo. So she includes the doting lover who wants to relive the romance of a generation ago, the Amelia-and-Dobbin courtship (complete even to colonial colonel), and the deserted wife waiting for her husband and meeting only the returned cat. Though the action works best when the cool characters deal with each other, it works next best when the discarded wife refuses to deal with anyone. What comes through is not so much pathos as an impatience that the novelist builds up in the reader. Ann and her colonel are clearly meant for each other. A marriage bureau would pair them instantly. Ann wants to recognize change and do the sensible thing, but cannot welcome it and finally cannot do it at all. The reader does not want to go on with page after page of this and only persists because he becomes involved in urging Ann to cheer up. This impatience finally becomes his memory of her—not anything about her looks, talks, visits, or even feelings.

Miss Murdoch also sees a significant conflict, being out of touch with possibilities, in Randall's father—but can only demonstrate at length his incompetence. Her attitude toward confusion and eccentricity differs from some of the best contemporary comic novelists'. Waugh and Henry Green see in oddities lovable touchstones of individuality in an organizing world. But Miss Murdoch has too much respect for being well-organized, however wrongheadedly, to sympathize deeply with the eccentric. She can be impatient with Ann, but only disrespectful with Hugh. The eccentric has proved even better than the rebel in conveying a contemporary sense of individuality, though, and, when Miss Murdoch's drama of forces lets up a little, she has none of this gratuitous individuality to fall back upon. Even her confused characters are too well integrated. (Though this rage for order both makes and limits the novelist of forces, Miss Murdoch stands out from her contemporaries by the amount and kind of confusion that she has been able to order.)

Primarily, two forces move *An Unofficial Rose:* a change from sulk to planning intelligence, eager to simplify choices by removing emotionalism and willing to apply modern insight to practical obstacles, and an exaltation of the power to reject. Randall carries the first line, in itself a shift from faith in the power of simple *no.* All the female principals—from the old writer through the wife to the child—carry the second. The mistress plays both sides. The common weakness in *A Severed Head* and *An Unofficial Rose* is that they work too hard—become too clever in the one case and too encyclopedic in the other—but they are working at something. They serve in Miss Murdoch's development to purge the sandcastle love for soft-headed emotional tangle. Both novels want to cut through to fundamentals. What are the real conflicts? What are the actual *choices* available? Together the two novels make the next stage of Miss Murdoch's development possible.

One talent above all others has enabled Miss Murdoch to keep on growing. She distrusts her own fantasies. Whatever part continental thought and fiction may have played in suggesting first questions to ask, her later novels have grown directly from their predecessors. Once she has defined a problem and given her answer to it, she then asks, what is wrong with that answer? What new problems does it give rise to? As she has herself approached middle age—"young" novelists almost always are middle-aged by the time critics take them up—she has refused to harden into fixed positions for meeting all events. She has not tried to continue the angry surprise of youth at the way the world goes, to judge all adult experience by the willful hopes of adolescence, or to degrade actual life by quasi-religious ideals—though every one of these elements appears at some time or another in her work. Her novels move forward by questioning both her own hard-headedness and her contemporaries' softness.

An Unofficial Rose lacks the strangeness of *The Bell* probably because it confines itself to standard real-life questions. For these Miss Murdoch typically uses standard real-English settings. *An Unofficial Rose* sympathizes in an orthodox way with the suffering of the rejected, and gives an unorthodox answer in idealizing the power of rejection to cut outworn ties and establish modes of life more in keeping with actual feelings. *The Unicorn* goes at still more fundamental questions. Lewis' *The Picaresque Saint* praises the sanctification of suffering as the major strain in contemporary fiction; on any count the line has been significant. So Miss Murdoch asks, how much do we dare honor suffering as such? If that question is partly directed at other writers, she asks herself a harder question, what does the power of rejection mean and how much can we idealize it?

In *An Unofficial Rose* the conflict between regrouping and rejection never quite joins itself. The representatives pursue separate courses. *The Unicorn* tells of a tug-of-war about these same issues. The unicorn herself is a static figure for the representatives of three main attitudes to struggle over. Seven years before the novel opens, Hannah Crean-Smith has fought with her husband at a cliff edge and thrown him over, failing to kill him but apparently gelding him. She has dealt with this violence in her personality by rejecting further experience and accepting sanatorium living in her remote "castle."

Three main positions contend for her loyalty. A young woman hired as a companion and teacher wants to cure by forcing her back to dealing with the world outside. A presumably successful bureaucrat comes on an annual vacation of tears and handpatting to indulge his own self-pity by inflating to Hannah the proportions of her suffering. The estate manager, a friend of her husband, wants to keep her in the controlled environment; he believes that she likes the restricted routine well enough and cannot deal with the upsets of everyday life. The novel begins from the question of what attitude to take toward these three views of a woman who has carried the power of rejecting experience near its ultimate extreme.

More literally, *The Unicorn* begins from landscape—one strange enough to satisfy any reader who had been hoping that Miss Murdoch would try something like *The Bell* again. But this landscapc does not ask for assent to its physical presence; it intends rather to call up memories of Brontë and Cocteau movies. Grand views, big black cliffs, lichen on rock, endless bogs in the backlands, a flood-destroyed village, a dangerous cove, a nineteenth-century "castle," an eighteenth-century house on a distant hill, a seldom-crossed river. Where the separated community in *The Bell* gardened and maintained relations with village and pub, the recluses living here survive on their own resources and do nothing. Again the very frankness of representation makes the scene work. The novelist counts on us to say simultaneously, "*Wuthering Heights*," and "frustrated will in retreat."

Hannah Crean-Smith—a combination mythical beast and Christ-figure, one character calls her—lives under the supervision of the politely domineering Gerald Scottow, aided by a staff, all of whom feel guilty whether successfully guilty of anything or not. Though she survives comfortably, drinks a great deal of whiskey, and reports only feeling numb, she is a *modern* unicorn for the outsiders because she "suffers" from her own impulses and acts; but Miss Murdoch undercuts their view by contrasting it with Hannah's apparent mundaneness. (Some critics complain that the unicorn fails to enchant the reader. But our suspicion that she is not worth the effort exerted for her is part of the effect; we need only believe that the characters project their own problems on to her.)

The strength of the novel comes not from the interest of characters, but from Miss Murdoch's bringing the contemporary revival of will squarely up against its strongest antagonists—the counter-will to passivity and the inadequacy of action to satisfy complex destructive needs. The landscape, like most primitive landscapes in literature, evokes intense feeling as opposed to the superficialities of society. The characters from outside choose this scene, and two brilliant letters alone convey what they are running from—a hard-surfaced world which expects the face of wit not merely to mask pain but to replace it. The egoist writers feel nothing much.

Thus even the sanest characters come to this backland searching for intensity, valuing sensibility. They identify with the unicorn because she seems guiltier than they and suffering more seriously. Effingham's temperament makes him want to admire from a safe distance; Marian's makes her want to take curative action. Gerald, presumably the villain, voices the counterweight of the novel to simple faith in will:

"You have imagined that you know our ills and you have imagined that you have the power to cure them. But neither is the case. . . . There are great patterns in which we are all involved, and destinies which belong to us and which we love even in the moment when they destroy us. Do you think that I myself am separated in any way from what goes on here, that I am free? I am part of it too. It does not belong to me, I belong to it. And that is the only way it can be here, because of the way the lives of several people are working themselves out, because of the pattern. That is what has authority here, and absolute authority. And that is what anyone must submit to, if they are to stay here, and what you must submit to, my Marian, if you are to stay here."

The excitement arises from shifting the play of these forces so rapidly that the one human being whom the reader can identify with, Marian, is always off-balance. In so far as the novel is *about* any single conflict, it is about trying to right this off-balance feeling by a "rational," active plan inadequate to the forces involved.

Gerald, another force who never becomes a character, appears as a counter-enchanter, Guilt personified and personable, eager to involve others in his "pattern." Instead of actions, we get reports. He has encouraged Hannah's adultery; revealed the relationship to her husband; become her jailer after the attack; and then idealized her as Queen Bee in a Hive of Guilt. Michael, in *The Bell*, is also the Antagonist for the central character, but the difference dramatizes the difference between the two novels. Both Michael and Gerald are organizers trying to shore up chaos, the one benignly and the other malignly. Michael works by persuasion and ritual, Gerald by force thinly surfaced with family spirit. (He welcomes Marian to the little group of guilty sufferers after her plan to free Hannah has failed.) Michael stands for a weak hope won amid painful experiences, Gerald for joining pain. But, just as Michael and Marian fail by overestimating the power of a simplified plan against the divisiveness of sensibility, Gerald also fails. Marian's scheme for freeing Hannah falters by coming up against "accident"—the spare woman's jealousy for her man—and, in larger terms, by having no more than a vacant idea of freedom to replace imprisonment. She has not faced the question of freedom-to-do-what—is, in fact, retreating from the very world she wants to force Hannah into.

Gerald understands and fears this vacancy. Against Hannah's anxieties and angers he opposes his charm, force, and cunning. But when the situation which brought on the original illness recurs, these talents become catalysts for the disease. The threat that the husband will return is only a threat, but it ruins the "pattern." Though Gerald seduces Hannah, cows the staff, and promises to take her away, close relationship is the heart of the threat to her. She has pushed her husband over a cliff and within a day shoots Gerald.

One of the most imaginative sections, though, deals with that day—when it appears that charm and energy will reestablish order against the chaos within so many of the characters. A series of aborted fairy tale endings occurs. Marian has an idyllic hour of love beside the salmon pool with the handyman. Effingham chases the spare woman to the edge of a tidepool. Gerald carries the limp Hannah to his room before the eyes of the paralyzed staff.

Realistically considered, it seems unlikely that Peter Crean-Smith is returning after seven years to revenge himself violently upon his wife, but re-emergent violence is what all the characters fear. They bear the inconveniences of "imprisonment" for that reason. The mere possibility leads to Gerald's agreeing to take Hannah away from the only conditions under which she can live. The reasons for the pattern hold, balance and love prove illusory, the violence subdued by force and confidence breaks out everywhere. When news of the final suicide comes as Marian and Effingham are returning to their own worlds, it seems only more of the same.

Miss Murdoch's earlier novels often suggested that *thanatos* was likely to prove stronger than *eros,* but *The Unicorn* lays out more accurately the reasons for thinking so. Here the affections appear miscellaneous, vagrant, distractable. Marian comes to the castle because she has at last given up hoping that her lover will marry her. But she is still looking. She looks at Gerald and gives up on him when people tell her he does not care for women. She shifts to the boy Jamesie, who proves under Gerald's shadow. She involves Effingham, but, when he seems another reluctant lover, goes to the salmon pool with a more loyal follower. None of these attachments reaches as deep as her aggressive wish to shock Hannah out of passivity.

Where love is shallow and miscellaneous, anger is deep and personal. The "saint" accepts numbness as delivery from inner violence, but in close quarters will turn in fear and hatred upon any lover—not merely her husband. Effingham's ineffectuality sends him on a suicidal trip across the bog. Hannah's hatred turns upon herself and she jumps over the cliff. Jamesie abets her out of anger about Gerald. In sum, the destructive impulses are focused and dependable, however long subdued; the affections are transient and all but impersonal.

Unlike its two predecessors, *The Unicorn* is not a knowing novel. Its dilemmas do not respond to sly answers. It slices through the pretensions of sensibility and sensitivity, even attacks them as unexamined values in the culture, without crediting will with the power to solve or the faith in itself to keep trying. From one point of view *The Unicorn* is a harsher version of *The Bell.* For all the contrast between Michael and Gerald, Gerald has also built an ordered refuge for people too sensitive to function in the ordinary world. Miss Murdoch has merely removed from him Michael's kindliness and Utopianism. Marian tries to restore the unicorn to a directionless normalcy from which she has herself fled. But, where the earlier novel treats the refugees sympathetically, the later one faces the dangers in "protecting" from an illness which has at its core anger and the fear of anger. Effingham's sympathy appears as self-indulgence, engaged in to prevent coming to grips with his problems. Gerald and the staff accept Effingham because he abets their life work of helping Hannah make a career of illness. Hannah *is* ill and does not want to get well, for that would mean facing the conflicts buried by the more or less benevolent conspiracy. And Marian, in trying to cure her, is making an indirect and over-simple attack on the anger which has led her too to withdraw from the outside world. Whatever the characters' differences as to method, everyone is fighting in the fog against a formless and omnipresent enemy within. By plotting positions and setting forces against each other, the novel tries to give shape to this nameless tension.

If Iris Murdoch and Bellow best represent the postwar spirit, what do they have in common? Certainly they are different enough. Even in her more painful discoveries she seems buoyed up by a confidence in the play of intelligence, sometimes to the point of playing with the reader. Bellow has to work harder to find intelligence doing any good against the "humiliating comedy of heart-break." But both novelists inherit under more hopeful circumstances the tensed will of wartime and depression, with its feeling for the value of high energy. Tying it to public action, though, creates too narrow an overlap with the essential needs of the personality. Both writers want to avoid becoming C. P. Snows. They do see two common possibilities: of continually realigning the impulses with "deepest wishes"; and of having the will turn in on itself and become its own torturer.

For Miss Murdoch, energy's first choices always go wrong. They are too ignorantly egocentric, too unaware of other people and forces. Restlessness, unashamedly and unquestionably existing, strives simultaneously to fulfil itself and "to be kindlier than we are." It has trouble finding objectives that are wholly satisfying or wholly practical—yet in its nature asks nothing less. And no stopping place ever lasts. Miss Murdoch explores the tensions, disappointments, and pleasures of a search that cannot end and often does not want to go on. For her, more than the technique of the novel blurs the will.

EIGHT

Conclusion

As 1930 marked the end of a generation, the present may be approaching the end of another. The recent past depends upon particular senses of deprivation and a corresponding willingness to be grateful for small favors. Its drama of shocks and attempted recoveries may seem less central to younger writers, who will have different things to recover from. A rising level of expectations could catch up with the novel too.

Meanwhile the story has told of struggles to merge the potentially antagonistic—sensitivity and aggression, imagination and realism, warmth and intelligence, integrity and applied knowledge. If the account given here is at all accurate, summaries of modern literature like Trilling's, where everything ends in Terror and withdrawal from society, bear little resemblance to the life in the best recent British and American novels. (Such views derive mostly from first-generation European writers and are extrapolated without test. Trilling's *Partisan Review* essay differs from what Edmund Wilson said thirty-five years ago, in *Axel's Castle,* chiefly in its substitution of terror for withdrawal.) The live fears, guilts, and hopes have contested with each other far more vigorously.

Things could conceivably have gone another way. The earlier heroes' self-analysis might eventually have applied insights that would have freed them from unrecognized aggressiveness and enabled them to act flexibly in a realistically charted world. Distinctions could have appeared more clearly between the uses of aggression and its mere acting out. The first-generation novelists had tried, like Freud himself, to bring consciousness to bear on unconscious self-deceptions and reluctances. The earlier writers in fact occupy themselves a great deal with inertia—hesitations to participate in *The Magic Mountain* and *Ulysses;* to change in *Swann's Way;* to recognize the failure of going ideals in *The Great Gatsby.* Their work thus includes the possibility of freeing the mind from its terror, apathy, and self-deception—making it more capable of managing itself and the world. Their interests in complex motive opens up a theoretical chance to be less outraged at others' conduct. Why then didn't the paradigm work out?

Hardened attitudes and discouraging events interfered. Post-romantic glorification of inner at the expense of outer increased a dualism of the self and the world difficult to reverse under changed circumstances. Going ideologies tempted with pleasant short cuts. The human tendency to eradicate newly discovered Error rather than to live with its ambiguities accentuated the drive for definiteness—for answers with immediate results. The depression heightened impatience. War gave focusing and coercing energy an emotional climate as well as a rationale. Yet the surprising character of what amounted to efforts at rebirth is not their violent rejection of the immediate past, but their will to incorporate it into a workable vision. The revolutionaries of the thirties were respectful. They and their successors have tried to develop a humanly acceptable but more angular personality, viable in the world yet maintaining a "civility" more readily compatible with passive ideals.

When writers after World War II reacted against crisis and tried to restore some earlier values, they came to the task with the accumulated headlong energy of a violently active century—and with a host of new prejudices about mismanagement of self and society. Their most convincing response has turned out to be an irritable jerkiness—a constant colliding between heroic assertiveness based in both *eros* and aggression, and an inherited ideal of sensitivity founded on a vulnerable, all-too-detached imagination and intelligence. The dissociation of *action* and sensibility has been an ongoing problem. And the discontinuity between both and result has by itself provided enough to be irritated about. Even without the shocks, psychology could hardly have forecast more than a continuing struggle between warmth and aggression. With the dislocations came a fiercer conflict.

The later writers have of course had to deal with the caution bred by the failure of so many one-piece answers. To take a less-noticed case, Iris Murdoch's canniness about love and sex play contrasts with the enthusiasm present, if not approved of, in *The Sun Also Rises* and *Point Counter Point*. Both she and Bellow instinctively know the difficulties of making a private peace with the world. Much second generation literature records disappointment in love and sex—partly because of the great demands being made on them to replace a supposedly disintegrating larger world. In Mink, Scobie, Jack Burden, and Lewis Eliot, the turn toward "heroism" in the public sphere follows defeat in the personal one.

So the fate of intensity-and-sensitivity in the past thirty-five years has been a shifting one. Elizabeth Bowen discovers it to be both a gentle effort to wrap the world in private sensibility and a ruthless will. The theatrical compromise of control by being looked at proves unsatisfactory. Faulkner analyzes the problem into compartments, expands its range, and edges toward a synthesis in play—which is only slightly available. (In Salinger this synthesis later reaches its fulfillment and meets its own new contradictions.) Warren and Greene interrupt the analytic process to show will asserting itself without having freed the psyche or tamed events enough to make conscious control a probability. When Bellow turns back toward the earlier vision with its private peace, he tries to see around and experiment with sensitivity to achieve a "natural" evolution into living the inspired life in the world. The more restless Iris Murdoch attempts to synthesize opposing values out of hand. At her best she shows a choice between excess and sour grapes, with an undistributed middle. (In these circumstances the absurd is as popular as it is because it seems the only balancing system. It combines the mixture of aggression and sensitivity with realistic awareness of self and situation. Without the awareness, the facts would seem demonic—and the absurd functions to show that they are not.)

As I have said, my aim has not been to capsulize novels under headings like Sensitivity and Aggression, but to show impulses not readily reconcilable working out in the concrete experiences of literature. The theatricality often referred to marks one significant interaction. For its basic drive is to essentialize, to focus energy, by writing sensitive imagination large upon the world. Near the end of *Mimesis,* Auerbach abandons his analytic tone for an almost bitter paradox about what literature like Virginia Woolf's, Proust's, and Joyce's will lead to:

> To be sure, what happens in that moment—be it outer or inner process—concerns in a very personal way the individuals who live in it, but it also (and for that very reason) concerns the elementary things which men in general have in common. It is precisely the random moment which is comparatively independent of the controversial and unstable orders over which men fight and despair; it passes unaffected by them, as daily life. The more it is exploited, the more the elementary things which our lives have in common comes to light. The more numerous, varied, and simple the people are who appear as subjects of such random moments, the more effectively must what they have in common shine forth. . . . It is still a long way to a common life of mankind on earth, but the goal begins to be visible. And it is most concretely visible now in the unprejudiced, precise, interior and exterior representation of the random moment in the lives of different people. So the complicated process of dissolution which led to fragmentation of the exterior action, to reflection of consciousness, and to stratification of time seems to be tending toward a very simple solution. Perhaps it will be too simple to please those who, despite all its dangers and catastrophes, admire and love our epoch for the sake of its abundances of life and the incomparable his-

torical vantage point which it affords. But they are few in number, and probably they will not live to see much more than the first forewarnings of the approaching unification and simplification.*

If Auerbach had extended his reading beyond the 1920's, he might have verified that his prophecy was already being fulfilled as he wrote. Imitators of the modern classics would have confirmed his forecast. As chapter one indicates, the expanders of sensibility reached the outer limits of their program more quickly than they might have expected to; only a few like Mann proved able to continue producing different *kinds* of detailed insight. The imitators conscientiously turned out more of the same kind. One man's consciousness playing on the daily resembled another's more than might have been hoped.

The early modernists easily rode down Old Guardsmen who did not want to work that hard sorting out interior detail. But these fogies were speaking, in the wrong language and at the wrong moment, for one side of a powerful ambivalence—the love and fear of the diffuse. The philosophical-logical-mythical framework of *Ulysses* does not really make the detail cohere so that the mind can hold it—for the reason that no ideas about experience available to Joyce had sufficient power to do so. Faulkner's compartments still scarcely satisfy the quasi-religious demand for unity of being. People would like, of course, infinite riches in a little room—and perfect working control. Finding the balance difficult, they alternate emphases. The early moderns took their excitement in multiplicity and were willing to pay the price of the fractured self. Since their rich interior also meant the amorphous interior, latent desires for unity remained a potential ally for any revisionist. After 1930 the wish for a personality angled enough to make its impact felt within and without created a pressure to align, by brains or force, the almost deliberately disordered impulses.

Theatricality became one of the important means. The word has pejorative connotations—exhibit, trick, prop—but the drive toward it was as sincere as any other when life is at stake. In this set of circumstances theatricality means self-conscious *choice, with em-*

* *Mimesis* (Princeton, N. J., 1953), p. 585.

phasis. Out of all his possibilities a character selects one or two "best" suited to his talents and desire for forcefulness. He concentrates on and more or less awarely heightens these, learns to convey them to a chosen public. The peripatetic masters of reverie in the first generation novels abroad give way to characters like Anna, Willie Stark and Judge Irwin, Snow's cards-of-identity men. The energized American hero begins to look more like universal man.

Theatricality grows out of two drives. The obvious one, partisanship, automatically dramatizes and polarizes. The more troublesome inner effect arises from the newness of the chosen role—and even of the problem it seeks to deal with. (Kenneth Burke saw in the thirties that "in the literature of transitional eras . . . we find an especial profusion of rebirth rituals, where the poet is making the symbolic passes that will endow him with a new identity."*) The difficulty does not derive, though, from the seriousness of the issue. Discrepancies between public and private role exacerbate Waugh's mere revolutionists of manners. Sheer recency of the new stance makes a character feel self-conscious and anxious about it—he needs to fit it into a body of ideas as Jack Burden does, is sensitive to ridicule as Anna is, is bewildered as Jago is by unfamiliar demands. The constant doubling of characters dramatizes the problem inherent in the particular stylization of personality. The opposing force appears in combinations like Portia and Anna, Jack Burden and Willie, the priest and the lieutenant, Crawford and Jago, Ratliff and Mink. Not only does making a rough fit between style and natural bent come hard, but choice with emphasis inevitably denies other admirable possibilities.

Theatricality becomes not merely a concept of self but a chooser of activity and scene. Novels of the thirties and forties are full of grand gesture—Willie Stark's purifying hospital, Portia's frantic renunciation, Quentin's and Scobie's suicides, the will to remain the last priest in Mexico, the unbreakable grasp for the mastership and its powers. Political action, relevant enough already, becomes

* "Freud—and the Analysis of Poetry," in *The Philosophy of Literary Form* (New York, 1957, rev. ed.), p. 234.

even more pervasive because it demands that half-articulate impulses be dramatized, stylized—as new deals or frontiers, great societies. Politics is one habitat of the naturally theatrical personality, and its alliance of individual with group fate softens the self-consciousness that bothers Anna.

But no novelist shows more than Graham Greene, who distrusts politics, the connection between theatricality and force. The effectiveness of his characters is forever in question; the power of his chaotic scene to impose itself on consciousness never is. His vultures, lying natives, meaningless night patrols, indifferent dentists, and silky betrayers have struck many readers as too much like the movies. They are, and intentionally so. Greene makes the modern popular theater become the ambiance in which his heroes live. And the effect is to focus sharply, to seek the essence of the irresistible milieu—to lift evils, out of their dailiness, to Evil. They become a Power, which the protagonist must oppose with his inadequate human resources.

As myth gives fluid consciousness a sort of center, theatricality gives coherence to the wish to make the mind a force and to locate its opponents. For theatricality shows more respect for the demands of specific situation and more suitability to individuals than myth, whose broad categories must satisfy with a very rough fit. The drive for control puts a new value on the highest precision possible—means a streamlining for action, a self-dramatization guided by what is needed for the best goal seen as within reach. The reception of *Finnegans Wake*, so disappointing to Joyce in 1939, indicates how far a new principle of coherence had replaced the old master's logic.

The impulse behind the theatrical hero resembles that behind the unconfident confidence man of contemporary tragicomedy, who also needs an angular personality. But in the comic protagonist, expediency and slyness provide a mode of operating and the resiliency needed to bounce back from reverses. The theatrical hero, though he may be expedient and may see around his chosen "identity," takes seriously his role as the best available to enlarge and organize the sense of self while trying for a partial control of the environment. He becomes valuable in a disturbed period struggling for piecemeal order and uncertain of its ability to achieve that.

Theatrical action is essentially an unconfident heroism. It takes head on the hardest problems and strives for pride against much evidence of incapacity and reluctance. Contemporary tragicomedy in the novel assumes the grounds for despair and the likelihood of obstacles, but stylizes both and expresses disrespectable but live hopes. The unconfident confidence man is willing to live from hand to mouth, but the exploring novelists, who want to hope only on the solidest basis, pick up and give full body to resistances within and without. The tragicomic writers can live less anxiously on shifting, unmapped terrain, or, like Powell and Hartley, can live off the feeling that there was solid ground here a few years ago and the ooze on top can't be too deep. So in its kind of novel theatrical action became the first fully developed answer to the threats of passivity and fragmentation. Since nothing fails like success and these are speedy times, its ascendancy did not last long. Its drive sometimes achieved a measure of control, always threatened, but at great cost in suppressing "irrelevant" aspects of personality. Later novelists, benefiting from the partly achieved control, bring out the suppressed evidence and concern themselves more with "deepest wishes."

These writers act on their predecessors' discovery of difficulties. For them, extreme styling for action sacrifies too much for too little. Play opens up the possibility of a more inclusive life—and resistance to play a formidable counterforce. Their revived hopes avoid the previous pitfall of passivity, and the possible sense of theatricality in new roles had already been acted out. It could seem an echo if not an absolute familiar. The generation after World War I—Fitzgerald, Waugh, Huxley—had already gone through the theatrical phase with play.

So, though the postwar novelists here resemble those of the twenties in historical position and response to wartime tensing of the will, they differ significantly. They are freer to experiment without looking over the shoulder for the effect on father. Their new games are more intellectual and complex. They involve more of the emotional life. And they are longer-term commitments, with much of the intervening energy of heroic aspiration behind them.

A last question remains. How good are these second-generation novelists? The book has tried to answer as it went along—saying that they are good at this, at that, and at something else. But in the present climate of disparagement and defense, the issue inevitably means a comparison with the early moderns. Though not the most profitable question, it ought not to be evaded.

The second generation has been nothing if not thorough in mapping its chosen terrain. For, in addition to the exploring novelists, there are the talented codifiers. Golding and Beckett, the best of these, concentrate on what in the explorers amounts to a counterpoint motif—the fear that energy, instead of going somewhere, merely spins its wheels. They make an art out of strain. By thus concentrating they help to absorb the threat. Golding in the long run accepts energy as a good thing in itself, the best available mark of humanity. Beckett leaves it as permanent tragicomedy. But they share a common esthetic problem. By positing the closed circle, they commit themselves to organizing the already recognized. Since at best novelists since 1930 have had a problem of flexibility and freshness compared to their predecessors, the willingness of the six major novelists treated here to expand into untried ways of coping with experience has at least given them points of test. In Beckett and Golding, though, the answer appears on page one. So both have had to keep devising startling, "experimental" beginnings and frameworks.

Beyond that, of course, they differ sharply. Golding is a moralist who minds getting dusty answers. Beckett does not. The exploring novelists push out trying to destroy and create simultaneously. The image of the raid recurs in their work—in Miss Bowen's skirmishing; Faulkner's and Warren's bushwhacking; Miss Murdoch's property-endangering Jake, Dora, and Marian; and Augie's hit-and-run strategy. However unproductive some of these attacks are, they reflect a response to tentative hopes, half-confidences in plan. But a writer like Golding feels more at home in the encircled fort. It offers the comfort of consistency as well as a Mithridatic cure for disappointment: everything that can occur has occurred already—and we have documents to prove it. Such a writer prefers life to be of a piece, even if a bad one, because it then at least has an understandable pattern. Better a slave to plan than to contingency. So Golding moves more openly than Iris Murdoch toward allegory. He looks for perfect, if unpleasant, orientation.

Golding too counterpoints his main theme. His moral preference is for striving to be kindlier than we are, but his talent is for showing the *strain* of applying energy and mind within an already lost conflict. He regularly shows great expense of spirit leading to bad results or little hope of achieving limited objectives. In *Lord of the Flies* he calls attention ingeniously to persisting Original Sin. *The Two Deaths of Christopher Martin* locates his central perception with great kinetic force. The hero, a selfish man, is blown off the bridge of a torpedoed destroyer. At the end an officer on the beach reclaims his body and says that he drowned instantly. But for two hundred pages between, Christopher Martin struggles through waves to an "uncharted" rock in midocean; inches to its top against the backward pull of the water; sets up house, water supply, and distress signal; hopes and waits and despairs; lives off the produce of the rock; and in a glorious moment purges himself of a three-week constipation. Christopher Martin is already dead, the circle is closed, and yet he struggles for two hundred pages as if he were alive. Strain has been his reality.

If the explorers and the codifiers sometimes seem opponents, though, they are also allies. The explorers, though they deal in intensely felt wishes, are not optimists. The codifiers are consolidating the findings of earlier explorers. And in so far as Golding and Beckett take a narrower view of human possibilities, they remind us that eternal recurrence does exist. The service of the codifiers has been to accept the wasteland with its original sin as a place where people can live, ruefully or comically. They too picture a resilient and energetic human animal, but, by failing to respond to the bouncier hopes of meaning in all this activity, they give a clear focus to what cannot be unlearned. Their warnings form the solid base camp for any forays beyond the perimeter. For all the calls for more joy in literature, any overwhelming amount of cheer would make people nervous nowadays. It would seem too detached from the threats that they have confidence in.

The issue of decline is finally transatlantic, not American. Few critics, if they actually pitted Faulkner against Hemingway, Warren against Dreiser, and Bellow against Fitzgerald, would see a sharp falling off. Decline appears most on the continent. Camus, Silone, Malraux, and Mauriac do not look too strong against Proust, Mann, Gide, and Kafka. Drama has provided Europe an apparently more appealing expression. England, then, becomes the real point of engagement. If Elizabeth Bowen, Greene, and Iris Murdoch seem more limited than Conrad, Lawrence, and Joyce, the British have also produced a great tragicomedy in Henry Green, Waugh, Cary, Hartley, and Powell and the far from contemptible codifications of Golding and Beckett. More fiction of near first rank, at least, has appeared in the second generation, and, taken together, the novelists plot their world from more angles than the first generation. The very crowding of talent has made preeminence hard to achieve. And tragicomedy, which the British developed before anyone had heard of the absurd, has swept the present so thoroughly that a book beginning with "serious" novelists has to end with Bellow and Iris Murdoch. They differ from many tragicomedians in being more fascinated with whatever frustrates a great expression of the self, but their superior confidence in fondling reversals nevertheless operates within the genre.

Finally, any superiority the first generation may have can hardly be a matter of sentences. The quotations scattered through this book match most comparable sets from the earlier novels. Despite their experimentalism, the first-generation writers do not even clearly excel in management; some contemporary structures are subtler and less obviously machined. The development of shorthand symbolism in the later works saves a good deal of encyclopedia reading. The second generation does excel in its effort at natural tone, and it has given a great deal more meaning and maneuver to scene. On dramatic action there can be no comparison except in America. The first generation abroad eschews it.

The great names have, though, two possible areas of superiority. As Frank Kermode has said in a lecture on the poets, the earlier novelists occupied almost all the possible revolutionary positions. So they automatically have more "flash," as Bellow's Leventhal would put it. And they may have an advantage in flexibility and scope of mind. The second generation has a problem in giving its activism the minute-by-minute freshness possible to fluid consciousness. Force operates along more fixed paths; dramatic action cannot match sheer play of mind in agility. In the long run the writers of the renaissance may appeal more to people who read books—partly because the authors think more like readers than like actors.

For the earlier novelists give humanity size. The crannies of character count. Later, events and actions have a size that reduces the human figure. Characters fear and concentrate so much on managing that people become closely identified with force and its results. The ultimate difference between generations is not sentence or structure, but problem. The recent past has had to deal more intimately with necessity, reversal of expectation, conflict of inherited wishes—and has had a less joyous confidence in its ability to meet its difficulties than the first generation had about meeting its.

So, if there must be a scorecard, mine shows this: the American novel has improved; the continental one has declined; the British has shown more range without developing quite the outstanding individual accomplishment of the earlier generation.

Aside from these ultimate judgments, the newer novelists have done a difficult thing. They have established an individuality different from highly successful fathers. They have met with intelligence and imagination the problems they had to meet. They have used what they could of the inheritance, ventured beyond, and mapped the world minutely. Like the physicists and economists, they know more accurately what they do know. And they got the novel moving again.

Finally, though, there is no competition. Is *The Adventures of Augie March* better than *Pamela*—or *Père Goriot*? Or *A Portrait of the Artist as a Young Man*? Rankings may make a good game, but who has a serious human stake in their decimal-place accuracy? The error in continuing to emphasize the comparison is that we cannot like a crab, or even a professor of nineteenth-century literature, go backwards. However much we may honor the concerns of an earlier time, we cannot duplicate its experience. So this book has concentrated on something we can do: look in likely places for what we really think and how we have come to think it.

Selected Bibliography: Recent Criticism

Listings include books of the last dozen years or so and articles on individual writers published since the latest critical work containing a good bibliography.

General Books

Allen, Walter. *Tradition and Dream: A Critical Survey of British and American Fiction from the 1920's to the Present Day.* London, 1964.

Allsop, Kenneth. *The Angry Decade: A Survey of the Cultural Revolt of the Nineteen-fifties.* London, 1958.

Baumbach, Jonathan. *The Landscape of Nightmare: Studies in the Contemporary American Novel.* New York, 1965.

Bellow, Saul. *Recent American Fiction, A Lecture. . . .* Washington, D.C., 1963.

Blotner, Joseph. *The Modern American Political Novel.* Austin, Tex., 1966.

Bradbury, John M. *Renaissance in the South: A Critical History of the Literature.* Chapel Hill, N.C., 1963.

Bulgheroni, Marisa. *Il nuovo romanzo americano: 1954-1959*. Milan, 1961.
Burgess, Anthony. *The Novel Today*. London, 1963. (Supplement to *British Book News*.)
Cowley, Malcolm. *The Literary Situation*. New York, 1954.
Daiches, David. *The Present Age in British Literature*. Bloomington, Ind., 1958.
Davidson, Donald. *Southern Writers in the Modern World*. Athens, Ga., 1958.
Dommergues, Pierre. *Les Êcrivains américains d'aujourdui*. Paris, 1965.
Edel, Leon. *The Psychological Novel, 1900-1950*. Philadelphia, 1955.
Eisinger, Chester E. *Fiction of the Forties*. Chicago, 1963.
French, Warren. *The Social Novel at the End of an Era*. Carbondale, Ill., 1966.
Frohock, W. M. *The Novel of Violence in America*. Dallas, Tex., 1957.
Fuller, Edmund. *Man in Modern Fiction*. New York, 1958.
Galloway, David D. *The Absurd Hero in American Fiction: Updike, Styron, Bellow, and Salinger*. Austin, Tex., 1966.
Geismar, Maxwell. *American Moderns: From Rebellion to Conformity*. New York, 1958.
Gerevini, Silvano. *Voci di letterature inglese contemporanea*. Pavia, 1958.
Gindin, James. *Postwar British Fiction*. Berkeley, Calif., 1962.
Hall, James. *The Tragic Comedians*. Bloomington, Ind., 1963.
Hardy, John Edward. *Man in the Modern Novel*. Seattle, Wash., 1964.
Hassan, Ihab. *Radical Innocence, Studies in the Contemporary American Novel*. Princeton, N.J., 1961.
Hoffman, Frederick J. *The Mortal No*. Princeton, N.J., 1964.
Holman, C. Hugh. *The Modes of Modern Southern Fiction*. Athens, Ga., 1966.
Hough, Graham. *Image and Experience: Studies in a Literary Revolution*. London, 1961.
Karl, Frederick R. *The Contemporary English Novel*. New York, 1962.
Kenner, Hugh. *Gnomon: Essays on Contemporary Literature*. New York, 1958.
Kermode, Frank. *The Romantic Image*. London, 1957.
Klein, Marcus. *After Alienation: American Novels in Mid-Century*. Cleveland, O., 1964.
Lewis, R. W. B. *The Picaresque Saint*. Philadelphia, 1959.
Lombardo, Agostino. *Realismo e simbolismo: Saggi di letteratura americana contemporanea*. Rome, 1957.
Mander, John. *The Writer and Commitment*. London, 1962.

Mizener, Arthur. *The Sense of Life in the Modern Novel.* Boston, 1964.
O'Connor, William Van. *The New University Wits and the End of Modernism.* Carbondale, Ill., 1962.
Podhoretz, Norman. *Doings and Undoings: The Fifties and After in American Writing.* New York, 1964.
Pritchett, V. S. *The Working Novelist.* London, 1965.
Rubin, Louis D. *The Faraway Country: Writers of the Modern South.* Seattle, Wash., 1963.
Stallman, Robert W. *The Houses that James Built and Other Literary Studies.* East Lansing, Mich., 1961.
Symons, Julian. *The Thirties: A Dream Revolved.* London, 1960.
Thorp, Willard. *American Writing in the Twentieth Century.* Cambridge, Mass., 1960.
Tindall, William Y. *Forces in Modern British Literature, 1885-1956.* New York, 1956 (rev. ed.).
Walcutt, Charles C. *Man's Changing Masks: Modes and Methods of Characterization in Fiction.* Minneapolis, Minn., 1966.
Ward, A. C. *Twentieth Century Literature, 1901-1950.* London and New York, 1957.

Saul Bellow

Binni, Francesco. "Percorso narrativo di Saul Bellow," *Ponte,* XXII (1966), 831-842.
Bradbury, Malcolm. "Saul Bellow's *Herzog,*" *Critical Quarterly,* VII (1965), 269-278.
Critique, VII, iii (1965). (Articles by James Dean Young, Robert D. Crozier, Allen Guttman, and James C. Mathis.)
Dickstein, Morris. "For Art's Sake," *Partisan Review,* XXXIII (1966), 617-621.
Donoghue, Denis. "Commitment and the Dangling Man," *Studies,* LIII (1964), 174-187.
Enck, John. "Saul Bellow: An Interview," *Wisconsin Studies in Contemporary Literature,* VI (1965), 156-160.
Fossum, Robert H. "The Devil and Saul Bellow," *Comparative Literature Studies,* III (1966), 197-206.
Galloway, David D. "The Absurd Man as Picaro: The Novels of Saul Bellow," *Texas Studies in Language and Literature,* VI (1964), 226-254.
———. "Moses-Bloom-Herzog: Bellow's Everyman," *Southern Review,* II (1966), 61-76.

Garrett, George. "To Do Right in a Bad World: Saul Bellow's *Herzog*," *Hollins Critic*, II, ii (1966).

Handy, William J. "Saul Bellow and the Naturalistic Hero," *Texas Studies in Language and Literature*, V (1964), 538-545.

Hoffman, Frederick J. "The Fool of Experience: Saul Bellow's Fiction," in *Contemporary American Novelists*, edited by Harry E. Moore. Carbondale, Ill., 1966.

Nathan, Monique. "Saul Bellow," *Esprit*, XXXIV, No. 9 (1966), 363-370.

Popescu, Petru. "Omil Oscilant: Debutul lui Saul Bellow," *Luceafărul*, IX (March 19, 1966), 1.

Tanner, Tony. *Saul Bellow*. Edinburgh, 1965.

Uphaus, Suzanne Henning. "From Innocence to Experience: A Study of *Herzog*," *Dalhousie Review*, XLVI (1966), 67-78.

Way, Brian. "Character and Society in *The Adventures of Augie March*," *British Association for American Studies Bulletin*, No. 8 (1966), 36-44.

Elizabeth Bowen

Brooke, Jocelyn. *Elizabeth Bowen*. London, 1952. (British Council pamphlet.)

Greene, George. "Elizabeth Bowen: Imagination as Therapy," *Perspective*, XIV (1965), 42-52.

Heath, William Webster. *Elizabeth Bowen*. Madison, Wisc., 1961.

Mitchell, Edward. "Themes in Elizabeth Bowen's Short Stories," *Critique*, VIII (1966), 41-54.

Rupp, Richard Henry. "The Post-War Fiction of Elizabeth Bowen," *Xavier University Studies*, IV (1965), 55-67.

Saul, George Brandon. "The Short Stories of Elizabeth Bowen," *Arizona Quarterly*, XXI (1965), 53-59.

Sharp, Sister M. Corona, O.S.U. "The House as Setting and Symbol in Three Novels by Elizabeth Bowen," *Xavier University Studies*, II, (1963), 93-103.

Wagner, Geoffrey. "Elizabeth Bowen and the Artificial Novel," *Essays in Criticism*, XIII (1963), 155-163.

William Faulkner

Absalom, H. P. "Order and Disorder in *The Sound and the Fury*," *Durham University Journal*, LVIII (1965), 30-39.

Alter, Jean V. "Faulkner, Sartre, and the 'nouveau roman,'" *Symposium*, XX (1966), 101-112.

Backman, Melvin. *Faulkner: The Major Years*. Bloomington, Ind., 1966.

Bleikasten, André. "Faulkner et le nouveau roman," *Les Langues modernes*, LX (1966), 422-432.

Bradford, Melvin E. "Faulkner, James Baldwin and the South," *Georgia Review*, XX (1966), 431-443.

———. "'Spotted Horses' and the Short Cut to Paradise: A Note on the Endurance Theme in Faulkner," *Louisiana Studies*, IV (1965), 324-331.

Brooks, Cleanth. *William Faulkner: The Yoknapatawpha Country*. New Haven, 1963.

Brown, Calvin S. "Faulkner's Manhunts: Fact into Fiction," *Georgia Review*, XX (1966), 388-395.

Campbell, Harry Moden, and Ruel E. Foster. *William Faulkner: A Critical Appraisal*. Norman, Okla., 1951.

Christadler, Martin. *Natur und Geschichte im Werk von William Faulkner*. Heidelberg, 1962.

Coughlan, Robert. *The Private World of William Faulkner*. New York, 1954.

Cowley, Malcolm. *The Faulkner-Cowley File: Letters and Memories, 1944-1962*. New York, 1966.

Dain, Martin J. *Faulkner's County: Yoknapatawpha*. New York, 1964.

Dickerson, Mary Jane. "Some Sources of Faulkner's Myth in *As I Lay Dying*," *Mississippi Quarterly*, XIX (1966), 132-142.

Dillingham, William B. "William Faulkner and the 'Tragic Condition,'" *Edda*, LIII (1966), 322-335.

Doyle, Charles. "The Moral World of Faulkner," *Renascence*, XIX (1966), 3-12.

Ford, Margaret Patricia, and Susan Kincaid. *Who's Who in Faulkner*. Baton Rouge, La., 1963.

Franklin, Rosemary. "Animal Magnetism in *As I Lay Dying*," *American Quarterly*, XVIII (1966), 24-34.

Gold, Joseph. *William Faulkner: A Study in Humanism, from Metaphor to Discourse*. Norman, Okla., 1966.

Gresset, Michel. "Psychological Aspects of Evil in *The Sound and the Fury*," *Mississippi Quarterly*, XIX (1966), 143-153.

Harrison, Robert. "Faulkner's 'The Bear': Some Notes on Form," *Georgia Review*, XX (1966), 318-327.

Hayes, Ann L., and others. *Studies in Faulkner*. Pittsburgh, Pa., 1961.

Hoffman, Frederick J. *William Faulkner*. New York, 1961.

———, and Olga Vickery, eds. *William Faulkner: Two Decades of Criticism*. East Lansing, Mich., 1951.

Holmes, Edward M. *Faulkner's Twice-told Tales: His Reuse of his Material*. The Hague, 1966.

Howe, Irving. *William Faulkner: A Critical Study*. New York, 1952, 1962. (Rev. and expanded.)

Howell, John M. "Hemingway and Fitzgerald in Sound and Fury," *Papers on Language and Literature*, II (1966), 234-242.

Hunt, John Wesley. *William Faulkner: Art in Theological Tension*. Syracuse, N.Y., 1965.

Kartiganer, Donald M. "The Role of Myth in Absalom, Absalom," *Modern Fiction Studies*, IX (1964), 357-369.

Kirk, Robert W. *Faulkner's People: A Complete Guide and Index to Characters in the Fiction of William Faulkner*. Berkeley, Calif., 1963.

Kowalczyk, Richard L. "From Addie Bundren to Gavin Stevens: the Direction from Reality," *California English Journal*, II, i (1966), 45-52.

Longley, John Lewis. *The Tragic Mask: A Study of Faulkner's Heroes*. Chapel Hill, N.C., 1963.

Malin, Irving. *William Faulkner*. Stanford, Calif., 1957.

Materassi, Mario. "Le prime prose narrative di William Faulkner," *Paragone*, XVIII, No. 196 (1966), 74-92.

Meriwether, James B. *The Literary Career of William Faulkner: A Bibliographical Study*. Princeton, N.J., 1961.

Millgate, Michael. *The Achievement of William Faulkner*. London, 1966.

Miner, Ward L. *The World of William Faulkner*. New York, 1952.

Nathan, Monique, ed. *William Faulkner par lui-même*. Paris, 1963.

Nilon, Charles H. *Faulkner and the Negro*. New York, 1965.

Nishiyama, Tamotsu. "What Really Happens in *Sanctuary*?" *Studies in English Literature* (Tokyo), XLII (1966), 235-243.

O'Connor, William Van. *The Tangled Fire of William Faulkner*. Minneapolis, Minn., 1954.

———. *William Faulkner*. Minneapolis, Minn., 1959. (University of Minnesota pamphlets on American writers, No. 8.)

Pearce, Richard. "Faulkner's One Ring Circus," *Wisconsin Studies in Contemporary Literature*, VII (1966), 270-283.

Robb, Mary Cooper. *William Faulkner*. Pittsburgh, Pa., 1957.

Runyan, Harry. *A Faulkner Glossary*. New York, 1966.

Skou-Hansen, Tage. "To slags kaerlighed," *Dansk Udsyn*, XLV (1965), 241-258.

Slatoff, Walter J. *Quest for Failure: A Study of William Faulkner*. Ithaca, N.Y., 1960.

Sleeth, Irene Lynn. *William Faulkner: A Bibliography of Criticism*. Denver, Col., 1962.

Smart, George K. *Religious Elements in Faulkner's Early Novels: A Selective Concordance*. Coral Gables, Fla., 1965.

Swiggart, Peter. *The Art of Faulkner's Novels*. Austin, Tex., 1962.

Thompon, Lawrance R. *William Faulkner*. New York, 1963.

Turaj, Frank. "The Dialectic in Faulkner's *A Fable*," *Texas Studies in Language and Literature*, VIII (1966), 93-102.

Vickery, Olga W. *The Novels of William Faulkner*. Baton Rouge, La., 1959 and 1964 (revised).

Volpe, Edmond Loris. *A Reader's Guide to William Faulkner*. New York, 1964.

Waggoner, Hyatt Howe. *William Faulkner: From Jefferson to the World*. Lexington, Ky., 1959.

Warren, Joyce W. "Faulkner's Portrait of the Artist,'" *Mississippi Quarterly*, XIX (1966), 121-131.

Warren, Robert Penn, ed. *Faulkner: A Collection of Critical Essays*. Englewood Cliffs, N.J., 1966.

Webb, James W., ed. *William Faulkner of Oxford*. Baton Rouge, La., 1965.

———. "Faulkner Writes *A Fable*," *University of Mississippi Studies in English*, VII (1966), 1-13.

Woodworth, Stanley D. *William Faulkner en France*. Paris, 1959.

Graham Greene

Allott, Kenneth. *The Art of Graham Greene*. London and New York, 1951.

Atkins, John Alfred. *Graham Greene*. London, 1957.

Barratt, Harold. "Adultery as Betrayal in Graham Greene," *Dalhousie Review*, XLV (1965), 324-332.

Boardman, Gwenn R. "Greene's 'Under the Garden': Aesthetic Explorations," *Renascence*, XVII (1965), 180-190, 194.

Davison, Richard Allan. "Graham Greene and L. P. Hartley: 'The Basement Room' and *The Go-Between*," *Notes and Queries*, XIII (1966), 101-102.

DeCap, Roger. "La Tradition puritaine dans la littérature anglaise: John Bunyan et Graham Greene, *Caliban*, N.S. l, i (1965), 129-145.

Dèchet, Ferruccio. "Suggestioni e limiti della tematicaldi Graham Greene," *Giornalo di Metafisica*, XIX (1964), 75-89.

De Vitis, A. A. *Graham Greene*. New York, 1964.

———. "Greene's *The Comedians*: Hollower Men," *Renascence*, XVIII (1966), 129-136, 146.

Evans, Robert Owen, ed. *Graham Greene: Some Critical Considerations*. Lexington, Ky., 1963.

Jones, James Land. "Graham Greene and the Structure of the Moral Imagination," *Phoenix*, No. 2 (1966), 34-56.

Kohn, Lynette. *Graham Greene: The Major Novels*. Stanford, Calif., 1961.

Kunkel, Francis L. *The Labyrinthine Ways of Graham Greene*. New York, 1959.

Lodge, David. *Graham Greene*. New York, 1966.

Marian, Sister I. H. M. "Graham Greene's People: Being and Becoming," *Renascence*, XVIII (1965), 16-22.

McCall, Dan. "*Brighton Rock*: The Price of Order," *English Language Notes*, III (1966), 290-294.

Mesnet, Marie Béatrice. *Graham Greene and the Heart of the Matter*. London, 1954.

Oppel, Horst, ed. *Der moderne englische Roman: Interpretationem*. Berlin, 1965.

Pange, Victor de. *Graham Greene*. Barcelona, 1964.

Pryce-Jones, David. *Graham Greene*. Edinburgh, 1963.

Sandra, Sister Mary, S. S. A. "The Priest-Hero in Modern Fiction," *Personalist*, XLVI (1965), 527-542.

Stratford, Philip, *Faith and Fiction: Creative Process in Greene and Mauriac*. Notre Dame, Ind., 1964.

Wilshere, A.D. "Conflict and Conciliation in Graham Greene," *Essays and Studies by Members of the English Association*, XIX (1966), 122-137.

Wyndham, Francis. *Graham Greene*. London, 1955. (British Council pamphlet.)

Iris Murdoch

Baldanza, Frank. "Iris Murdoch and the Theory of Personality," *Criticism*, VII (1965), 176-189.

Byatt, A. S. *Degrees of Freedom: The Novels of Iris Murdoch*. London, 1965.
Dick, Bernard F. "The Novels of Iris Murdoch: A Formula for Enchantment," *Bucknell Review*, XIV (1966), 66-81.
Gregor, Ian. "Toward a Christian Literary Criticism," *Month*, XXXIII (1965), 239-249.
Hall, James. "Blurring the Will: The Growth of Iris Murdoch," *ELH*, XXXII (1965), 256-273.
Hall, William. " 'The Third Way': The Novels of Iris Murdoch," *Dalhousie Review*, XLVI (1965), 306-318.
Heyd, Ruth. "An Interview with Iris Murdoch," *University of Windsor Review*, I (1965), 138-143.
Martin, Graham. "Iris Murdoch and the Symbolist Novel," *British Journal of Aesthetics*, V (1965), 296-300.
Petersen, Jes. "Iris Murdoch," *Dansk Udsyn*, XLV (1965), 196-203.
Wolfe, Peter. *The Disciplined Heart: Iris Murdoch and Her Novels*. Columbia, Mo., 1966.

Robert Penn Warren

Bohner, Charles H. *Robert Penn Warren*. New York, 1965.
Bradbury, John M. *The Fugitives: A Critical Account*. Chapel Hill, N.C., 1958.
Casper, Leonard. *Robert Penn Warren: The Dark and Bloody Ground*. Seattle, Wash., 1960.
Cheney, Brainerd. "Is There a Voice Unheard in Warren's Book Who is Speaking for the Negro?" *Sewanee Review*, LXXIV (1966), 545-550.
Cowan, Louise. *The Fugitive Group: A Literary History*. Baton Rouge, La., 1959.
Justus, James. "The Mariner and Robert Penn Warren," *Texas Studies in Language and Literature*, VIII (1966), 117-128.
———. "The Uses of Gesture in Warren's *The Cave*," *Modern Language Quarterly*, XXVI (1965), 448-461.
Longley, John Lewis, ed. *Robert Penn Warren: A Collection of Critical Essays*. New York, 1965.
———. "Robert Penn Warren: American Man of Letters," *Arts and Sciences*, Spring (1965), 16-22.
Moore, L. Hugh. "Robert Penn Warren, William Styron, and the Use of Greek Myth," *Critique*, VIII (1966), 75-87.
Scott, James B. "The Theme of Betrayal in Robert Penn Warren's Stories," *Thoth*, V (1966), 74-84.

Stewart, John L. *The Burden of Time: The Fugitives and Agrarians.* Princeton, N.J., 1965.

Strandberg, Victor H. *A Colder Fire: The Poetry of Robert Penn Warren.* Lexington, Ky., 1965.

Warren, Robert Penn. "*All the King's Men:* The Matrix of Experience." *Yale Review,* LIII (1964), 161-167.

Index